# ART FORMS OF INDIA

# ART FORMS OF INDIA

*Editor-in-Chief*

**Swami Chidatman Jee Maharaj**

**ANMOL PUBLICATIONS PVT. LTD.**

**NEW DELHI - 110 002 (INDIA)**

**ANMOL PUBLICATIONS PVT. LTD.**

**H.O.:** 4374/4B, Ansari Road, Daryaganj,
New Delhi-110 002 (India)
Ph.: 23278000, 23261597
**B.O.:** No. 1015, Ist Main Road, BSK IIIrd Stage
IIIrd Phase, IIIrd Block,
Bangalore - 560 085 (India)
*Visit us at*: www.anmolpublications.com



*Art Forms of India*


First Published, 2009
ISBN 978-81-261-3638-4



PRINTED IN INDIA

Printed at Mehra Offset Press, Delhi.

# Contents

*Preface* *vii*

1. Dances of India 1

2. Indian Music 105

3. Theatre and Cinema of India 153

4. Indian Paintings 171

*Bibliography* 241

*Index* 245

# Preface

India colourful and vibrant, a land as diverse as its people. A mosaic of faiths, cultures, customs and languages that blend harmoniously to form a composite whole. One of the world's oldest living civilizations—which gave to the world—the concept of zero, the primordial sound Aum..., Yoga and Buddhism.

She is old. She is young. The two diametrically opposite, different yet unique and dynamic faces of India coexist even at this turn of the millennium. With a history of heritage, learning and civilisation dating back to almost 5000 years or perhaps even more, the modern India presents itself as an ideal country. From snow clad mountains to breezy sparkling blue sea side. From arid deserts with shifting sand dunes to lush green country sides. From ancient relics and architectural ruins dating back into antiquity to modern cities, India has it all.

To the north it is bordered by the world's highest mountain chain, where foothill valleys cover the northernmost of the country's maximum states. Further south, plateaus, tropical rain forests and sandy deserts are bordered by palm fringed beaches. Its southernmost tip is the meeting point of three Oceans.

India is a land of staggering contrast with a mingling of the tradition and modernity that is an unique experience to be in India. One will forever remember the stay in this wonderful Homeland-a land truly of mystery and enchantment. Only India can offer such an astonishing variety of contrasts.

She has given birth to numerous spiritual leaders and founders of some of the popular religions of the present day world. India probably has the most religious diversity in any country. It's the birthplace of Hinduism, Buddhism, Sikhism and Jainism and is among the few places to have a resident

Zoroastrian population. India with her veritable treasure trove of culture, mysticism, philosophy, art, music and architecture to name a few. Much of India's classical music is devotional and the North Indian Hindustani and South Indian Carnatic streams are distinct and both have a complex 'raga' framework. The legacy of dance in India is tremendous. The classical dances of India are numerous such as Kathakali of Kerala, Bharatnatyam of Tamil Nadu, Kuchipudi of Andhra Pradesh, Manipuri and Odissi from Orissa are the prominent dance forms in this country that sways to an altogether novel beat. The Yakshagana, nautanki and puppetry are ancient folk forms that live on till date. The earliest specimens of Indian painting are the ones on the walls of the Ajanta Caves dating back to 2nd century BC. The Mughals had a huge impact on Indian art. The influence of Persian art brought placid garden scenes, illustrations from myths, legends and history into Indian art. Word craft, handicrafts, architecture and sculpture all contribute to this rich and varied domain. Indian literature, both in English and in the vernacular, is ever more popular around the world.

The book aims at presenting perspectives of different aspects of Indian culture. It has topics on Indian classical music and dance, painting, ayurveda and yoga which are traditional and indigenous system of physical and mental wellbeing, language, philosophy and excellence achievements by Indian in the different branches of science and social sciences. It also includes our ancient religious and classic literature.

It is hoped that this book will be welcomed by the general readers as also scholars who are interested in the Indian heritage.

—*Editors*

1

# Dances of India

It is said that the gods created dance as a device for entertainment. Later, in order to please the gods, human beings enacted the tale and glory of the gods. Thus began a cycle of celebration manifested in the joyous abandon of movement and music.

Over a period of two millennia, dance in India acquired a set grammar, which led to a certain codification of technique. Thus were sown the seeds for Bharata Muni's celebrated treatise on dance, the *Natya Shastra*. Bharata's Natya Shastra (believed to be penned between second century B.C. and second century A.D.) is the earliest available treatise on dramaturgy. All forms of Indian classical dances owe allegiance to Natya Shastra, regarded as the *fifth Veda*.

The fascination for Indian dance all over the world is indicative of the deep-felt needs to use the human body to express and celebrate the great universal truths. Indian dance does just that in a heightened, reverential form. Also, since dance is physical and visual, it illuminates India's culture in a direct manner, playing on the sensibilities of the onlooker.

Thus, those who are attracted to India will find the idiom of dance the best introduction to India's rich ethos and traditions.Indian Dances illuminate & express India's culture in a direct manner, playing on the sensibilities of the onlooker.

India offers a number of classical dance forms, each of which can be traced to different parts of the country. Each form represents the culture and ethos of a particular region or a group of people.

There are many types of dance in India, from those which are deeply religious in content to those which are danced on more trivial happy occasions. Classical Indian Dances are usually always spiritual in content, although this is often true also of Folk dances. The most popular classical styles seen on the Indian dance stage are Bharata Natyam of Tamil Nadu, Kathakali and Mohiniattam of Kerala, Odissi of Orissa, Kathak of Uttar Pradesh, Kuchipudi of Andhra Pradesh and Manipuri of Manipur.

Indian mythology, legends and classical literature provide the themes of the Indian dance, both of the classical and folk variety. The classical dance is based on rigid rules and dance discipline. Its forms include Bharata Natyam, Kuchipudi, Odissi and Kathak as also a tradition of dance-dramas—Kathakali, Kutiyattam, Mohiniattam, etc.

Indian dance is divided into nritta—the rhythmic elements, nritya—the combination of rhythm with expression and natya—the dramatic element.

Nritya is usually expressed through the eyes, hands and facial movements. Nritya combined with nritta makes up the usual dance programmes.

Indian classical dance is the embodiment of a whole range of expressions, which include fantasy and yogic discipline. The different forms represent the meeting point of three arts: music, drama and dance. Though highly defined and codified, they are perceived primarily as a form of worship, as homage to the almighty. Their classicism lies in the continuity of an unbroken history of over five thousand millennia, one which overwhelms yet inspires.

Using the body as a medium of communication, the dance programmes. Nritya comprises abhinaya, depicting rasa (sentiment) and bhava (mood). To appreciate natya or dance drama, one has to understand and appreciate Indian legends. Most Indian dances take their themes from India's rich mythology and folk legends. Hindu gods and goddesses like Vishnu and Lakshmi, Rama and Sita, Krishna and Radha are all depicted in classical Indian dances.

Each dance form also draws inspiration from stories depicting the life, ethics and beliefs of the Indian people. It is said that Brahma-the Creator, created Natya, taking literature from the Rig Veda, song from the Sama Veda, abhinaya or expression from the Yajur Veda and rasa or aesthetic experience from the Atharvana Veda.

It also contains deliberations on the different kind of postures, the mudras or hand formations and their meanings, the kind of emotions and their categorisation, the kind of attire, the stage, the ornaments and even the audience. All dance forms are thus structured around the nine Rasas or emotions, Hasya (happiness), Krodha (anger), Bhibasta (disgust), Bhaya (fear), Shoka (sorrow), Viram (courage), Karuna (compassion), Adbhuta (wonder) and Shanta (serenity). All dance forms follow the same hand gestures or Hasta Mudras for each of these rasas. The dances differ where the local genius has adapted it to local demands and needs.

## The Origins of Indian Dance

The Natya Shastra was created in the beginning of Treta Yug by Brahma on the request of Indra and other devas as an object of diversion (Kridaniyaka). As the lower castes (Sudras) were not entitled to listen to the four Vedas (Sama, Yajur, Rig and Atharava), Brahma created the Natya Shastra as the fifth Veda which was open to all, irrespective of caste and creed.

Prior to the creation of the Natya Veda, Brahma entered a yogic trance in which he recalled the four Vedas. He drew the recitative (Paathya) from the Rig, songs (Geeta) from the Sama, histronic representation (Abhinaya) from the Yajur and sentiments (Rasa) from the Atharva. These aspects are the four main constituents of the Natya Veda. When the Natya Veda was ready, the Gods expressed their inability to practise it, and Brahma passed it to Bharata Muni and his one hundred sons who were asked to practise it. The dance was first seen at the Flag Festival of Indra to celebrate the victory of the Devas against the Daahavas. Shiva learnt the Tandava (masculine) form of the dance, whereas Parvati, his consort learnt the Lasya (feminine) form.

### *Nataraja*

One of the most enduring symbols of India is the figure of Nataraja-Shiva (The King of Dancers). Shiva's cosmic dance is believed to encompass creation, preservation, and destruction and this idea has been embedded in Hindu thought and ritual since the dawn of civilization. He holds a small drum (Damaru) in his upper right hand. His lower right hand shows the fear-negating gesture (Abhaya), his upper left hand is in half-moon pose (Ardhachandramudra) which holds a tongue of flame which is the fire (Agni) that finally destroys the world and is then quenched in cosmic waters. Thus the hand holding the drum and the one holding fire balance the forces of creation and destruction. The second left arm is held gracefully across the chest (Gajahastamudra) with the hand pointing to the uplifted foot, denoting favour or grace for the devotee.

### *Elements of Indian Dance*

***Abhinaya:*** Abhinaya is common to all Classical Indian dances. Abhinaya is the expressional aspect of dance, or nritya. In contrast to this, Nritta is composed of only pure dance and will feature striking and aesthetic poses, but will have no expressional meaning and symbolism. Abhinaya has been analysed in the Natya Shastra and has been categorised into four types:

- Angika or physical, using movements of every part of the body to convey meaning, with hastamudras (hand gestures), mandis (postures) and even the walk of the dancer.
- Vachikabhinaya or vocal/verbal, used formally today by members of the orchestra or supporting, non-dancing cast.
- Aharyabhinaya or external, expression, mood and background as conveyed by costume, makeup, accessories and sets.
- Satvikabhinaya or psychological, shown by the eyes in particular and as a whole by the entire being of the performer, who feels the mood, the character and the

emotion as emanating from the self, not as an act or practical presentation.

***The Navrasas:*** In addition, the navrasas, or nine emotions, give all dance a completeness that allows the dancer and the rasikas (audience) to experience the full beauty and meaning of the lyrics and the movements they are portrayed by. These emotions are expressed in the eyes, the face, subtle muscle shifts and the body as a whole. They are:

*Hasya (happiness),*
*Krodha (anger),*
*Bibhatsa (disgust),*
*Bhayanaka (fear),*
*Shoka (sorrow),*
*Veera (courage),*
*Karuna (compassion),*
*Adbhuta (wonder) and*
*Shanta (serenity).*

### *Slokas Specific to Classical Dance*

*Slokas* or verses which are full of wisdom are central and common to the traditional way of life; that is, life as per the Vedas. Thus it is only natural that we find many verses that pertain to the art of dance. Below it is presented only two, but these are very widely known throughout India and although appropriate to dance, they can fit in happily to all aspects of life.

In Bharata Natyam, as in many other dance forms there is an oft-repeated sloka:

*Guru Brahma*
*Guru Vishnu*
*Guru Devo Mahesvaraha*
*Guru Sakshaad Parambrahma*
*Tasmay Shri Guruveh Namaha*

*Aangikam Bhuvanam Yasya*
*Vachikam Sarva Vangmayam*

*Aharyam Chandra-Taradi Tvam Namaha*
*Sattvikam Shivam*

The sloka can roughly be translated to mean:

*Lord Brahma, Lord Vishnu, Lord Shiva, (My) Guru*

*I bow to you, the ultimate Lord/Guru:*
*You, whose limbs are the Universe,*
*You, the Originator of all speech,*
*You, whose adornments are the moon and stars,*
***You are The Truth.***

***The Natya Krama***

The following sloka is:

*Khantaanyat Lambayat Geetam*
*Hastana Artha Pradakshayat*
*Chakshubhyam Darshayat Bhavom*
*Padabhyam Tala Acherait*
*Yato Hasta Stato Drushti*
*Yato Drushti Stato Manaha*
*Yato Manaha Stato Bhavom*
*Yato Bhavom Stato Rasaha*

This means:

*Keep the song in your throat*
*Let your hands bring out the meaning*
*Your glance should be full of expression*
*While your feet maintain the rhythm*

*Where the hand goes, there the eyes should follow*
*Where the eyes are, the mind should follow*
*Where the mind is, there the expression should be brought out*
*Where the expression is, there the rasa or flavour will be experienced (by the audience).*

## Bharata Natyam

Bharata Natyam is one of the oldest dance forms of India. It was nurtured in the temples and courts of southern India since ancient times. Later it was codified and documented as a performing art in the 19th century by four brothers known as the Tanjore Quartet whose musical compositions for dance form the bulk of the Bharata Natyam repertoire even today. The art was handed down as a living tradition from generation to generation under the Devadasi system under which women were dedicated to temples to serve the deity as dancers and musicians forming part of the elaborate rituals.

These highly talented artists and the male gurus (nattuvanars) were the sole repository of the art until the early 20th century when a renewal of interest in India's cultural heritage prompted the educated elite to discover its beauty. By this time the Devadasis had fallen upon evil days due to lack of state patronage and changed social mores. The revival of Bharata Natyam by pioneers such as E. Krishna Iyer and Rukmini Devi Arundale brought the dance out of the temple precincts and onto the proscenium stage though it retained its essentially devotional character.

Today Bharata Natyam is one of the most popular and widely performed dance styles and is practised by male and female dancers all over India. Due to its wide range of movements and postures and the balanced melange of the rhythmic and mimetic aspects lends itself well to experimental and fusion choreography. Degree and Post-Graduate courses covering the practice and theory of Bharata Natyam as well as the languages associated with its development are available at major universities of India.

It has been aptly said that Bharata Natyam is a symbol of beauty and aesthetic perfection. As a philosophy, it is a search of human soul for ideal. As a religion, it is the man's quest for the Supreme and the desire to unite with the Ultimate. As a science, it is to attain the perfection of body technique and corporal movement and as poetry, it is the symbol of rhythmic lyricism.

Bharata Natyam, has been one of the oldest and the richest classical dance of India. It's antiquity lies about 3000 years ago with a mythological as well as a historical origin. It was initially known as Sadir-attam (court dance) and also Dasiattam (performed by the daasis-the servants of God).

In its popular connotation, the name Bharata Natyam is understood in two ways:

- It is the dance (natyam), that beautifully blends the three elements-'Bha'-Bhava (from expressions), 'Ra'-Raga (from musical melody) and 'Ta'-Tala (from rythm).
- The name 'Bharata' is after the great author of the treaties, "Natya Shastra" (an encyclopedia on Dance, Drama and Music).

As in any classical dance form, Bharata Natyam requires total dedication, vigorous practice and full concentration. A basic training of minimum 6 years is required to present a full recital on stage. It requires a mastery over the technique of movements to achieve grace, balance, suppleness, physical endurance and a faultless sense of rhythm.

***Dance as a form of Worship***

The intimate association of dance with religion and as a ritual, a form of worship in the temples is well established. The institution of the Devadasis, servants of the God, contributed in perpetuating and preserving the art. In ancient times, the system of dedicating young dancers to the temples as devadasis seems to have prevailed. Dance has special mention in two important Tamil works Silappa Dikaram and Manimekhalai of the Sangam age (500 B.C-500 A.D).

The sacred texts of the Shaivagamas prescribed the mode of worship and referred to the consecration of dancing girls in the service of the gods. The temples were not only places of communication between man and God, but also strongholds of the Arts.

In the beautiful Nata-Mandapas (dance-halls) of the magnificent temples, the devadasis used to perform ritual dances as votive offerings to the presiding Deities.

***Various Steps***

As in any Indian Classical Dance, Bharata Natyam too requires vigorous practice, hard work and full dedication. In order to achieve the balance, grace and mastery over the technique, one has put in her/his best effort, dedication, faith and interest. The Bharata Natyam Training begins with a *Namaskar*. Then some exercises are done to warm before learning the basic steps *(Adavus, Korvais)*. The Bharatnayam dancer uses the hand gestures as her language of expression *(Abhinaya)*. Gradually, the student is taught the various items beginning from simple to complex *(Margam)*. And when the Guru thinks that the student is ready, her first public performance is done *(Arangetram)*.

***Namaskar:*** The training begins with the learning of a prayer and a Namaskar. The disciple first pays her salutation by saying a prayer to Nataraj/Mother Earth and then performs the traditional Namaskar to Mother Earth, the God, the Guru and the audience. She bows to Mother Earth when she touches the floor and prays to God when she keeps her hand in 'Anjali' hasta (that is, joined as in doing Namaste in Indian tradition) a little above her head. She prays to the Guru when her 'Anjali' hasta is on her forehead and to the audience when her 'Anjali' hasta is on chest. Namaskar is done to ask permission and forgiveness from Mother Earth for stamping her. This salutation is done before and after every dance session, be it a recital or a class.

***Adavus:*** Then the disciple is taught the basic steps called the '*Adavus*'. But before that it is always a good practice to do some Exercises to warm up and help the body in achieving flexibility, balance and poise in the basic positions and movements. While carrying out the Adavus, special importance is paid to the 'Angashuddha', that is, correct posture of the limbs which includes the 'Nritta hastas'; the 'Paadabhedaas'; 'Taalashuddha', that is, accurate rhythm; then the 'Taandava' (strong movements) and the 'Laasya' (graceful movements). The style of these Adavus vary with each Guru and Sampradaya (tradition). There are about hundred variations of Adavus which are practised before the main items are taught. Then these

Adavus are combined to form the *Korvais* or Jethis, that is a group of Adavus in varied permutation and combination. The Korvais are in turn combined to form the *Teermanams* (sequence of Korvais) and *Aridis* (endings with the repetition of particular adavus for three times on special rhythmic syllables).

There are varieties of Adavus like Tattadavu, Natadavu, Tatta Mettadavu, Kattadavu, Kudittamettadavu, Maiadavu, Mandiadavu, Jati, Nadai and many more....The posture is always half sit that is 'Ayata' or 'Aramandi' except in cases where mentioned otherwise. After the teachings of Adavus, the main items (Margam) are taught beginning with Alarippu, Jatiswaram and so on.

***Margam:*** Margam means a path or a course followed. It is one full definite course where in dance items are performed in a traditional order. The items that are included are Alarippu, Jatiswaram, Shabdam, Varnam, Padam, Tillana and Sloka or Verse. According to some scholars, it does not mean that these are the only items that can be performed but any traditional dance item or any song which can give scope for the exposition of Nritta and Nritya at their best can be included. Therefore, Pushpanjali, Kauthukam (Kauvutvam), Mallari, Javalis and others are also found in the repertory of certain schools of Bharata Natyam.

In early 19th century, the four famous and great musicians, nattuvanars, dancers, poets of Tanjore, namely, Chinnaiya, Ponnaiya, Shivanandam and Vadivelu (1777-1832) have created and propagated the present format of a Bharata Natyam recital from the traditional Sadir Natya or Dasiattam. According to the great legendary dancer T.S. Balasaraswati, "The traditional order of the Bharata Natyam—alarippu, jatiswaram, shabdam, varnam, padam, tillana and sloka or verse, is the correct sequence for revealing the spiritual through the corporeal."

She has compared the Bharata Natyam Recital to a grandly structured Temple: *"We enter through the Gopuram (outer hall) of Alarippu, cross the Ardhamandapam (half way hall) of Jatiswaram, then the Mandapam (great hall) of Shabdam and enter the holy precinct of the deity in the Varnam. In dancing to the Padams, one experiences the contentment, cool and quiet of entering the sanctum from its external precinct. It is akin to the juncture when the cascading lights of worship are withdrawn and the drum beats die down to the simple and solemn chanting of sacred verses in the closeness of God. Then the Tillana breaks into movement like the final burning of camphor accompanied by a measure of din and bustle."*

***Arangetram:*** A minimum of 6-7 years is required to know the technique and learn the Margam. That is when the dancer is ready to give her first performance in public. This is called as the 'Arangetram'. Arangetram is a Tamil word, 'Aranga' meaning a raised floor and 'Etram' meaning climbing or entering. After taking the training from her Guru, the dancer is sort of qualified and is introduced in the field of Performing Arts. In real sense this is just the beginning of a dancer's life and there is a along way to go. It is a great and a prestigious event for the Guru as well as the shishya the student. It is the test of the Gurus teachings as well as the test of talent and virtuosity of the student dancer.

## *Language of Gestures*

The language of dance is conveyed through the gestures. In the abhinaya items which mostly consists of lyrics, poetry or a narrative set to music and rhythm, the sahitya (lyrics) is interpreted by the dancer through a series of *Angika abhinaya*.

That is, through hand gestures and movements of eyes, eyebrows, eyeballs, etc. and through the expression on the face. Through the feet, the tempo (laya) is followed. Thus we see that the whole of body acts as a vehicle to express and reach out to the audience. These parts are categorised as Anga, Upaanga and Pratyanga. The hand gestures are the focal point of language.

Hence the student dancer is taught all hand gestures, Drishtibhedaas (movements of eyes), Grivaabhedaa (movement of neck), Shirobhedaa (movement of head), Padabhedaa (various movements and positions of leg and feet) and so on, in the form of slokaas which are in Sanskrit. The movements of hand gestures have been grouped under those of single (asamyukta hasta) hand gestures and those of double (samyukta hasta) hand gestures. These primary hand gestures can be used to as they are or suggestively to represent things, places, rivers, animals, human beings, relationships or to convey ideas and emotions or they can be used as symbols.

The movement of head, eyes, eyebrows, etc., especially help in conveying the bhaava and rasa, that is the mood and the inner emotions. Thus in words of Dr. Kapila Vatsayan, "through hand gesticulation, the universe can be comprehended". Today most of the Bharata Natyam dancers follows more or less the 'Abhinaya Darpanam' as a reference for 'Angika Abhinaya'

***Costume and Jewellery***

***Costume:*** The costume of Bharata Natyam has been developed from time to time. The costume that were prevalent earlier have been improvised and designed according to the needs and aesthetics. But the most commonly used styles include the Skirt/Sarree style and the Pyjama Style. Some also use the normal sarree and stitch it temporarily for the dance purpose. The most beautiful part of the costume is the knife-pleated fan which is either knee length or mid-calf length and links the two legs of the pyjamas. This fan opens up whenever the dancer takes the basic Bharata Natyam posture of aramandi.

***Jewellery:*** The specific jewellery that is used for the dance is called as the Temple jewelry which is made of semi precious stones and metal. It consists of Maattal and earbells for the ear, Kasumalai (coin necklace made of 'panchdhaatu'), Muthu maalai (long necklace), Necklace (small), Bangles, Talaisaamaan (head set, sun-surya prabha and moon-chandra prabha), Flowers (Jasmine ring and Kanakambaram (orange flowers), other hair decoration, Nose ring, Chalang (Ghungroos-ankle bells-of brass meatl) and Waist band (kamar patta). The raakodi is worn at the top of the head which provides as an anchor for the flowers worn by the dancer. The hair is mostly plaited and tied to a beautiful fringe called the kunjulam.

## Kathak

*Kathak* is one of the *classical dance* forms of India (originally from North India). It is a narrative dance form characterised by fast footwork (*tatkar*), spins (*chakkar*) and innovative use of *bhav* in *abhinaya*. It has today a form that has been influenced at various times in the past by mythological narratives by *kathakas*, temple dances, the *bhakti movement* (both Vaishnavism and Shaivite), and Persian influence of the Mughal courts in the 16th century onwards; and these elements are readily discernible. Performers today generally draw their lineage from two major schools of Kathak: the Jaipur *gharana* and the Lucknow *gharana* (born in the courts of the *Kachwaha Rajput* kings and the *Nawab* of *Awadh* respectively); there is also a slightly less prominent Benaras *gharana*.

### *Origin*

This dance form traces its origins to the the nomadic bards of ancient northern India, known as Kathaks, or story-tellers. These bards, performing in village squares and temple courtyards, mostly specialised in recounting mythological and moral tales from the scriptures, and embellished their recitals with hand gestures and facial expressions. It was quintessential theatre, using instrumental and vocal music along with stylised gestures, to enliven the stories. With the advent of Mughal culture, Kathak became a sophisticated chamber art. Patronised by art loving rulers, the practitioners of Kathak worked at refining its dramatic and rhythmic aspects, delighting elite audiences with their mastery over rhythm and the stylised mime.

The technique of Kathak today is characterised by fast rhythmic footwork set to complex time cycles. The footwork is matched by the accompanying percussion instruments such as tabla and pakhawaj, and the dancer and percussionists often indulge in a virtuoso display of rhythmic wizardry. The dance movements include numerous pirouettes executed at lightning speed and ending in statuesque poses. The interpretative portion, based on tales of Radha and Krishna and other mythological lore, contains subtle gestures and facial expressions. Lucknow, Benaras and Jaipur are recognised as the three schools, or gharanas, where this art was nurtured and where the interpretative and rhythmic aspects were refined to a high standard.

**Various Steps**

All compositions are performed so that the final step and beat of the composition lands on the 'sam' or first beat of the time-cycle. Most compositions also have *'bols'* (rhythmic words) which serve both as mnemonics to the composition and whose recitation also forms an integral part of the performance. Some compositions are aurally very interesting when presented this way. The *bols* can be borrowed from *tabla* (*e.g. dha, ge, na, tirakita*) or can be a dance variety (*ta, thei, tat, ta ta, tigda, digdig* and so on).

Often *tukras* are composed to highlight specific aspects of the dance, for example gait, or use of corners and diagonals, and so on. A popular *tukra* type is the *chakkarwala tukra*, showcasing the signature spins of Kathak. Because they are generally executed on the heel, these differ from *ballet's* pirouettes (which are properly executed on the toe or ball of the foot). The spins usually manifest themselves at the end of the *tukra*, often in large numbers: five, nine, fifteen, or more, sequential spins are common. These *tukras* are popular with audiences because they are visually exciting and are executed at great speed. Other compositions can be sub-divided:

1. *Vandana* the dancer begins with an invocation to the gods.
2. *Thaat* (the first composition of a traditional performance; the dancer performs short plays with the time-cycle, finishing on sam in a statuesque standing (thaat) pose);
3. *Aamad* (from the Persian word meaning 'entry'; the first introduction of spoken rhythmic pattern or *bol* in to the performance);
4. *Salaami* (related to Ar. 'salaam'—a salutation to the audience in the Muslim style);
5. *Gat* (from the word for 'gait, walk' showing abstract visually beautiful gaits or scenes from daily life)
6. *Kavit* (a poem set on a time-cycle; the dancer will perform movements that echo the meaning of the poem)
7. *Paran* (a composition using *bols* from the *pakhawaj* instead of only dance or tabla bols)

8. *Parmelu* (a composition using *bols* reminiscent of sounds from nature, such as kukuthere, jhijhikita, etc.)
9. *Tihai* (usually a footwork composition consisting of a long set of bols repeated thrice so that the very last *bol* ends dramatically on 'sam')
10. *Ladi* (a footwork composition consisting of variations on a theme, and ending in a tihai)

### *Gharanas*

Kathak, passed down from *guru* to *shishya*, has developed different styles, called *gharana* especially during the pre-independence period. Some well known *gharanas* are:

***Lucknow Gharana**:* The *Lucknow Gharana* developed in the courts of the Nawab of Awadh of Lucknow is characterised by its *nazakat* and *khubsurti*. *Abhinaya* plays a very strong role in this style. It is known for the improvised *abhinaya* of Birju Maharaj and Shambhu Maharaj.

***Jaipur Gharana**:* The *Jaipur Gharana* developed in the courts of the Kachchwaha kings of Jaipur, is characterised by strong rhythmic elements. This style explores different *talas*, and provides a vigorous and forceful form.

***Benaras Gharana**:* The *Benaras Gharana* is the style developed by Janakiprasad. It is characterised by the *natwari bols*, which are different from the tabla and the pakhawaj *bols*. This style uses the twelve *natwari bol* based compositions exclusively. There are differences in the *thaat* and *tatkaar*, and *chakkars* are kept at a minimum. Though the style developed in Benaras, it flourishes today from Bikaner.

### *Innovation within Tradition*

***Kathak Yoga:*** Kathak Yoga is a technique created By Pandit Chitresh Das, within the tradition of Kathak, bringing harmony of mind, body and soul where the dancer recites the chosen Taalam, singing the melody of the chosen Taalam, and dances precise mathematical footwork and Chhakars (pirouettes) all at the same time. In traditional Kathak, there is a singer who recites the given bol to guide the dancer. But in Kathak Yoga, one has to dance the mathematical bol pattern without assistance and recite the basic taalam, which requires the dancer to know the mathematics of the dance bols precisely.

***The Music of Kathak***

Kathak can be danced with a wide variety of music. Here are some of them:

1. Slokas *(Sanskrit / Hindi)* and Bhajans (devotional songs for Hindu Gods and Goddesses).
2. Classical and Light Classical Songs *e.g.* Thumri, Dadra, Kajri, Hori.
3. Film songs preferably based on Ragas
4. Darbari and Ghazals *(mainly Urdu)*—songs based on love, admiration, infatuation, seperation, etc.
5. Pure Classical type *e.g.* Paran, Tukda, Gat Nikas, Jugalbandi (a friendly competition), Sawal-Jawab (footwork with tabla or pakhawaj) and demonstration of different Beats.
6. Tarana based on different Ragas.
7. Songs written by Ravindra Nath Tagore and Kazi Nazrul Islam *(Bengali)*
8. Folk Dances from different states of India *e.g.* Bhangra, Dandia, Garba, Machua, Chhau, etc. and also gypsy dance. They have a unique style but they can be blended with kathak.
9. Dance Dramas *(mainly Hindi)* example, topics chosen from the epic Mahabharata which was composed by Vyas Deva and describes the story of Vedic era. The other great composition is the epic called Ramayana written by Valmiki. It describes the story of Rama (a representative of God Vishnu), the king of Ayodhya. Rama's wife Sita was abducted by Ravana, the demon king of Sri Lanka. Rama fought a war against Ravana and defeated him. Ramayana presents the ideology of king Rama and his love for his country; Shakuntala, Krishnaleela, etc.
10. Any musical (classical) composition *e.g.* Sitar, Sarod, Violin, Sarengi, Israj, Dilruba *(String instruments)*,

Sehnai, Flute *(Wind instruments)* and Tabla, Pakhawaj, Naal, Dholak *(Percussion instruments)* based on an ancient or modern theme *(preferably on* India*)*.

11. Kathak (specially footwork) can be blended with Tap dancing

***Kathak Costumes***

- Kathak is a wonderful blend of Hindu and Muslim culture. The costumes are very gorgeous for both Hindu (Lahenga-Choli) and Muslim-(Churidar-Kameez-Vest) called Angrakha.

## Kathakali

Kathakali (Malayalam) is a form of Indian dance-drama. It originated in the Indian state of Kerala during the 7th century C.E. The Raja of Kottarakara is the earliest exponent of this art. It is considered to be one of the oldest dance forms in India. It is a spectacular combination of drama, dance, music and ritual. Characters with vividly painted faces and elaborate costumes re-enact stories from the Hindu epics, Mahabharatha and Ramayana. Kathakali is featured in the award-winning Indo-French-German produced film *Vaanaprastham*. Kathakali is traditionally performed in the Hindu temple, but nowadays may also be seen in theatre performances. Kathakali is considered to be a combination of five forms of fine art:

- Literature (Sahithyam)
- Music (Sangeetham)
- Painting or make up (Chutti)
- Acting (Natyam)
- Dance (Nritham)

Kathakali, literally meaning 'story-play', is a dance-drama originated in the 17th century in Kerala, one of the smallest states in India lying on the west coast of the Indian peninsula. However, its roots could be tracked back even to the earlier times. *Koodiyattom*, the only surviving form of Sanskrit theatre in India has been preserved in Kerala for centuries, now, by a small community called *Chakyar* as a part of their hereditary temple service. *Krishnanattom*, another form of dance-drama considered fore runner to Kathakali in its origin, is performed even today at the famous Sree Krishna temple in Guruvayoor as an offering to the Lord. Besides these two forms, elements from martial, ritualistic, socio-religious arts have also influenced in the making of Kathakali. Though Kathakali is only 300 years old, a great deal of enrichment and refinement has taken place in every aspect of its technique during this short period. Scholars are of opinion that Kathakali is the result of a fusion between all Indian theatre tradition represented by *Koodiyattom* and the indigenous tradition of folk dance forms.

It was one of the *Rajas* (Chieftain) of Kottarakkara, who wrote the first play intended for Kathakali performance. They form a cycle of eight stories based on *Ramayana*. The performance for each story was designed to last for six to eight hours. The performed stories were then known as *Ramanattom* (play pertaining to Rama), which later came to be called as Kathakali. Stories based on other epics and *puranas* were added to its repertoire in later period.

A vivid picture of the nature of performance of Kathakali in the past is not known. However, it is said that in the beginning the actors themselves used to sing the text while performing. Masks were elaborately used for some characters and percussion was limited to a *Maddalam* (two headed barrel shaped drum), a *Chengila* (metal gong) and *Elathalam* (a pair of cymbals).

Among the better known Kathakali play writes are Kottarakara Thampuran, the author of the above mentioned Ramayana Stories; Kottayam Thampuran, who wrote four stories based on *Mahabharata*; Irayamman Thampi, who was both a good poet and composer, accredited three stories; Unnayi Warrier, the author of *Nalacharitham* (Story of King Nala); and Vayaskara Moosad who wrote one of the popular stories—*Duryodhana Vadham*.

***Structure of the Performance:*** In olden days Kathakali performance mostly took place on a temple premises or at the house of a local land lord. For a typical performance, a simple temporary *pandal* (canopy made of thatched roof) at a height of 101/2 feet will be erected. A minimum of 12 feet-square (144 sq. feet) is needed for the acting area. A green room will also be located close to the stage. The stage will be decorated with coconut leaves, bunches of areca nuts, etc. The only source of light is a big bell metal lamp placed down the centre stage. The level of the stage used to be the same as that of the ground where people used to squat while witnessing the performance.

*Kelikottu* at about 6 'o' clock in the evening will announce the performance of the evening. *Kelikottu* is a brief passage of drumming involving *Chenda* (a cylindrical drum), *Maddalam*, *Chengila* and *Elathalam*. The actual performance will begin only between 9:00-10:00 PM. *Arrangukeli* will announce the beginning of the performance. This is a passage of drumming, which is followed by *Thodayam*, a piece of abstract dance at the same time are invocatory in nature. *Thodayam* is performed by junior actors in the group with simple makeup. Recitation of *Vandanaslokam* (Prayer Song), followed by *Purappad*—traditionally a preliminary item introducing the main character of the story in full costume and makeup.

However, nowadays it is mostly Krishna and Balarama who are presented, sometime with their spouses in this introductory dance. Next is the *Melappadam*, which is a musical piece where vocalists and the drummers are given opportunity to show their skill without depending on the actors. Then the story or part of the stories proposed are enacted which may last till dawn. The end of the performance is marked by a piece of pure dance called *Dhanasi*.

***Techniques:*** Kathakali is a dance-drama in which a high degree of stylisation is seen in the method of acting, presentation, makeup and costuming. Realism is limited only to certain characters. The acting mode of Kathakali in its totality can be better understood in terms of four fold scheme of historic representation given in Natya Shastra. They are:

1. *Angika*—pertaining to the body and its limbs.
2. *Vachika*—relating to the vocal including proper pronunciation, modulation of voice accents and percussion.
3. *Satvika*—representation of psychic condition.
4. *Ahraya*—costume, makeup, stage props, etc.

***Angika Abhinaya:*** This involves the whole body of the actor and included an elaborate scheme of facial expression, mime, gestures, accompanied by their appropriate movements, poses and attitudes. Dance passages known as *Kalasams* have an important role to play in Kathakali. While sustaining as a pure dance, it is also meant to enhance the appropriate *bhavas*. Hand gestures is another integral part of *Angika* since the interpretation of the text is mainly conveyed through this. *Hastalakshna Deepika* is the regional text on the *Hastas* (hand gestures) mainly used in Kathakali.

***Vachika Abhinaya:*** One of the distinguishing characteristic of Kathakali is that the actors do not speak. *Vachika* (drama text in the form of verses and songs) are recited and sung by vocalists. These songs are explained and interpreted in details by actors through an elaborate method of *angikabhinaya* which consists of highly codified gestures, facial expression, and body movements. The vocal music in Kathakali although based on the *Karnatic* (South Indian) system has developed a distinct regional style called *Sopanasangeetham*. Its main aim is the evocation of the appropriate, dramatic mood and sentiments.

***Satvika Abhinaya:*** A highly stylised technique in the invocation of *bhava* has been developed in Kathakali. This is called *Rasabhinava*. Indian dramatic theory explain 9 kinds of basic sentiments, *Rasa* with a corresponding *sthayi bhava* (emotional stayi mood). They are:

| ***Rasabhinava*** | ***Sthayi Bhava*** |
|---|---|
| *Sringara* (EROTIC) | *Rati* (LOVE) |
| *Hasya* (COMIC, HUMOR) | *Hasa* (LAUGHTER) |
| *Karuna* (PATHETIC) | *Soka* (SORROW) |
| *Raudra* (FURIOUS) | *Krodha* (ANGER) |
| *Veera* (HEROIC) | *Visaha* (ENERGY, HEROISM) |
| *Bhayanaka* (TERRIBLE) | *Bhayam* (FEAR) |
| *Atbhutam* (MARVELOUS) | *Vismayam* (ASTONISHMENT) |
| *Sandham* (SERENE) | *Sama* (TRANQUILLITY) |

Through a systematic process of practice an actor gain a full control of the facial muscles which enables him to express the bhavas. Apart from the above sets of emotional moods *Natya Shastra* lists another set of 8 moods which is called *Satvika Bhavas* compared to *Angikabhinaya* this is more subtle and involuntary. Through an internal discipline an actor develops his ability in mastering this action technique. This will help the actor to go deeper into the characterisation of the role in proper situation in the play.

***Aharya Abhinaya:*** The makeup and costuming is another important factor of the dance-drama. Such an elaborate system is rarely found elsewhere.

The characters in Kathakali are types. As such characters are classified under 5 major types. According to their nature. They are:

- *Pacca* (green)-heroic, divine *e.g.*:-Krishna, Arjuna.
- *Kathi* (knife)-heroic but lustful with arrogant. *e.g.*:-Duryodhana, Ravana.
- *Tadi* (beard)-red, villainous and evil. *e.g.*:-Dussasana
- *Kari* (black)-a demoness.
- *Munukku* (shining)-all females (expect demoness in their original form). Brahmans, sage, messengers, charioteer.
- *Teppu* (special make-up)-birds, bheeru (coward), etc.

A major part of the face makeup is done by the actor himself. However, specially trained artists are entrusted to apply *Chutty* (framing the face with white paper and rice paste). Design vary according to the type of a characters. A close observation on *Aharya* aspect of Kathakali would reveal the highest level of aesthetic imagination conceived by our predecessors. This short note on Kathakali could be summarised as such that the theatre form is a combination of dance, music, percussion, acting and painting thus make a total theatre in its completion.

***Makeup:*** Kathakali makeup is an elaborate process lasting for 3 hours. It helps in giving a super human look to the actors. The make up of the male character other than the saint, is tedious. The Makeup is directly applied to the face and it does not obstruct the full expression of face and eyes.The colouring material used is made from various stones and powder which are mixed with water or coconut oil and ground into fine paste.

The actor lies flat on a matted floor and the expert starts drawing "the designs" on the face. The most elaborate part of the make up is the chutti (a series of white ridges built up from the chin to the either side of the cheek). After face part make up the actor stands up to put on the costume.

The skirt is a well starched and pressed into frills garment. Before the skirt is put on, the actor ties 20 to 40 pieces of short cloth around the waist by the help of a large cloth twisted rope in order to give the skirt a oval shape. He then puts the jacket, etc. The actor is profusely ornamented with garlands of beast, armlets, cupped mirrors, etc. The head dresses are huge and large.

The make up colour also plays an important role in Kathakali. According to sastras colour symbolism has got significance. They reflect certain categories of emotions and gunas (attributes). The classification and nature of character are as follows.

*Green represents Sattivika nature*

*Red represents Rajasic nature*

*Black represents Tamasic nature*

Yellow represents Sattivika & Rajasic nature Green goes with godliness, white with spirituality, red with ambition and violence, yellow with passivity, and black with evil.

***Mudras***

Mudras are gestures of hands which imparts the expression of thought and emotion. This mudras are prevalent from the time of the vedas and still used by the priests while chanting manthras. In Kathakali stories conveyed by mudra from tragedy to exultation. Each mudra has got a different meaning. Depending upon the context the meaning changes. The actor should learn about 600 mudras during training. The alphabet of the hand, as mudras are, form a complete vocabulary of more than 500 words which most commonly occur in a dance story and which describe concrete objects or express an emotional situation or relate an incident in simple words.

### *Aesthetics*

In Kathakali each dance gestures is accompanied with some bhava, the ultimate climax is rasa. Rasa literally the essence, maybe explained in simple terms as aesthetic outcome of mood in a relishably enjoyable form. There are nine rasas. They are as follows

- Sringara
- Hasya
- Karuna
- Raudra
- Bhayanaka
- Vira
- Bibhatsa
- Adbhuta
- Shanta.

### *Origin and Development of Kathakali*

It was believed that *Kathakali* was conceived from *Krishnanaattam*, the dance drama on the life and activities of Lord Krishna created by the Zamorin of Calicut. The reason for that is said as follows: Once *Kottarakkara Thampuran* the Raja of Kottarakkara who was attracted by the tone of the *Krishnanaattam* requested the Zamorin for the loan of a troupe of performers on the eve of some festive occasion. Due to internal feuds and political rivalry between them, the Zamorin refused to send the performers and insulted with the remarks: "It is useless to depute the troupe, because Kottarakkara Thespian's court would be neither able to appreciate nor understand anything of the highly artistic *Krishnanaattam* and the high standard of the performance". Here the political rivalry between the two chieftains leads to the art rivalry.

So *Kottarakkara Thampuran* initiated a parallel mode of entertainment, which he called *Raamanaattam* which was later transformed into *Aattakatha*, and yet later into *Kathakali* while

*Krishnanaattam* based on the story of Lord Krishna's activities, *Raamanaattam* described the complete story of Lord Raman. *Krishnanaattam* was written in Sanskrit, "the language of the Gods". *Raamanaattam* was in Malayalam, the language of the people. By the end of the seventeenth century, the finished product of *Raamanaattam* was placed before the world under the tittle *Kathakali. The* costume of *Kathakali* has been much influenced by *Chaakkyaar koothu* and *Koodiyattam* the two older forms of dramatic representations in vogue in Kerala.

The history of their origins dates back to the period of *Perumals, i.e.* much earlier to the introduction of *Raamanaattam*. The whole scheme of *Abhinaya* (acting) and the use of *Mudras* (hand poses) and gestures were bodily adopted in *Kathakali* from them in addition to its borrowing and refinement of facial makeup and costume. The use of colour, costume, and makeup present a unique show and create an unearthly atmosphere. *Kathakali* became more attractive and popular than the *Chaakkyaar koothu* and *Koodiyattam*.

Moreover, its performance was not restricted to the precincts of the temples. *Kathakali* had a golden period between 1665 AD and 1743 AD. Remarkable contributions were also made by *Kaartika Thirunal*, the king of Travancore, to Kerala's literature, art and dance. His efforts were also directed to popularising *Kathakali* among the people. He instituted a tradition of arranging *Kathakali* performances at various festivals and on the Navaratri night. *Kathakali* employs the four abhinayas, viz *Sattvika*, expression of thoughts by the efforts of the mind (*Bhaava* and *Rasa*).

*Aangika*, conveyance of ideas by the movements of the various parts of the body (gestures).,*Vaacika*, spoken words, singing, shrieking, etc., and Aharya, the dress and deportment. As in earlier dramatic forms, *Raamanaattam* players also sang the *padas*. But for the vigorous *Kathakali*, demanding tremendous physical exertion, singing by the actors was exacting and tiring. A change in the practice was conceived by Prince *Vettathu Thampuran*, who introduced a few fundamental innovations. He provided seperate singers and introduced the *chenda*, a percussion instrument, to announce a performance and give background sound effect. This drum's powerful and penetrating sound heightened the acting of supernatural characters appearing on the stage in hideous and fantastic make-ups. The religio-theatrical reforms brought *Raamanaattam* performances outside the temples for the enjoyment of all sections of the community.

Masks were replaced by makeup; *Mudras* were accentuated, a variety of percussion instruments and characteristic costumes were introduced; singers and musicians formed an independent part of a show.Symbols of the hand have played an important role in the art of *Kathakali*. With the help of *Mudras*, the hand poses are called in Sanskrit, a whole literary expression is reduced to elementary notions. There are sixty-four basic hand poses which connote five hundred words, while the alphabet of the eyes express emotions. Their permutations can be employed to convey any number of meanings requiring any detailed explanation in the modern concept of story-telling. In the art of *Kathakali*, all emotional qualities, and psychic conditions acquire remarkable outward manifestation and *mukhabhinaya* (facial mime) is cunningly, sometimes lightly employed. While the *Kathakali* use elaborate similes and hyperboles, and fingers permute into *mudras* to represent words of comparison such as like, as if and same as, the eye-balls roll evanescently to tell the miracles.

The face becomes the open drama in which the story is drawn in successive shades and touches of lineament.According to the theme, a *Kathakali* song suggests the use of a particular *Bhaava* and *Rasa* (aesthetic delights) and the dance and mimicry are rendered most effectively in harmony with these aesthetic appeals.

The powerful music heightens the moods of the actor and adds life to acting. He dances to the melodies of the song and executes the various passages with well-defined *Padaghats* (foot work). It provides scope for the amplification of an emotion and the abridgement of the climax of a story. The powerful footwork trembles the earth below and cuts short the final action. As *Kathakali* is a story-play, interpreting a *drisya kaavya*, its various contrasting characters are presented.

There are good and bad characters, demons and gods, wordly and unwordly role-types according to their castes, quality and nature. Each group is distinguished from the other by specific make-ups. The makeup of *Kathakali* character is peculiarily native to the Kerala folk-art. In folk theatrical varieties, huge marks and make-ups were as much prevalent during the historic span of time. Elaborate makeup heightens dramatic effects. Colour symbolism reflect certain categories of emotions and *gunas*.

The green colour represents *Saattvika* reveals godliness, white represents spirituality. Red represents *Rajasic* reveals violence. Black represents *Tamasic* reveals evil. Yellow represents the combined character of *Saatvika* and *Rajasic*. Thus *Kathakali* characters are grouped into five major role-types, each having a specific makeup and costume. These role types are *Minukku*, *Paccha*, *Katti,taadi* (has three varieties, *viz. Veluppputaadi*, *Chuvannataadi* and *Karupputtadi*) and *Kari*. *Minukku* is the polished variety of facial makeup consisting in smoothening the actor's face with a coating of a mixture of yellow and red pigments.

The composition obtains 'a self' (or natural skin) complexion colour. It reflects the characters usually found in Brahmans, Rishis and Virtuous women. The eyes and eye-lashes are painted and contours elongated with the black unguent and greasy collyrium. Sometimes the face is decorated with white or cream colour dots, running from the cheeks to the fore-head in a bow-shape. The lips are reddened and the forehead is decorated with a caste mark. This colour scheme serves to give a symbolic glow of piety to a devotee character. Women role-types are given delicate touches of the make-up.Paccha or pre-dominantly deep green face role-types, are Gods, celebrated mythological heroes, and virtuous personages, symbolising inner refinement poise, heroism and moral excellence. This include heroes of a play and noble characters, Indra, Krishna, Rama, Lakshmana, Bharata, Satrugnan, Harischandra and Nala.

The front part of their faces is given smooth deep green base on which *chuttis* (white rice-paste curves) run from the centre of the chin,covering the lower jaw, to either side of the face. The eyes and the eye-lashes are painted black and the lips bright red. It assumes the shape of a broad-blade saber or of a sweeping curve of a bow. The forehead, above the bow-tie shaped painted portion, is covered by a red ribbon of the gilded head gear. Kattias compared to *paccha*, the makeup of *Katti* role-types is complicated.

This term literally means the knife, because in its makeup the shapes of colour positions resemble sharply bent daggers. Evil, demoniac and fierce characters standing against the hero of a play. *Pratinayakaas* such as *Asuras* (the enemies of the God's) ambitious and arrogant *Ravana*, *Keechaka*, *Kamsa* and *Dussaasana* are distinctively treated with this makeup. Their faces are given a foundation with green colour, the sides of their noses are painted in red.

The red paint round the nose rises up to the forehead above the eye-brows. It is like a patch, an upturned moustache, covering the upper jaw. Its border lines are treated in white. On the green base of the rest of the face, a *chutti* runs along the jaw-bones from the middle of the cheek. Two white knobs, called *chuttippuvus*, are placed on the face. These vary in size with the degree of the fearsome appearance of some demoniac characters like *Ravana* and *Dussaasana*, two long protruding canine teeth(called *dhamshtras*)are perched on either side of the mouth. These drop over the lower lips. *Katti* makeup characters stand in a singular position. taadi (Beard)Those who have the *taadi* makeup are again, good godly and evil-demoniac.

To differentiate one from the other, three taadi make-ups are in vogue: *Veluppu taadi* (white beard), *Chuvanna taadi* (red beard) and *Karuppu taadi* (black beard) In these make-ups white chutti is not planted on the face. Veluppu taadiIt consists of a white beard and a fur coat. It is a realistic makeup for characters like *Hanumaan*, the son of God *Vaayu*, and other monkey sages and warriors. The upper half of the face-the neither part of the eyes-and lips are treated with a black ointment. The chin at the middle is decorated with a white rosette, bearing a red dot within. Red paint is applied to the lower part of the lower lip, up to the chin. A thin coating of *chutti* decoratively encloses the black-end part of the face and meets the *chuttinata*-the hem of the head dress.

Another white pattern develops on either side of the cheeks and circling the red spots, starting from the base of the green painted nose. On the tip of the nose and the forehead two oval-shaped spots are given in red. Chuvanna taadi is given to hideous characters. The face is painted red, with black contour lines drawn round the eyes, lips and chin. This adds to the ferocity of less evil characters like *Baali*, *Sugriiva*, *Kaalakeya* and *Dussaasana*. The eye-brows and lashes are not elongated, no *chutti* is applied to the *Chuvanna taadi*.

The face is dubbed in red and treated with black lines. Around the eyes, almost a square patch of deep black colour is provided to give to the eyes a fiendish look of a evil designer. Lips painted in black, are given a hilly curve to give the role type a lucid image of a beastly character. Running from the upper lip are two white paste bristled rows throwing the black patch round the eyes in bold relief and adding ferocity to the fiery red eyes, and demarcating the black portion from the remaining nether part of the face is red. *Chuttippuvus* (white blobs) on the tip of the nose and the fore-head are bigger in size than those put on by *kathi* characters. It is the most impressive of all make-ups in *Kathakali*. Karuppu taadi the third type of bearded characters makeup is with a black beard and coat. These characters include *Kali*, *Kaattaalan* (hunter), brigands and robber chieftains. In their makeup, the face is first coated with black unguent.

The eyes are bracketed within oval-shaped white border lines, the area between two such lines being painted in red. Small white bristles adorn the ridges. Lips are in red. The tip of the nose bears a *chuttippuuvu*. Kari reveals the vile and evil characters, such as *Suurpanakha* and *Simhika*. Their faces are painted in black and the cheeks have a red crescent in the middle. A pair of *damshtraas* are provided. Shiva in the role of *Kiraata* (hunter) is also given this type of the makeup. A remarkable feature of the *Kathakali* makeup is the reddening of the white of the eyes of all characters by putting in a few young seeds of *chunda puuv* (sollanum pubescence) crimson eyes stand in contrast to the colour scheme of the face. The practice is usually followed in *pacha* and *minukku* faces. Makeup in the 'Green room'*Kathakali* makeup is an elaborate process lasting for over three hours.

It helps in giving a super human look to the actors. Whether it is a man's makeup or the woman's, the work is conducted by a makeup expert. Paints used in Kathakali makeup are freshly prepared and applied to ensure correctness of rhythmic curves and precision. The makeup of the male characters other than saints is tedious. The role-type lies flat on a matted floor and the expert starts drawing 'the designs' on the face with a thin rod. The face part being complete, the role type gives the finishing touches himself. Thereafter he stands up for putting on the costume. The skirt is a well starched and pressed into-frills garments. But before the skirt is put on, the actor ties 20 to 40 pieces of short cloth round his waist by the help of a long cloth twisted rope in order to give the skirt an oval shape. He then puts on the jacket, etc.

The finishing touches to the costume are given by the costume attendant. The actor is profusely ornamented with garlands of beads, armlets, cupped mirrors, etc. Fully decorated, the actor gives the last minute touches to his makeup with the help of the cupped mirror. His head-dresses are huge and often unwidely. These are tied by an attendant. The last part of the costuming is the tying up of the anklet bells. Women fancy to have the silver paijaebs (an ornament) and then tie the bells. In the case of male characters a decorative woolen is tied immediately above the anklet and the bells fixed on a leather pad or tied right below the knee. *Kathakali* makeup traditions today widely differs from what it was in the seventeenth century. An intensive dance training is needed to make the body flexible and supple in order to respond to unusual forms weaved in the course of dancing. To achieve fluidity, a *Kathakali* pupil undergoes extensive and vigorous training from an early age.

A complete alteration in the behaviour of the body is effected. Massages and oil-baths are an essential aid to awaken muscles, joints and nerves and to control their behaviour. Between the age of 11 and 14 years the pupil goes to an *Aasaan*, the teacher of a *Kalari* (a kind of gymnasium) and offers to him *daanam* (a present) either in cash or in kind clothes and with his *guru-diksha* (benediction) he enrolls himself for training. *Kathakali* performances are not confined to a temple's courtyard; they are held in the open under the sky. Before a performance begins, *chendakkaaran* the instrumental musician, beats the drum to announce the news that a dance-drama will be held shortly. This nervous and insistent tattoo' is called *Ke'likottu*. The village folk-men, women and children begin to assemble and crouches on the land in a circle around *chendakkaaran*.

The night's 'stadium' has the covering of a clear, star-studded sky; cool breeze rustling through the jagged patterns of palm fronds, children wandering back and forth aimlessly or running to a hawker or pestering their mothers or aping a character of a previous play; people discussing a role-type, an actor, a character, a story or a matter of current or religious interest.

And those among the audience who are tired from the day's hard work on their fields go back and sleep until they are awakened by a relative or a friend or by the noise from the stage, to witness the favorite hero play or a climatic battle scene. In its indigenous form, Kathakali has no stage in the modern sense. The centre of the stadium is the stage provided with a huge brightly polished brass lamp of coconut oil. The audience sits in darkness.There are no back-curtains, no stills, no sceneries. But behind the lamp there is a simply designed 'tirasila', a rectangular silk curtain, held by two members of the troupe.

Actors who have to appear first stand hidden behind it. During scenes the curtain is dropped to the ground and removed by the two men. The job over, these men go about on other errands of the stage, like pouring oil in the lamp-well, adjusting the thick wicks which constantly threaten to gutter and burn out, arranging the banana tree trunk support against the wicks gliding down in the well, and assisting the actors on odd jobs. The stage is also provided with a small stool. This is used for many purposes. For instance, in the 'curtain look' the actor stands on it; on other occasions an actor may rest on it. Musicians stand in a half circle behind the actors. They number four to twelve. Musicians do not wear any special costume.

They are normally bare-chested. The actors are profusely dressed mostly in billowing skirts, crowned with massive head-dresses and provided with the accessories of the face and finger nails. The 'actresses' are adolescent boys, for they are nearest to femininity and have simple dress. In the repertoric of its technique Kathakali has seven items to be presented in the following sequence: 1. *Todayam*-the basic nritt; 2. *Purappaadu*-debut of the hero and the virtuous character; 3. *Tirano'kku*-'curtain look' by evil characters and demons; 4. *Kummi*-permeable for the female character's appearance; 5. *Kathakali*-the main play; 6. *Kalaasham*-a passage of vigorous dance which serves as a hyphen between two pieces of verse-play; and 7. The concluding benediction dance The dance drama begins with the call of the drum which has rent the air at night.

The audience is alerted. *Tirasiila* is drawn by two men. Music begins. Drummers display their cleverness. Religious songs are sung. They purify the atmosphere. And dancers are behind the curtain. The preliminary dance behind the curtain is commonly refused to as *Purva-ranga* by *Bharata* in the *Natya Shastra*, in the language of *Kathakali* it is called *Todayam*. The basic technique of *Kathakali* lies in *Todayam*. *Purappaadu* or the debut, signifies the first appearance of a character on the stage. It is a piece of a preliminary dance. It serves to announce the virtuous qualities of the hero. If a demon is to appear violent drumming of high pitch drums is incessant. The curtain is drawn as high as the arms of the attendants can stretch.

The whole atmosphere is surcharged with earth-shaking and hair raising activities. The sound of quick and heavy foot steps can be heard from behind the curtain. Its synchronisation with the sound effect of the drums heightens the climax. The entire climate forebodes that a terrific personality is about to appear. Suddenly a coloured canopy appears over the curtain and a rumbling growling noise is heard. Drums burst into shattering sounds. Here is a shrick, and there a groan. But before the eyes can catch the character, fingers are seen rising in the centre of the curtain. The left hand fingers are covered with long thimbles.

The two hands are kept about three feet apart. They clutch the curtain. Fingers glide across its top. There is deafening drumming; but no singing.To the accompaniment of the drums, the anti-hero shakes the curtain violently, and breathless the audience catches an occasional glimpse of the top of a glittering head-dress, which seems to be gyrating madly in some internal whirlwind. He pulls the curtain towards him; then plugs forward and fans flames. With gusto, the fire illuminates the character's face and enables the audience to spot him out by his weird makeup. The feverish pitch of excitement over, the curtain is dropped and the whole figure of the character emerges after a great deal of suspense. The curtain is pulled off the stage from its right wing.

Thus develop *tiranokku* or 'curtain look'. For male anti-heroes *Tiranokku* is prescribed and for female characters there is another standard dance called *Kummi*. In it gestures and movements are modified and smoothened to lend gentleness and elegance. so much necessary for feminine characters. Paces are slow; roles are passive and subsidiary. *Kalaasams* are pure dance passages performed in pure *taandava* style. They punctuate two verses; two scenes. It is here that in *Kathakali* an important role of *nritt*a is discovered. From the sequence detailed *Kathakali*'s basic characteristic of a dance-cum-drama is unfolded. How the various limbs of *sangiitha* have been synthesised to bring about an underlying unity of all Indian dramatic arts in *Kathakali* is unique. It is the only form of the histrionic arts in India, which adumbrates in principle, the three essentials of the Sanskrit drama, *naatya*, *nritya* and *nritt*.

Aivarnaatakam *Aivarnaatakam* is one among the popular rural dramas of Kerala. It is also known as *Aivarkali* and *Pandavar kali*, which means the play of the *Pandavaas*-the five heroes of *Mahabhaaratha*-and is performed by the *Viswakarmas* which enfolds five communities consisting of *Aasaari* (Carpenter), *Muusaari* (Brassmith), *Kollan* (Blacksmith), *Tattaan* (Goldsmith) and *Kalthachan* (Mason). This ritualistic art form is performed in almost all important temples of Kerala. Today it is found in central Kerala. In Trichur District *Vilkurupas* also enacted this art form. It is performed on a tara or a raised platform in a beautifully decorated pandal with a five-wicked *Nilavilakku* (bell-metal lamp) at its centre. The *Nilavilakku* is crowned with multi coloured flowers. *Kulaavazha* or plantain trees with full bunch of ripe plantains are erected on both sides of the Tara.

In some villages, they have permanent platforms for the performance of Aivarnaatakam. Permanent platforms are found in the villages such as Adattu, Olarikkara, Pallippuram, etc. near Bhagavathi temples. The performers describe to the audience the details of the stage and other decorations in their songs.

The performers numbering five or more with their leader called *Kaliaasaan* enter the performance area after ritualistic bath, with sandal paste on their foreheads, chests and upper arms. They are dressed in white dhoti and have a towel wrapped around their heads. The dancers gather around the lamp carrying small sticks with small bells attached at one end called *Ponthi* and offer their prayer to their deities.

After *Ganapati Pooja*, they bow to their leader and the *Nilavilakku* and start the dance by singing devotional songs. Aivarnaatakam is divided into three parts namely *Vattakkali*, *Parichamuttukali* and *Kolkali*. *Vattakkali* means the dancing in a circular form round the *Nilavilakku*. *Parichamuttukali* is the second part of *Aivarnaatakam*, where sword and shield are used.

The dance gradually grows vigorous and powerful and is accompanied by varied songs sung by all the dancers led by their leader. Besides *Ponthi*, only *elathaalam* is used for musical accompaniment with the singing, the dancing rises to a crescendo of rhythmic fervour and the dancers swish around, feet in step and the sticks striking perfect time. It is the third item of Aivarnaatakam. After this performance the group leader switches on to its prose version called kavitham which gives elucidation of the song sung. *Kavitham*, one of the highlights of *Aivarnaatakam* is a rhythmic prose rendering of the play.

The *Aasaan* ask questions to the audience to test their knowledge in the epics and he himself gives answers to the questions. *Aasaan* gives the synopsis of this story to the audience. *Aivarnaatakam* is performed during the night. Even three whole nights may not be sometimes enough to complete a story. The contestants have the freedom of choosing their actors for performance.

At the conclusion of the performance, the people conduct pooja. Both the actors and spectators like fruits as a token of the blessings given by Saraswathy, the Goddess of wisdom. This ritualistic dance is reminiscent of an ancient legend connected with *Mahabhaaratha*. On hearing that one of her devotees, *Karna*, had been killed by the *Pandavaas* in battle. *Bhadrakaali* is determined to annihilate them.

Lord Krishna who is a friend of the *Pandavaas*, comes to know this and he directs them to sing praises of the goddess and to propitiate her, The legend has it that Lord Krishna transformed himself into a lamp and prompted his friends to sing and dance in praise of the Devi.

The Devi finally becomes pleased and blesses them. *Aivarnaatakam* was an effective mass media for transmitting morally oriented stories of epics in the villages of Kerala, particularly to the artisan class and the Harijan community. 1. Chummar Choondal, Aivar Natakam, NBS, Kottayam, 1976.2. Festivals of Kerala, Tourist Dusk, Cochin, 1993.

Chaakyaar koothu *Chaakyaar koothu* is one of the plays performed in temples. This is enacted in the special dance hall called *Koothambalam*, connected to the temples. It is performed by people belonging to the *Chaakyaar* community. The word *koothu* is derived from the Sanskrit term, *Koordanam* which means 'dance'. The *Chaakyaar* community is a group which earns its livelihood by performing *Chaakyaar koothu* and *Koodiyaattam*. There are many versions regarding the origin of the term *Chaakyaar*, The *Chaakyaars* are believed to be people who have been ostracized from the Namboodiri Brahman Community. The women of the community are called *Illottamma*.

The *Chaakyaar koothu* consists of two parts of which one is action and the other narration. In the earlier days, the action part of it was known as *koothu*. There are different types of *koothu*, known by different names like *Mantraangam koothu*, *Anguliiyaangam koothu*, *Parakkum koothu*, *Matta Vilaasam koothu*, etc. When more than one actor performs on the stage, it is called *Koodiyaattam*. If the actors are not more than one, it is called *Chaakyaar koothu*. *Chaakyaar koothu*, is the narrration of Puranic stories by the *Chaakyaars* who wear the attire of a joker and tell the story humourously. Nobody knows how ancient this art form is. It is however clear from *Chilappatikaaram* that even during the reign of *Chenkuttava Perumaal*, *Chaakyaar koothu* was performed. The *Koothambalam* constructed for the perfomance are edifices built according to Bharata Muni's *Natyasaastra*.

It mentions three types of theatres which are rectangular, quadrangular and triangular. The *Koothambalam* of Kerala has a green room inside at one end. Just in front of the green room is the stage. The remaining portion is left for the audience to sit. The musical instruments used for *Chaakyaar koothu* are *Mizhaavu*, *Kuzhittaalam*, *Itaykka* and *Sankhu*. Of this *Mizhaavu* is the most important. It is said that *Mizhaavu* can be made from copper, bell-metal, or granite. Nowadays only *Mizhaavu* made of copper can be seen. *Mizhaavu* is a huge pot upto one's waist. Its mouth is tied firmly with animal skin. The sound of the *Mizhaavu* is more majestic as its size increases. The *Chaakyaar* adorns his face with the usual caste mark on the forehead (*pottu*), In addition soot and turmeric too are smeared on the face. There is a huge earring called *Kundalam* on one ear.

On the other ear, he wears betel leaves and geranium flowers as earrings. A pleated costume is worn. He wears girdle and bangles. The head is tied with a red cloth. *koothu* is a combination of dance and humour. As soon as the *Chaakyaar* comes to the stage and offers his salutations, a dance known as *Chaari*, starts. This dance is an offering. Hence there should be no mistakes in it. Later, prose and verse are recited and meanings given. Initially, *Chaakyaar koothu* was only storytelling. Each word is pronounced very slowly and in a special tune which is called Bharu Method. This special kind of pronunciation is found only in the speech of the *Chaakyaars* on stage. This special sound and clarity of speech are efficient to attract the attention of the distracted among the audience. It is audible, and the meaning can be grasped by the hearer. In the Sanskrit Dramas enacted in Malayalam, not only Sanskrit and its Prakrit are used but also Malayalam and its Prakrit.

In plays where there is the clown (*Viduushaka*) the *Viduushaka* speaks in Malayalam. He first pronounces the Prakrit sounds, which he is supposed to utter, and later speaks similarly in Sanskrit and again explains it in Malayalam. One can hear old Malayalam forms from the *Viduushaka*. The actor enlivens his narration with *Thaandava* dance, gestures and bodily postures derived from *Natya Shastra*. Combined with mime and gestures and interspersed with occasional dances, the narrative is made dramatic. The actor never misses an oppurtunity to make humourous and witty statements about political and social situations. He has the license to ridicule the audience according to his own imagination or discretion. Nobody could object or protest.Criticisms of contemporary events or personalities also figure in the narration. References 1. Narayana Pisharoti. P. *Kalaalo'kam*, Kerala Sahitya Academy Trichur 1989. 2. Vishnu Namboodiri M.V. Folklore *Nighantu*. State Institute of Languages, Trivandrum;2000. 3. Festivals of Kerala Tourist Desk, Cochin 1993.

*Kaakkaarissi Naatakam Kaakkaarissi Naatakam* is a popular entertainment among the backward communities of Kerala. This art can still be seen in its original flavour and style in the village of Nedumangadu in Trivandrum district. In the southcentral region of Kerala, it is found in Kurumpala, Karakkat, Karunagapally, Panthalam, Cheruvally, Ambalapuzha, Mankombu, etc. Here it is presented by the *Paanar* and *Kummaalar* communities. In Kilimanoor and Nedumangadu it is presented by *Kurava* and *Ezhavas*. Though there is a community called *Kaakkaalas*, they never take part in the performance or presentation of the play. Begging is considered as their legitimate profession with palmistry and lizardology – predictiing the future by interpreting a lizard's movements and sounds. This art form is spread all over the state, but they differ in certain respects from place to place. The main object of *Kaakkaarissi Naatakam* is to make the public aware of the poverty, misery and suffering of the communities. Legends about *Kaakkaalas* There are many legends about the origin of the *Kaakkaala* tribe.

One of them traces their beginnings to *Garuda*, the king of birds and the divine vehicle of *Vishnu*. Once *Garuda*, furious with mankind, gobbled up the entire human race, including all Brahmans. But later when his mother, *Vinata*, explained to him the sin involved in killing and eating up the Brahmans, he was filled with remorse. As a penance, he regurgitated what he had swallowed and threw up the Brahmans. Thus they were brought back to life. These Brahmans were called *Kaakkaalas*, from *Kaakkuka* – to regurgitate – in Malayalam. Another legend links this nomadic tribe with *Shiva* and *Paarvathy* – the parents of the world – who came on earth in order to redress the complaints of the suffering among the human race. They manifest as *Kaakkaalan* and *Kaakkaalathy*, the male and female respectively of the *Kaakkaakan* community.

The present–day *Kaakkaalas* are believed to be their descendants. The northern variation of *Kaakkaarissi Naatakam* is called *Paanarkali*, became it is performed by members of the *Paanar* community. Performance of *Kaakkaarissi Naatakam*. According to tradition the performer starts with the chief character named *Sundarak Kaakkaan* entering the arena and exchanging conversation with the audience. He invites the female players named *Kaakkaathimaar*, and when they enter, the play begins. Besides there characters, *Vedan*, *Thampuraan*, *Kuravan*, *Kurathy*, wild tiger, etc, also figure in the enactment.

Usually, the play takes place on a raised platform. The performance starts with *Naarada*, the celestial sage, informing *Shiva* and *Paarvathy* about the suffering humanity on earth. The *Kaakkaathimaar*, female characters, dance and invoke the presence of *Kaakaan*, the male character. He emerges from the crowd carrying a naked torch and enters the area with vigorous, rhythmic steps. He is accompanied by *Thampuraan*, representing an upper caste man, who shoots a volley of questions at the *Kaakkaan* who,through his crisp replies, tells the story and, at the same time, sarcastically comments on the arrogance of the higher castes.

The *Kaakkaan*, who is wholly absorbed in the rhythm of his steps, is interrupted by the *Thampuraan* who reminds him that he should first offer praises to Lord *Ganapati*. After the eulogy in accordance with the *Thampuraan*'s request, the *Kaakkaan* invites the two *Kaakkaattis* to the stage. The women quarrel and the *Kaakkaan* is totally lost. Through the dire helplessness of the *Kaakkaan*, the pitiable plight of a husband with two wives is humorously portrayed. In the second act, the *Kaakkaan* makes his reappearance as the *Sundara Kaakkaan*, a snake charmer. He goes snake – hunting into the deep jungle, blowing on and swaying his pipe to the rhythm of the snake's movements. Unfortunately the snake bites him, and he falls down unconscious. Meanwhile, the *Kaakkaattis* anxiously await the return of their *Kaakkaan*. Alarmed at the delay, they go searching for him with *Alakësan*, their brother. After they have travelled many a weary day through the thick woods, they find him at last, lying unconscious, and the *Kaakkaan* is saved.

The mastery of the staging lies in the fact that without any sets, the jungle, the Kaakkaan's abode, and the search are all conjured up through the performer's words and movements. The most important element in the next scene is the appearance of a *velichapaadu*, an oracle, and his prophetic pronouncements under divine dispensation. A band of professional thieves pray to their tutelary goddess before setting out on one of their nocturnal exploits. The spirit of the goddess enters the body of one of the thieves and thus he becomes a *velichapaadu*.

In that movement of divine enlightenment, he knows the truth about all the thefts that may have taken place in the near part. He reveals these secrets to the other thieves in the course of his inspired utterances. The aim of this episode in to warn the public of the doings of professional thieves haunting the area. During earlier days, these plays were enacted in the centre of a large level ground lighted with petromax lamps.

In many scenes, the actors went into the midst of the spectators thus giving them a feel and thrill of actual participation. Costumes are rustic, with the females wearing colourful clothes and the *Kaakkaan* in simple black. *Vedan* and *Kuravan* smear charcoal over their bodies. In the southern region, the *Kaakkaan* is painted jetblack and designs in white dots are executed on the surface. Turmeric and rice powder are also employed for makeup. Harmonium, *ganjira*, *elathaalam and mrudangam* are the musical instruments used. Stage props are not used in the performing stage.

There is no regular script for the performance of *Kaakkaarissi Naatakam*. Though essentially a ritual entertainment, its performance is not limited to rustic audiences. Puranic stories form the main themes of this drama but in presenting these stories, current problems are skillfully incorporated into the narration. Till 30 years ago, *Kaakkaarissi Naatakam* enjoyed considerable popularity. Then followed a period of gradual degeneration. Of late however the art form is being revived and is slowly regaining its place in the rural society.

## Kuchipudi

*Kuchipudi* is a classical dance form from Andhra Pradesh, a state of South India. Kuchipudi is the name of a small village in the Divi Taluq of Krishna district that borders the Bay of Bengal and with resident Brahmans practising this traditional dance form, it acquired the present name.

With the dance form attaining perfection by the time of Golconda king Abdul Hassan Tanesha, Kuchipudi Brahmans are said to have received 600 acres (2.4 $km^2$) of land as an endowment from Tanesha for the great presentation before him.

Siddhendra Yogi is said to be the first scholar to give it the current form of dance drama. *Bhamakalapam* is one of his celebrated compositions. He also reserved the art to males by teaching it to young Brahman boys of the village. However, in modern times, the art has been dominated by women.

The performance usually begins with some stage rites, after which each of the character comes on to the stage and introduces him/herself with a daru (a small composition of both song and dance) to introduce the identity, set the mood, of the character in the drama. The drama then begins. The dance is accompanied by song which is typically Karnatic music. The singer is accompanied by mridangam (a classical South Indian percussion instrument), violin, flute and the tambura (a drone instrument with strings which are plucked). Ornaments worn by the artists are generally made of a light weight wood called *Boorugu*.

Some of the well-known people in this tradition are Dr. Vempati Chinna Satyam, Vedantam Lakshminarayana, Tadepalli Perayya, Chinta Krishna Murthy, Padma Sri Vedantam Sathya Narayana Sarma, Pasumarthi Venu Gopala Krishna Sarma, Raja Reddy and Radha Reddy, Mrinalini Sadananda, Nilimma Devi, Anuradha Nehru and "Hamsa Awardee" Sarala Kumari Ghanta.

The Kuchipudi Arts Academy, was established in Chennai by Dr. Vempati Chinna Satyam specifically for kuchipudi training. Many of Dr. Vempati Chinna Satyam's students became famous names themselves; Some of his illustrious disciples include Shobha Naidu and Manju Bhargavi.

There are now a number of Kuchipudi teachers, choreographers and dancers in North America; Most of them have trained under the master teacher Dr. Vempati Chinna Satyam. Some of the well known teachers in North America are Sasikala in Atlanta, Kamala Reddy in Pittsburg, Ratna Papa in Texas, Himabindu Challa in the San Francisco Bay Area and Sandhya Atmakuri in Detroit.

The name Kuchipudi denotes both the dance style that has come to prominence since the 50s and the tiny, remote village where it was born. Kuchipudi, little known outside a few villages skirting it, has no come to occupy a very significant place on the dance map of India, though it has yet to acquire the prestige and acceptability it fully deserves. Situated in the Krishna district of Andhra Pradesh, it is 32 miles from Vijayawada.

Its particular location proved very fortunate for its people and its art. Kuchipudi has a great history. Six miles away from it lies Srikakulam, the ancient capital of the Satavahana Empire (2nd century BC). The rulers of the Satavahana dynasty were great patrons of art. From the inscriptions found here, on the temples of Andhra Vishnu, which was the most sacred shrine of those days, it is evident that no fewer than 300 devadasis consecrated to the deity, received royal patronage. The sculptures excavated in this area have crystallised into stone the effulgent grace of those women whose dance was an act of worship.

As any other art form, dance also enjoyed the patronage of rulers prior to the advent of Kuchipudi style in its present accent, because of the prevalence of the devadasi system. In course of time, unfortunately devadasis became the victims feudal abuse. In later years, Buddhism flourished at two particularly prominent centres. Nagarjuna, the great exponent of Mahayana school, liver near Kuchipudi during his early years. Ghantasala, another place five miles away, was a great Buddhist pilgrim centre from the 2nd century AD to the 14th century. It was prosperous port too; tempting traders from far away countries till the Krishna River changed her course.

Movva, the birthplace of Kshetrajana, the great composer of devotional Padams, is about two miles away from Kuchipudi. From all this can be surmised that the location of the Kuchipudi village has been, over a long period spanning twenty centuries, historically as well as culturally most important with a halo around it. The whole vicinity of Kuchipudi was filled with flavours of art.

As empires rose and fell in the Andhra territory, religions also shared their fate. The Satavahana Empire declined and with it the Vedic religion that the rulers practised received a setback. Buddhism rose to greater importance and held way till about the 4th century AD. That is till it was replaced by Jainism under the Easter Chalukyas. In order to propagate their religion, these Jain rulers exploited all the available dance forms patronising liberally both the classical and Margi style of devadasis-some of the whom by then had degenerated into Rajanartakis or court-dancer and folk or Desi style rooted in the soil.

The Chalukyas gave away to the Kakatiyas of Waranagal by about the 12th century. Originally Jains, the Kakaitya rulers took to the Pasupata Virasaiv cult under the influence of Basava. In 1230 AD a powerful ruler of the Kakatiyas, Kakati Ganapati Deva, invaded divi and subjugate the ruler, Jayappa of the Ayya dynasty and later appointed him commander of his own elephant corps. An ardent lover of dance in all its many slandered forms, Jayappa wrote and excellent treaties on the subject, entitled Nritta Ratnavali.

The Kakatiya rulers, being followers of the Virsaiva cult, used the local dance forms to spread their own religion. Palkuriki Somanatha an eminent poet of the Kakatiya court listed all these dance forms in his book, Pandittaradhyacharitra, in Telugu. The Muslim ruler Mohammed bin Tughlak, invaded Warangal and humbled the Kakatiyas. In course of time, Viranarasimha III, ruler of neighbouring kingdom of Kalinga, annexed the region around Srikakulam and renovated the Andhra Vishnu temple. Being a devotee of Lord Vishnu and having renovated the temple of Lord Jagannatha at Puri, he decided to propagate vaishatvism in the Srikakulam region once again.

With the raise of Vaishnavism, the prevalent cult of Virasaivism declined. He was also great lover of art and patron of dance. Anand Tirtha, the great devotee of Lord Kirshna preached his Vaishnava cult through out his region, even persuading two ministers of kalinga court, Sobhana Bhatta and Syama Sadtry, to become his disciples. They came to be known as Padmanabha Tirtha and Narahari Tirhta respectively. Narayana Tirtha became regent after the demise of the Kalinga ruler, Bhanu deva, in 1227 AD. In this capacity, he visited Srikakulam, which was then part of Kalinga Empire. He stayed there for 11 years propagating the Krishna cult. Jayadeva's Getthagovindam enriched the local devadasis and Rajannartakis.

One of the disciples of Narahari Bhatta, Gopalakrishna Saraswathi, lived in this region. He composed many songs on the Leela of Lord Krishna as did Lilasuka, composer of Sri Krishna Karnamrita. At this time about the 14th century AD, the worship of Krishna held complete away from the minds of local people and the dancer reelected this feeling of total devotion to the Blue God. Into this prevailing atmosphere of Krishna-Intoxication was born a boy name Siddhappa. He was an orphan.

But the villagers knew him to be a Brahman. A kind landlord performed his Upanayam (sacred thread ceremony). Later Siddhappa married but hardly remembered his infant Instead of her young handsome bridegroom, she saw an ascetic, dressed in the ochre robes of hermit. Siddhappa now remembered his promise and rose above all temptations of sensuality. Now before his eyes, appeared Lord Krishna and Sathyabhama. From that movement on, he saw in all women, including his wife, the image of Sathyabhama who lover her Lord passionately and possessively claiming him exclusively for herself and refusing him to share him even with his Pattamahisihi Rukmini. "Satya" in the "Truth" for the realisation of whichever seer and saint had been meditation, from time immemorial.

Thus Siddhappa, released from his family ties, came to be known as Siddhappa or Siddhendra Yogi. He began to propagate the Bhama cult, also known as Madhura Bhakti, like Satyabhama, every devotee imagines Lord Krishna to be the Supreme Lover, the Lokabharata, and himself to be cast in the image of Satyabhama, longing to unite with Sri Krishna and keep him entirely to herself. Song after song poured out of the heart, at the separation from her divine lover, into these inspired works.

The songs compiled together became the vehicle of a dance drama of unsurpassed beauty and came to be called Bhamakalapam. The Bhamakalapam songs were so enchanting and so full of rich imager that the temple dancers and court dancers residing at Srikakulam and Ghantasala were eager to learn them and dance to their tunes and lines. But Siddhendra Yogi feared that, since the theme centred to the romantic love between Sri krishna and Satyabhama and since the dancers already excelled in the art of portraying the Sringara rasa or romantic love, they may exaggerate the sentiments and destroy its lofty spiritual ethos. Naturally he decided to initiate only young and good-looking Brahman boys into the art.

He taught them the Bhamakalapam Song. He overcame the objections of their families to this unprecedented step by assuring them of salvation—an assurance that was further strengthened by a letter from the head of the math of Udipi offering them his patronage. He made these few families take a vow that at least one male child born into each one of them would devote the entire life time to singing and dancing the glory of the lord. Bell tied around the waist of the new-born boy symbolises this vow.

- Asthana Vidwan by Sri Venkateswara Temple (Pittsburgh)
- T.T.K.Memorial Award by the Madras Music Academy
- Kalidas Puraskar by Government of Madhya Pradesh
- Kalai mamani by Govt. of Tamil Nadu.
- The Mayor of Miami presented the Golden Key award to him in 1984
- The Mayor of Dayton, Ohio declared September 25,1994 as Vempati Chinna Satyam Day
- The Mayor of Ghana, Ohio declared April 27,1984 as classical Indian Kuchipudi Ballet dance Drama and The Mayor of Atlanta declared 3rd November 1994 as Kuchipudi Dance Drama Day.
- The Mayor of Cleveland conferred honorary citizenship on Dr. Vempati.
- The Mayor of Memphis declared September 24, 1994 as 'Ramayana Day' and the Key to the city was awarded to him.
- Gold medal was presented to him by the President of Tunisia at the Cartage Festival. Citations and Honours conferred at the Avignon Festival, France in 1995.

***Invocation***

A dance in praise of Rabindranath Tagore's Chandalika, Kuchipudi art, and the members of the orchestra Chandalika awakens early in the morning and tends to her chores. She hears the call of flower sellers in the market and goes in search of them. When Chandalika approaches them, high cast women intervene and forbid the flower sellers to sell to her, an Untouchable girl, Similarly, Chandalika is shunned while trying to buy milk from the milkmaids and bangles from the bangle sellers. Chandalika is at first bewildered and hurt, Then becomes filled with fury and rages at the injustice and oppression committed by society. Hurt and angered by this encounters, Chandalika becomes depressed.

Her mother, Maya, Finds her daughter's listlessness difficult to understand. She scolds Chandalika, urging her to tend to her daily chores and work. Chandalika expresses her frustration to her mother, asking why she had ever been born an untouchable, blaming god and her mother for her plight. "Why was I born in to this life of isolation?" She asks. Unable to understand her daughter, Maya leaves, perplexed. A weary Buddhist monk, Ananda, enters and sks Chandalika for some water to quench his thirst. Legend has it that the monk was Ananda, The principal disciple of the great Buddha himself, the Enlightened One. Chandalika refuses initially to serve Ananda, saying her low Chandala Caste forbids her from serving someone as fortunate and blessed as he.

To her surprise, he rejects this explanation, saying that all human beings are created equal in the eyes of the God. He calmly asks her to judge herself by her own standards rather than the artificial standards of an unjust society. These were revolutionary wards to Chandalika, yet they articulated the same feelings churning within her heart. Entranced by these words, she serves him water from the well. Ananda proceeds on his journey, and Chandalika is at first unwilling to accept that her encounter with the monk was real. Seeing the water bucket placed in a different location, near where thought she had seen the monk, convinces her that the conversation with Ananda had been real. Chandalika filled with a sense of renewed life, freedom, and joy, dances in ecstasy. The encounter with Ananda has transformed Chandalika. She is brimming with gratitude and love for him. He has become her world, her only focus, and her reason for living.

## Manipuri

Manipuri one of the six classical dance styles of India, the others being *Bharata Natyam, Kathak, Kathakali, Kuchipudi,* and *Orissi*. It is indigenous to Manipur, the northeastern state of India and the indigenous people of this valley were said to be the dance-expert *Gandharva's*, mentioned in the epic Ramayana, Mahabharata and other religious scriptures.

Manipuri dance is purely religious and its aim is a spiritual experience. Development of music and dance has through religious festivals and daily activities of the Manipuri people. Not only is dance a medium of worship and enjoyment, a door to the divine, but indispensable for all socio-cultural ceremonies. From the religious point of view and from the artistic angle of vision, Manipuri Classical Form of dance is claimed to be one on the most chestiest, modest, softest and mildest but the most meaningful dances of the world. The most obliging aspect of Manipuri culture is that, it has retained the ancient ritual based dances and folk dances along with the later developed classical Manipuri dance style. Among the classical categories, '*Ras Leela*'—a highly evolved dance drama, choreographed on '*Vaishnavite Padavalis*' composed by mainly eminent Bengali poets and some Manipuri Gurus, is the highest expression of artistic genius, devotion and excellence of the Manipuris.

### *History of Manipuri Dance Forms*

It is stated that the indigenous people of the valley were the Gandharva's mentions in the *Ramayana* and Mahabharata. The dance patterns in Manipur must have a link with the Gandharva's Culture—which is mythological believed to excel over all other dance forms.

### *The Gandharva Culture of Mahabharata*

Manipuri dance—as the name suggests, originated in Manipur, the northeastern state of India—a paradise on earth when the nature has been extra-generous in her beauty. Love of art and beauty is inherent in the people of this land from time immemorial. The people of Manipur are well-known for their high cultural sense. They are very religious minded exclusively attached to Sri Krishna and Sri Radhika, who are always in their thought. And it is difficult to find Manipuri girl who cannot sing or dance. Not only girls but boys too excel in art and culture. Dancing as a profession for few classes of people is unknown to the simple people. Every Manipuri can dance without additional effort and considerable time. A young Boy plays the rule of Krishna in the Ras Lila. This child seemed to be too young to dance. Surprisingly most of the dancers do not have a formal training.

It is stated that the indigenous people of this valley were the dance-expert Gandharva's, mentioned in the epic Ramayana and Mahabharata. The Aswamedha Parva of Mahabharata refer to the defeat of Pandava's at Manipur and the identification of Babhrubahana, the son of Arjuna and Chitrangoda, the soul daughter of the Gandharva king Chitrabahana. Babhrubahana, the legendary King of Manipur played a vital role in the formation of the existing professional caste and races of Manipur. The dance patterns in Manipur must have a link with the Gandharva's Culture—which is mythological believed to excel over all other dance forms. Among the classical categories, 'Ras Leela'—a highly evolved dance drama, choreographed on Vaishnava Padavali's, is the highest expression of artistic genius, devotion and excellence of the Manipuris.

### *Manipuri Dance is Categorically Vedic-Aryan in Character*

The history of Manipur says that different clans of the Indo-Vedic and Mongoloid people lived side by side in Manipur for centuries. Now it assembled in her the major folks of the east and the west-the Meiteis and the Bishnupriya Manipuris. Orthodox Bishnupriya Manipuris consider themselves to be the genuine Vedic decent, who according to them, came to Manipur valley from Dvaraka and Hastinapura, just after the Mahabharata war, which happening before the 9th century B.C. as generally accepted by modern research. The Meitheis, on the other hand, differentiate themselves as mongoloid group of people. But some orthodox Meiteis believe that they are the descendants of group of people coming from Mithila (Videha) which is the eastern frontier of Aryan culture for a long time.

Referring to the people of Manipur E.T. Dalton in his book "Descriptive Ethnology of Bengal", states that, "..And, this hordes overrun a country (Manipur) that has been previously occupied by the people of Aryan blood known in the western India and to the Bards." Also while explaining the appearance of the Manipuris, Dr. R. Brown says "although the general facial characteristics of the Mannipuris are of Mongolian type, there is great diversity of features among them, some of them showing regularly approaching the aryan type" (Imperial Gazetteer of India, 1908, Vol 17, page 126).

So certainly there was a bulk of Vedic people from the north-west of India had entered into Manipur valley in the pre-Christian era. If we talk of the history in respect of the Aryan population, their migration, settlements and cultural penetration and the development of political institutions in Manipur Valley, there are a little source of information's about this. Ancient temples like the Vishnu temple of Bishnupur, Govindaji temple in Imphal, the Kohima stone, old palaces and other related buildings and structures provide us little more historical information's. G. E.Geraini, in his work, Researches on Ptolemy's Geography, indicated the establishment of an Indo-Vedic state by the Bishnupriya Manipuris in the remote period in Manipur. He states, "From the Brahmaputra and manipur to the tonkin gulf, we can trace a continuous string of petty states ruled by those scions of the ksatriyo race, using the sanskrit or pali language in official documents and iscriptions, buildings, temples and monuments of old Hindu style and employing Brahman priests at the propitiatory ceremonies connected with the court, and the state".

The Manipuri Dance and Music of international repute basically centre round Krishna Bhakti and is indeed a great contribution of the Gandharva's and the Vedic immigrants to Manipur as per expressions found in Ashoka's Pillar inscriptions.

### *Mongoloid Elements*

The other race in Manipur, the Meitheis, moved in from Chinese territory and this is reflected in the name. Meithei means, in Chinese, 'people of this country', *i.e.*, Chinese territory.

"It is quite probable that the kalachaias are the first cultural race in possession of the Manipur valley," wrote Rajmohan nath in' The Background of Assamese Culture'. R.M. Nath also held that-"The Meitheis were the later immigrants."

The Meitheis brought with them the experience and momentum of an ancient civilization. They probably had superiority in numbers and gradually they gained ascendancy. Manipuri folklore tells of an adventurer named Poireiton who came form' the land of death' and taught the locals many wonderful things. This mythical figure may have been an enterprising Meithei. It is also possible that Poireiton wasn't a single person. It may have been a common name for the early settlers.

It is evident by a number of sources that China supplied some earlier racial elements that attributed to the development of the Indo-Chinese culture in Assam. The Accounts of Shung Shu (420-479 AD) recorded the Chinese's subduation of manipur valley, and also establishment of their suzerainty over Kapily valley which is to be located in Modern Nowgaon. Referring to the Chinese or Mongolian racial elements in the Manipur valley, Arther Pelliot (Deux Itineraries) stated that the Chinese invaded the valley in about 700 AD.

The Chinese called the people of the valley as Khalachas, *i.e.* the son of the wide lake (Loktak) and described them as highly civilized. Interestingly, the Meiteis of the Mongolian stock and later comers to Manipur used to call the Bishnupriya Manipuri as Khalachaya. E. T. Dalton held that by degrees the Meiteis became more powerful in Manipur. It encouraged them to introduce matrimonial relations with the indigenous people undoubtedly with the Vedic Aryan people, and it now merged into totally a new origin, *i.e.* Indo-Mongoloid Culture.

However, as mentioned in the Meitei sacred scriptures and texts, a most comprehensive dance form popularly known as *Lai-haraoba* mirrors the pre-vaishnavite culture and other types of solo, duet, group, etc., within its body.

Lai-Haraoba (Merry Festival of the Deities) is the festival of the recollection of the creation stories played by all these deities with the first origin of this universe and evolution of the plants and animals through the will of *Atiya Shidaba*, the Supreme God of the Meitei sanamahi's.

### *A Remarkable Example of Cross-Cultural History*

The people of Manipur and Bengal provide a most interesting example of cultural and aesthetic fusion. The story begins in the 15th century when religious developments from Bangladesh reached Manipur. By the mid-Seventeenth century a full repertoire of songs and dances of Bangla origin took root in Manipur. This was aptly named 'Bangladesh Pala'. Gradually the main centre of Bangladesh's distinctive school of the Kirtan-based songs and dances shifted to Manipur and has remained there ever since as an essential part of Manipuri culture.

The most obliging aspect of Manipuri culture is that, it has retained the ancient ritual based dances and folk dances along with the later developed classical Manipuri dance style. Among the classical categories, 'Raas Leela'—a highly evolved dance drama, choreographed on 'Vaishnavite Padavalis' composed by mainly eminent Bengali poets and some Manipuri Gurus, is the highest expression of artistic genius, devotion and excellence of the Manipuris.

### *Contribution of Rabindranath Tagore*

Rabindranath Tagore, the world poet, was a great patron of the Manipuri dance and culture. He also deserves a honorable place in the style and regarded as the "pioneer of Manipuri dance and culture". It was he who popularised the style with its high zenith among the people of the world. The world poet was fascinated with the lovely and charming Manipuri Rasleela at Machhimpur, a Bishnupriya Manipuri locality in the modern Sylhet District in Bangladesh in 1920. He immediately decided to open a new department of Manipuri Dance in his Shantiniketan in Calcutta. Consequently, he invited Guru Senarik Singha Rajkumar,—a native of kalijar downtown Silchar of Assam and Guru Nileshwar Mukharjee of kamlganj thana of undivided Sylhet district. Both of the Gurus belonged to the Bishnupriya Manipuri Community, and with them the new department of It was an epoch making events in the history of Manipuri Dance and within a decade in crossed its regional as well national fields and became a reputed international style.

***Ritualistic, Recreational, Religious and Temporal***

The traditional Manipuri style of dancing preeminently embodies delicate, lyrical and graceful movements which enhance the audience in its beautiful and colourful costumes and presentation. The Manipuri dance whether folk, classical or modern, is devotional in nature. The folk dances of people captivate the beholders with their exotic costumes and simple but graceful rhythm. Their folklore is rich in quality. The dances are ritualistic and recreational, religious and temporal. The ritual dances are performed at a particular rite or ceremony or sacrifice and these dances naturally have a spiritual and religious basis. From the religious point of view and from the artistic angle of vision, we can claim that the Manipuri Classical Form of dance is one on the most chestiest, modest, softest and mildest but the most meaningful dances of the world.

The Gandharva's dance skills are mentioned in the Ramayana and Mahabharata and other Hindu Puranas. In Mahabharata, there is reference to Manipur in at least four different places – once in Adi parva, twice in Aswamedha parva and once in Mahaprashthanik parva. According to the Mahabharata, the ancient name of this country was 'Meckley' and this is the name that was used when King Gaursham signed a treaty with the British in 1763. In 1876, the king of Manipur used the same name referred to his kingdom which is documented in the treaty with the British Government.

Scholars have different opinions as well as views regarding the exact location of the Mahabharata Manipur with the recent Manipur. In the Allahabad stone pillar inscription of Samudra Gupta (4th century AD) there is no mention of Manipur, although the neighbouring kingdoms are named. In old assamese records, Manipur is mentioned as Magloo or Moglai. The Burmese call the country a Cassey or Kassay. McCulloch described that "The name Manipour accounted for by the Munniporie, who quote the Mahabharata in confirmation of its accuracy. They gave the same form Muni, a jewel. This jewel formerly in the possession of the Rajas of the country ages ago.

The country was at one time named Mahindrapore, but one Rajah by the name Manipur was in existence before the birth of Babhrubahana, and Mahindrapore or Mahindra Parbhata was the name of the hill, situated but a short distance to the east of the capital". On the other hand G. E. Geraini's Researches on ptolemy's Geography and The Gaits History of Assam compiled by Prof. Padmanath Battacharjee, stated that Bishnupur was the ancient capital of Manipur and Imphal come into existence in much later period than that of the city of Bishnypur.

Dr. Dinesh Chandra Sen (Brihod Bongo, 1935), Shri Ochchutcharan Chaudhury Tatvanidhi (Srihotter Itibritta, 1905,), Shri Janokinath Bosak (Manipur prohelika), L. Ibubghal Singha (Manipura), Sri Sena Singha (Prachinadhunik somkhipta Manipurer Itihas), Shri Mukundalal Chowdhury (Manipurer Itihas), Shri Mohendra Kumar singha (Manopurer Prachin Itihas), Shri Krishnamohon Dhar (Purbabango O Assam, 1909) and some other Indian scholars and historians idientified the present Manipur to be that of the epic as described in the Mahabharata, in their writings and articles.

The inhabitants of Manipur did identify them as "Manipuris" since past centuries. The land Manipur was formerly divided into small territories occupied by different clans, namely, the Khumals, the Moirangs, The Angoms, The Luwangs, the Ningthoujas, etc. The territories were after the names of the respective clans. Besides there are 70 Lokei (Ningthou–Khongya or members of Royel Family), Lempa Lokei (Thakcham), Moirango Lokei (Moirang –them) are the dominating groups. Each of the Lokei have their distinct ethnic identity (Gotros). So different clans of the Aryan and Mongoloid people lived side by side in Manipur for centuries.

Conversion of Meiteis in Hinduism by Shri Santidas Babaji in 19th century at the instance of the king Shri Pamhaiba was aimed at linking the with the Aryans, the mainstream of people of Manipur and their language too with Sanskrit. The Aryans, the followers of Lord Vishnu denied to accept the initiation by

Shri Santadas Babaji and the others (accepted). And thus the Manipuri people – Aryan and Kuki-chin group have been classified and renamed as Bishnupriya and Meiteis their language too. Culturally, the Meiteis and Bishnupriyas cannot be distinguished from each other. Both these two clans developed a homogeneous culture, and the concept of the one community grew among them.

By analysing the root of establishment of Hindu dynasties in upper Burma, we can see that all the Hindu dynasties settled in Upper Burma had to come across Manipur from the western and northern India by road as Manipur was only the gateway of Far East. The beauty of the land Manipur, lake Logtak and its surrounding areas also might have attracted them and some of them settled there and reigned there for years together.

Manipur or Meckley is actually on a tableland surrounded by hills. In the plains beside the loktak lake lived a race of people who had sharp Indo-Aryan features and used a language which was similar to the Kamrupi tongue rather than the Burmese-Chinese group. For centuries these Aryan people have been called 'Khalachai' which in southern Chinese dialect means 'Children of the wide lake' (Kha=Lake; La=Wide; Chai=Children) as described by Shri R. M. Nath in "The Background of Assamese Culture", Page 86-87, 2nd Edn, 1978. Statement by Late L Iboonghal singha, Rtd. District and sessions Judge of Manipur in a monthly Magazine "Ritu", 1959, page-21: "Arther Paliot in his History of China stated that the chinese invaded Manipur in about 700 A.D. and won over the war. They called Manipuris as khalachais or sons of the wide lake (Loktak) and described them as highly civilized". The Chinese inroads over the valley was authenticated in the writings of Hien-Tasng, the great Chinese traveller who has visited the court of Kumar Vaskar Varma of Kamrupa in the 7th Century A.D.

Manipuri is the classical dance from the Manipur region in the northeast. The past and origins of this dance are not clear as many myths and legends are associated with it. The Manipuris consider themselves the descendants of the Gandharvas who were the legendary musicians, and dancers in the celestial courts of Indira. The earliest records of this dance form date back to about 100 AD. It was King Bhagyachandra of 17th century who established Manipuri dance on a scientific basis. It was he who innovated Ras Leelas (dance dramas) and Sankirtan (form of invocation). He also designed the beautiful Manipuri dance costume. Some other beliefs also exists like that of the Meitei tribes of Manipur, they believe that when the earth was newly formed it was lumpy and to make it soft and firm the seventh Lainoorahs danced on the earth by pressing their feet very gently. That is the secret behind the delicate steps of Manipuri dance.

Slow and gracious movements differentiate Manipuri from other dance styles. The delicate arm movements and gentle foot work characterise this dance. The Vaishnava faith brought along with it the origin of the Manipuri dance. The repertoire is dominated by the themes from the Vishnu Puranas, Bhagvata Puranas, and Geeta Govinda.

The female 'Rasa' dances, based on the Radha-Krishna theme feature group ballets and solos. The male 'Sankirtana' dances performed to the pulsating rhythm of the Manipuri Dholak are full of vitality. Manipuri dance is very much religious and associated to Vaishnava cult of Hinduism. The art form primarily depicts episodes from the life of Vishnu. This style is multifaceted, ranging from the softest feminine to the obviously vigorous masculine. Dignified grace is to be found in every aspect and the range it offers in technique, rhythmic and tempo makes a Manipuri recital an absorbing and exhilarating experience.

### *Dance Style*

The technique of Manipuri dancing is based on an interesting principle of compensatory movement with the objective of achieving rounded movements and avoiding any jerks, sharp edges or straight lines.

The Manipuris are completely ignorant about the use of dance for the sake of dancing and contract system. From the sacred texts, we can point here some characteristic features of Manipuri dancing which are as under:

(1) The place where dance are held are sacred. It is considered to be a crime or sin to violate the rules. Anytime, anyplace is not good enough.

(2) Dances are devotional or ritualistic rather than entertainment of the eyes. It is a *Sadhan-Bhakti*-kind of devotion to God for both the dancers and onlookers.

(3) The dressing is so designed as to free them from any stimulus, excitement to the opposite sex. Dance is but the rhythmic expression of action and activities of life on the upper part of the body.

(4) The artist never looks at any person or audience as a mark of concentration to the Lord surrendering the outward world and illusions of *Maya* and also giving up all lust, greed, anger, envy, hatred and pride of the dancers.

(5) The steps of dancing are very much acute and complex and never show outward feeling of lust and amorous play.

### *The Techniques*

The technique of Manipuri dancing is based on an interesting principle of compensatory movement with the objective of achieving rounded movements and avoiding any jerks, sharp edges or straight lines. If the right hand is outstretched towards the right, for example, the body is tilted towards the left in order to offset the right side thrust. The movement towards the right has been balanced and subdued by one towards the left. This particularly contrasts with the technique of Bharata Natyam, in which, in the same example, the effort would generally be to emphasis the movement to the right. It is this aspect which imparts to Manipuri an undulating and soft appearance. This impression of softness actually hides a very tough regimen of body control.

### *Feet Movement*

Similarly, the feet never strike the ground with a sound on impact, as this would interfere with the delicate flow of the body movements. The knees and ankles cushion the landing so that no sound ensues. Manipuri dancers do not even wear ankle bells, whose purpose is after all to accentuate the beats tapped out by the feet.

***Taal's and Matra's***

The *Taal's* in Manipuri dance generally similar to those of the dance forms in north India. There is considerable number of characteristics that are not distinguishable with the Bangladesh Kirtana.

Taal
Matra
Taanchep-4
Tintaal Mel-3
Mel Kup-6
Tintaal Macha-7
Moitaal Surfunc-10
Tall Jao-12
Chari Taal-7 or 14
Ponchom Sowari-15
Raaj Mel-7
Meitaal Suryok -10
Rupak-6
Tintaal Achouba-8

***Mudra's (Hand Movements)***

The Mudra's or hand movements in Manipuri dance are quite different from other classical dance forms. From Bhagyachandra's *Govinda Sangit Leelabilas* and the book *"Laithok Laikha Jogoi"* the following Mudra's are found:

O-songyukta (single hand): *Potaka, tripotaka, ordopotaka, kotokamukh, sondongsa, mrigashirsha, hongsashya, olopollob, bhruksa, angush, ordhochandra, kurak, mushti.*

Songyukta (Double hand): *Shangkha, Chakra, onjoli, Taksa, Paas, korkot, Somput, rombhasum, pushpaput, kukil, shoshtik, sook.*

### ***Musical Instruments***

Dances are very much based upon the cymbals (*kartal* or *mangkang*) and the cylindrical drum known as *Manipuri mridang* or *pung*. Unlike other classical, dances where the instrument is merely used as an accompaniment, the *pung* and the *kartal (manjira)* are actually used in the dance. Manipuri is unique among the classical Indian dances in that the instrumentation is a central part of the dance, rather than as a side accompaniment. The main musical instrument in Manipuri dance is Kartal or cymbal. Another important instruments is the *Dhak* or *Pung* (mridanga or dram). *Dhak, Kartal, Mangkang, and Sembong* are the soul of Manipuri Sankritan music and Classical Manipuri Dance.

It assumes an important ritual character, an indispensable part of all social and devotional ceremonies in Manipur,- the instrument itself becoming an object of veneration. *Manzilla*, used by the female performers, is similar to *kartal*, but different in nature and smaller in size. There are of course may be considered as resultant instrument of traditional Manipuri and Hinduised Manipuri culture. The musical instrument which is Manipuris own is *Pena*, a string instrument which is played by fiddling somewhat similar to *Ektara* of Bengal. Often, The use of *Baashis* and *Harmoniums* are found in Manipuri Dance.

### ***Dance Costumes***

The Ras costumes and ornaments of Sri Radhika and the Gopies are colourful and handsome. The skirt the present day Ras dancers wear is modeled on the one the Maharaja Bhagya Chandra (1763-1798) saw in his dream.

The costumes in Manipuri dance is very colourful, attractive and very richly bedecked. The female dancers wear a dress called "*patloi*". The lehenga is called "*Kumin*" with mirrors and zari work intricately woven into beautiful designs. It is layered with a transparent silk or "*Pasuan*". The choli is also embellished with zari, silk or gota embroidery. On the head, covering the face, they wear a transparent odhni, through which the expression and emotion on the face of the dancer can easily he seen. Gopis usually wear a red dress while Radha stands out in green attire. The male dancer, who is Krishna, wears a saffron dress.

Ras costumes and ornaments of Sri Radhika and the Gopies are colourful and handsome. The skirt the present day Ras dancers wear is modeled on the one the Maharaja Bhagya Chandra (1763-1798) saw in his dream.

Here is List of Costumes and some terms related to the costumes and ornaments used in Manipuri Dance:

- *Potlei:* Ras costume of *Sri Radhika* and the *Gopi*s, designed by the *Potlei-setpa*'s who rent them for the performance at some rates.
- *Koknaam:* A gauze at overhead, embossed with silver *Jari*.
- *Meikhumbi:* A transparent and thin vail thrown over the head.
- *Kumin:* An Embroidered brightly colored silk skirt.
- *Pasuan:* A short flair of silver gauze over the kumin.
- *Khaon:* Rectangular embroidered piece with belt.
- *Koktombi:* Cap covering the head.
- *Thabret:* A griddle round the waist.
- *Khangoi:* Small rectangular belt over the Pasuan.
- *Leitreng:* Golden ring round the head.
- *Chura:* Made of peacock feathers, wired on top of head.
- *Feichom: Dhooti,* a saffron dress.
- *Ghungur:* Ornament for the foot.

***Movements***

The dancer begins with the movements known as the chali. It is a movement which suggests basic ways of walking and covering space. The dancer moves first to the front and back with hands held horizontally at the chest level and then moves these hands vertically in an up-and-down direction. She then covers space in side-ways walking, ending by weaving circles and spirals. In these basic movements, the various types of bhramaris are introduced, the two distinct varieties being the uplai and the longlai. These lais whether in lasya or in tandava as ways of covering floor-space; usually is side ways movement followed by a semi-circle. They are the finale of the dance cadences and are often executed in multiples of three as in the tikai of the other dance styles. Sometimes a spiral movement in vertical space is executed, where the dancer treats her body like a screw and weaves a spiral vertically from a higher level to lower level. While doing so the dancer also takes a circle or a spin. This is very difficult movement has a graceful fluidity, sometimes mistaken for imprecision. The achongha of jumping movements are characteristic of the tandava portions of the dance.

The basic movements of the chali are connected together to form the various types of parengs. The parengs are cadences of movements in a given metrical cycle. The metrical cycles are many and in-beats and the cross-beats are complicated, requiring a high sense of precision. All the lais are used in parengs and different types of talas are employed, especially the rajmela, the seven beats (rupaka), 15 beats (panchamsvari) and the 16 beats (tintala). The first three bhangis and the bhangi pareng achongba, the Vrindavan pareng and the khurumba pareng are known as the lasya cadences. They are used in common rasa portions of the dance. The three other bhangis have a common adjestive gostha which stands for the tandava bhangis. They are used by actors while presenting the character of Krishna in the rasa dances. Three such bhangis are prescribed, namely the gostha bhangi pareng, the gostha Vrindavan pareng and the gostha Khurumba pareng. The last one is rarely performed and seems to have gone out of vogue.

The dance has a highly complex technique of movement and tala. The dance is not restricted to solo numbers. Manipuri is the only classical style in which we find exquisite survivals of compositions, such as the hallisaka, the charchari and other forms mentioned in classical Sanskrit literature. In the rasa dances, we find that all the four types of pindis mentioned by Bharata can be seen.

***Technique:*** Manipuri has a flow and a grace which contrasts from the precision of the South Indian styles. This impression of ease and fluidity results from an unusual treatment of the body. The vertical line of the body is never broken The body merely curves itself into a figure of 8. The positions attained are thus relaxed and controlled rather than sculpturesque. An effort is made to connect two parts of the body through beautiful curves. There are no sudden transitions from particular horizontal sutras as in Bharata Natyam. The knees are kept close together and the body is held upright but without any tension. The torso is not treated as a unit, but is divided into two distinct parts above the Katisutras, the chest and the waist.

Neither unit is used singly because the bend of any part by itself would mean creating an angle. Thus, the chest and the waist, although moving in opposition, are always connected. The effect is of the slow drawing of a curve in the shape of "S", but is never a simple bend. The neck and the head follow this principle but the head never moves horizontally. It also executes a figure 8 in space. The arms and hands follow the pattern of the lower limbs and the torso. They too are never tense nor are they even in acute flexion. They are held, in a naturally relaxed manner away from the body in a semi-circular curve. The wrists plays an extremely important part in the movement of the hands and the fingers, because it is the wrists which give the movements of the fingers a unique fluidity. A basic movement is the gradual closing in an opening out of the fingers; while the wrist attempts to execute a lateral figure.

The face is placid and without any exaggerated facial expressions. This controlled, but not unduly severe or austere, expression is sustained throughout the performance. In the Lasya portions the dancer does not and cannot lift her foot away from the ground above the level of the knee. The release from the ground is invariably characterised by a sweep of the ground, a gliding movement almost touching the floor rather than a movement where the foot is lifted high above the ground. The situation changes considerably in the tandava portion known for its agility, verve and high leaps.

The basic position in tandava is no longer the closed feet with knees bent in front leaving no space between them. There is nearly a four tala distance between the two feet and the knees are bent in front. In the tandava portions, the torso is occasionally treated as a separate unit and side bends are frequent. There are many sitting positions and many spirals and turns known to the dance styles, both in lasya and tandava. In lasya, the sthanakas or various positions once again attempt to limit space and although women dancers change the level throughout a performance, there is hardly ever much space between the two feet.

In the tandava portions, the sthanakas take the form of positions known as the Vrischika Karnas of the Natya Shastra tradition. There are few leg extensions in the lasya or tandava portions. Hip movements are not allowed in the tandava and lasya portions. There is one type of thigh or pelvic movement known to the dance style. It is an up and down movement and it is achieved through knee dips and through a suggestion of a hop on the toe. The manner of covering space in Manipuri, is expressive of its grace and delicacy. The dancer covers floor space also in figures of 8 and then the foot is lifted to cover space, it invariably touches the ground by a slight toe movement rather than flat foot or the heal. The Kunchita foot or the agratalasanchara foot of the Natya Shastra is seen repeatedly in this dance style.

### *Music, Costumes and Ensembles*

The musical accompaniment to Manipuri dances is played on an instrument rather like a guitar called the khol, and the mridangam. But sometimes the singing is done by a group whose members do not join in the dance. When the drummer and the dancer together execute certain quick talas, each in his own medium, the tempo of the dance increases and the quick rhythmic pattern is enchanting to watch. The costumes are very picturesque. The women wear a tight-fitting conical cap of black velvet or other material, trimmed with a border of synthetic pearls, under a thin white veil. Modern dancers often discard the cap in favour of a bun on top and to the side of the head, and haloed with flowers. The choli or tight fitting bodice is usually of velvet with tight sleeves trimmed with gold embroidery. The gagra or flounced skirt is of a striking colour, yellow, red or green and usually of silk with a wide border at the bottom of the skirt consisting of a design of sequins. Tiny square, round or oval mirrors are scattered all over the skirt, which has a transparent Muslim garment over it, embroidered with silver thread. As the dancers swirl round, the flashing mirrors reflecting the light produce a striking effect.

The male dancer wears a dhoti with embroidered bands across his chest ending in flaps that fall over both hips. In the Ras-Leela, Krishna is gorgeously attired in a pleated dhoti of gold or yellow silk, the chest being covered with glittering necklaces while wristlets and armlets adorn the arms.

The Rasa dances go on for several hours at a stretch. The honeyed melodies Meera, Krishna's disciple are also greatly in vogue. The ritualistic dances have Krishna as the central figure. Manipuri dancers firmly believe that when they dance the gods descend to earth to join their revelry. The name Lai Horaopa signified 'sporting or making merry with the gods. Girls, gaily dressed, begin the dance with offerings of flowers and fruits. The men then join in and pick their partners. Actually this dance is the Shiva-Parvati done in the Manipuri technique. It is very robust.

The animism of the Manipuris, preceding their conversion to Hinduism, has left its stamp on their dance art and in the Lai Hairobi it is pronounced. This is an annual ceremony performed in every village for the purpose of propitiating its Lai, *i.e.* god's seat or the dwelling of Lam.

### *The Repertoire*

The repertoire of Manipuri dances can be divided into three or four broad categories. This would not include the whole group of dances which one would call tribal or folk. The first group would comprise the pre-Vaishnava dance forms or dance rituals. Closely related to this group would be the Thang or the martial ritual dancers of Manipur, all these belong to pre-Vaishnava state of Manipuri culture.

The second group would constitute the dance and the dance music sections of the various jatras in Manipur. The Holi Pala, the Khumbak Ishei and other numbers today presented on the stage are part and parcel of these seasonal festivities.

The third group would constitute the different types of Sankirtana traditions. Part and parcel of these Sankirtana was the group dancing, the various types of walking or group forms executed either through clapping or through the playing of small cymbals called Manjira or large cymbals called Kartala.

A fourth group may be considered for the ballad forms which have both a vocal as also a miming aspect to them. Among these would be the presentation through solo duet rendering, in the forms known as the Wariliba, the Haiba Thiba, etc.

A most important part of Manipuri repertoire is recognised by the generic term Jagoi. At the artistic level, the Jagoi can be considered as the main type of art dance. Jagoi represents those sections of music and dance from amongst the Sankirtanas which could be presented outside the ritual parameters. The traditional gurus of Manipur have divided the Jagoi into several sub-categories such as the Pungalola Jagoi, the Motkanba Jagoi and just Lila. There is a further sub-division which is made by adding the adjectives Nupa or Nupi-Nupa standing for man and Nupi for woman. Amongst the further divisions are the Cholam, the Kartala Cholam, the Mridang Cholam, the dance of the Ghosta lila (also called the Shanshenba Jagoi) and the Spear dances.

Ras Leelas and Sankirtans are the highly developed dance-forms revealing the high aesthetic religious feeling of the people of Manipur. Ras Leelas go on for 8 to 10 hours in the temple courtyard from dusk to dawn. The religious people of Manipur shed tears of joy experiencing it as the real spirit of the Lord. All the technical elements mentioned in the Sangeet Shastras are found in Ras Leelas, such as Nritta (Pure Dance), Nritya (Interpretative dance) and Natya (Theme expressed through four kinds of Abhinaya). In Sankirtan, male dancers with kartal and Mridang wear white dhotis and turban creating a serene and dignified atmosphere. In the festival dances, women wear the hand-woven and embroidered Phanek with strips and white thin scarf. There are various types of cholams. The cholams are both lasya and tandava.

***Kartal Cholam:*** It is a Tandava dance of cymbals. It is performed, by the male dancers only. Their feats are in intricate talas or timing on the Kartals (large cymbals). An essence of harmony is achieved with the rhythmic tunes of mridang. The dancer shows the dexterity by making jumps radiating in semi circular ways, making strength-full movements with speedy whirls and turns with the exact Tala of the music. The dancer imitates the natural movements of Kapote (crane), Mayur (peacock), Khanjan (bagtail) and Hansa (swan) in perfect accuracy of movement and sound.

***Manjira Cholam:*** This Tandava dance is performed in temples during Jholan Yatra. A beautiful dais is formed in the Mandapa hall of the Govindaji temple. The idols of Radha and Krishna are placed on the dais. The music party of the temple sits before the deities and then this dance is performed in their presence in reverence to the god and goddess.

***Pung Cholam:*** It is a Tandava drum dance generally performed by a male dancer in the temple square on some special occasions. The dancer performs with a mad frenzy of speed with bends and turns holding the drum and producing the music simultaneously. Sometimes the drum sound is produced by imitating the sounds of Nature.

There are other cholam dances such as the Duff cholam and the Kanjira cholam. Amongst the Kartali dances are the clapping items performed only by women as the Nupi Khumbak ishei and the Nupa khumbak ishei. These are group dances in which a number of interesting group formations can be seen and the dance is built on clapping of hands at cross rhythms to be basics rhythm played by the accompanying pung. All the cholam and Kartali dances are pure nritta. There is not abhinaya, not is there any song accompaniment.

The Thang haiba and the Takhew sauba or the sword and the spear dances which belong to the tandava category have now become part of the artistic repertoire. Originally these were performed either in the contact of ritual magical performances or as a sequence in the Lai Haraoba. When incorporated as an artistic number, these are called thangta jagoi.

The Nupi Jagoi or the women's dance is the graceful variety and is divided into two main sub-divisions. The first Bhangi Jagoi and the second Punglol Jagoi. *i.e.*, that which is performed only to the mnemonics of the Pung the Manipuri Mridangam. The Bhangi Jagoi is marked by seriousness of purpose, a slow tempo and a very careful delivery of movements which are controlled and restrained. It comes under the category called the smitanga. The Punglol Jagoi is executed in a fast tempo, a metrical pattern and a repetition ending in triplets of three. All these should be considered both of the male and the female as pure abstract dancing without mime or abhinaya. This is the nritta repertoire of Manipuri dancing. It must be remembered that none of these numbers are dissociated from the repertoire which have mentioned in the context of the sankirtana and the jatra dances

***Lai Horaoba:*** Lai Haraoba is performed all over Manipur, but chiefly at Moirang village in the memory of princess Thoibi and her lover Khamba. Lai Haraboa is an annual festival, a ritual and a dance-drama performance all rolled into one and lasting for many days. It is also performed to appease the local deities. It is performed on the outskirts of the village in front of the shrines of the deities of the forest called Umang lies. Lai Haraoba literally means "merry making of gods". The participants of this dance and music mela begin to assemble on the village green in the afternoon and enjoy the festival till sun set everyday in May. The main participants are the priests and priestesses called maibas and maibis respectively. The males disguise as ancient Manipuri warriors and heroes and the women as princess, dance together in a roaming fashion to reveal and re-enact the story of the creation and continuity of the universe. The dance movements present a strange mixture of suggestiveness, ludicrous and wed revelry.

The music that accompanies the dance consists of drums, flutes, gongs, manhiras and pena which has a bunch of tiny bells tied on one end of its bow. The bells produce a subdued tinkling sound in combination with the sombre and rather sad melody of the instrument proper, which resembles the music of a Sarangi. The dancer do not put on ankle bells. It seems the episodes of Khamba-Thoibi romance were incorporated in the dance-drama afterwards. These episodes have been narrated in the Manipuri epic.

Five different varieties of the Lai Haraboa are known and these are associated with different venues such as Kanglai, Moirang, Kakaching, Andra, and Chakpa. The festival begins with a procession going to a nearby river or a pond-like the leaders of the village invoke the spirits of the waters. The leaves-one placed facing the sky and the other covers the first leaf. The ritual symbolises the emergence of life from eternal water. Ritually, a seed is put within the two leaves. The procession returns with a filled pitcher from the pond and the leaves placed above it

***Rasa:*** The Rasa dances of Manipur are lyrical narrative and not dramatic. The rasa dances have a structure and technique which can distinguish them from any other type of dance in Manipur. Bhagya Chandra Maharaj or King Jai Singh is considered the composer of at least three of the four Rasa dances known to Manipur. The Rasa dances are performed on particular occasion and in particular season.

First and the foremost is the Vasant Rasa for the full moon day of Holi. The Vasant Rasa is invariably preceded by the Natapala or the group of men dancers who play the drum and sing. Thereafter there is the presentation of a particular raga in this case, Vasant Raga by women singers now called sutradhari. Here the singing sets the tone of the presentation of the rasa. A particular mood is invoked and the players and the audience become prepared to transport themselves into the world of Lord Krishna in Vrindavan. Thereafter, there is the description of Vrindavan sung by the sutradhari and followed through dance by a group of young dancers.

The next sequence is Vaishnava Vandana. The most exciting part of the rasa is the entry of the young Krishna, normally played by a young girl. Thereafter is the presentation of the main themes in the case of Vasant Rasa. It is the theme of the gopis playing Holi with Krishna.

The Kunj Rasa is performed sometime in August coinciding with what is known as the full moon or rakhi or rakhi purnima. The theme of this rasa is drawn from the Srimad Bhagvata. It revolves round the mutual hide and seek of Radha and Krishna. The rasa is performed in a special group and it recreates the dance of the gopis with Krishna.

A third rasa called the nritya rasa which was created by Maharaja Chandrakirti in the nineteenth century can be performed at any time. Here dance, rather than the story or the theme is more important. These dances are performed generally at night in the dancing halls attached to the temples. The halls are profusely and tastefully decorated with garlands, flowers, flags, buntings, etc. on the occasion. Truly classical in spirit, the Rasa-dances are full of devotional fervour and are performed to the singing of songs and Kirtans and to the accompaniment of Khol or mridanga, manjira and bamboo flutes. Their liquid beauty lyrical quality, restrained and rhythmic swaying, swinging and spinning almost at one place, with hands, close to the body, coupled with soft vocal and instrumental devotional music lend the performance a uniqueness which defies description.

Besides these rasa dances, there are the Lilas. These Lilas also constitute an important part of the repertoire of the Manipuri dances. The Gostha lila recreates the play on Krishna and Balarama; Krishna and Yashoda and the dancers of Krishna with his companions. The main singer for the gostha lila is a man and not a woman.

In the ulukhala rasa, the birth of Krishna, Putna Vadh, etc. including makhan chori are presented. The Vaishnavite flavour lives and vibrates in the hearts of every Manipuri and truly through the rasa dances and the presentation of the lilas Vrindavan is called in every heart in far of Manipur. Their sophisticated pieces of opera with libretto musical scales, ragas, talas, giving enough scope for pure nritta abhinaya and the combination of both singing and dancing. The Maharasa concentrates on the love quarrel between Radha and Krishna. The theme is based on the story of the Bhagvata Purana. The gostha or the Gopa Rasa is performed in Tandava style by Lord Krishna with Gopas. The killing of Asuras, etc. is shown in the dance.

## Mohiniattam

Mohiniattam is derived from the words "Mohini" and "attam". Mohini means a beautiful woman and attam means dance. So this dance is an exquisite feminine style with undulating flow of body movements. The theme of the dance is generally "sringara" or love. Delicate themes of love are performed with suggestive abhinaya, subtle gestures, rhythmic footwork and lilting music.

After almost virtual extinction early this century, it is gratifying to note, that Mohiniattam survived its difficult phase and emerged as a full fledged dance form and credits itself to be one of the most exquisite dance styles of India.

Mohiniattam means Mohini's dance. Mohini according to Indian mythology, is a very beautiful woman who attracts people instantly and was an enchantress, thus it is the dance of the enchantress. It is also believed that Lord Vishnu had disguised himself as 'Mohini' with an intention to slay Bhasmasura and also during the churning of nectar from the ocean. But the basis of this dance is not seduction alone. It also signifies transformation of Lord Vishnu into a female form and also the concept of 'Ardhnareeshwara', *i.e.* male and female as one. Like many other dance forms, this was also restricted to the Devadasis.

The first reference to Mohiniattam is found in 'Vyavaharamala' composed by Mazhamangalam Naryanam Namboodiri, assigned to the 16th century A.D.

In the 19th century Swati Thirunal, the king of erstwhile Travancore, tried to encourage the development of this dance style. But after him, Mohiniattam suffered heavily owing to the exploitation by the Satraps and the Landlords. Poet Vallathol revived it and gave it a status throughout Kerala through

Kalamandalam founded in 1930. Kalamandalam Kalyaniamma, and Chinnammu Amma, the last links of a disappearing tradition, nurtured aspirants in the discipline at Kalamandalm.

The theme of Mohiniattam is love and devotion to god. Vishnu or Krishna is more often the hero. The spectators could feel his invisible presence when the heroine or her maid details dreams and ambitions through the circular movements, delicate footsteps and subtle expression.

The dancer in the slow and medium tempos is able to find adequate space for improvisations and suggestive bhavas. In format, this is similar to Bharata Natyam. The movements are graceful like Odissi and the costumes sober and attractive. It is essentially a solo dance, but nowadays Mohiniattam is performed in groups also.

The repertoire of Mohiniattam follows closely that of Bharata Natyam. Beginning with Cholkettu, the dancer performs Jathiswaram, Varnam, Padam and Thillana in a concert. Varnam combines pure and expressionful dance, while Padam tests the histrionic talent of a dancer and Thillana exposes her technical artistry.

The basic dance steps are the Adavus which are of four kinds: Taganam, Jaganam, Dhaganam and Sammisram. These names are derived from the nomenclature called Vaittari.

Mohiniattam maintains realistic make-up and simple dressing. The dancer are attired in a beautiful white and gold bordered Kasavu saree of Kerala. Mohiniattam like many other form, follows the Hastha Lakshandeepika, as a text book for Mudras, or hand gestures. The style of vocal music for Mohiniattam as is generally seen, is classical Kamatic. The lyrics composed by Maharaja Swati Tirunal and Irayimman Thampi are in Manipravala (a mixture of Sanskrit and Malayalam). Till recently, Thoppi Maddalam and Veena provided the background music of Mohiniattam. These have been replaced in recent years by the Mridangam and Violin.

Some of the exponents of this dance form are Chinnammu Amma, Kalyani Kuttiamma, Kanak Rele, Sunanda Nair, Deepti Bhalla and Bharati Shivaji.

### *The Dance of the Enchantress*

This Indian classical dance form—Mohiniattam—comes from one of the South States of India, Kerala. And the mere mention of Kerala brings up in one's mind the wondrous and incomparable beauty of its landscape. The scenic backwaters where the palm fronds fill up the Kerala skyline moving gently and gracefully in the breeze, the boats bobbing up and down gently, gracefully and in perfect tune with nature and its rhythm.

A Mohiniattam dancer immediately reminds you of this scenic beauty in her dance. The movements are beautiful and lyrical and they are always in an unbroken chain, from one movement very gently and gracefully merging into another. Though the movements are swaying and gentle the presentation comes out with a tremendous and strong impact leaving the spectator in an atmosphere of grace, charm, vitality and a forceful vivacity.

The graceful and long limbs of a Mohiniattam dancer brings before your eyes the vision of the palm fronds swaying and dancing in the breeze and the movements are like those of a boat bobbing up and down in the back waters. There is a tremendous amount of force that a Mohiniattam dancer brings out in her performance without which the performance would be lacking in its lustre but this tremendous energy is released in a very controlled and graceful manner which can be achieved only with discipline, hard work and (bhakti) or devotion to the art form.

Also, another feature that influences Mohiniattam is the simplicity of dressing by the people in Kerala which is visible in the costume of the dancer. White is a favourite colour of the people basically because of the hot and humid climate, and a Mohiniattam costume is always white or off white with gold or red border. The hair is tied in a bundle on the left side with white flowers (mogra) around it, with a simple ornament tied on the bun.

The jewellery used for the neck is a 'choker' and a kasimala (coin chain). For the ears a dancer wears a "toda' which is circular like a coin and has dangling earrings with it known as "jhumka". The face is done up with an exaggerated eye make up to help her express her emotions. The eyes reflect immediately the mental state of the situation or character the dancer is representing and a description of Mohiniattam cannot be complete without the mention of the nayanabhinaya or the use of the eyes, eyebrows and eyelids.

But at the end of it all the transformation is tremendous. The merrily dancing eyes and the fluttering of the eyebrows of the dancer all create a devastatingly mischievous atmosphere. The sweet smelling of the flowers, the gentle, swaying movement of the torso in perfect harmony with the music and the bewitching personality of a Mohiniattam dancer all take us to the highest aesthetic order "the atmosphere of enchantment.

The Indian mythology mentions a few times when Lord Vishnu (one among the trinity of Gods-Brhma, Vishnu, Mahesha) assumes the form of Mohini to save the Gods from their clash with the asuras or demons. In one instance when the Gods and demons were churning the mighty ocean for the pot of nectar (amrita), with the serpent Vasuki twined around the mountain Mandaragiri. The ocean brought out all the treasures buried in its depth, while the devas (gods) and asuras (demons) churned on and on. Finally when the pot of nectar appeared, the demons true to their nature grabbed it. The universe would be in total darkness if the demons had their way. It is at this moment the Lord, assumes the form of Mohini to save the Universe from the hands of the demons and total darkness.

The tinkling sound of bells, the sweet smell of flowers, the divine being, the beauty unparalleled-The Enchantress. The one, who could take your minds away from the present to another world of beauty and charm. The lotus eyed one dancing gently and gracefully filling the atmosphere with unsurpassed heavenly beauty. The demons true to her instructions shut their eyes to relinquish and behold the beauty they envisioned. She is Mohini the celestial dancer, one who has come to enchant.

Until, a few decades ago it was presumed that in India there were only four classical dances. Bharata Natyam, Kathak, Manipuri and Kathakali. But then due to the pioneering works of great gurus (teachers), dancers and scholars the dance forms of Mohiniattam, Kuchipudi and Odissi were discovered in their native settings and brought out into the urban stage, much to the delight and wonderment of the lovers of dance.

There is a considerable amount of disagreement among scholars regarding the antiquity of Mohiniattam. Most of them agree that it was during Maharaja Swati Tirunal's rule in the 16th century that Mohiniattam achieved its refined form. The Maharaja of Travancore was a great patron of arts and he encouraged artistes, singers, dancers from all over the country to come and perform in his court. During this time he also invited the Tanjore quartets from Tamil Nadu who were great Bharata Natyam nattuvanars (or teachers) who brought with them dancers and thus influenced the already present local dance form. The Maharaja was a great bhakta or devotee of Lord Padmanabha and wrote and composed in Hindustani as well as Kamatic innumerable kritis, padams and varnams in his praise. The Maharaja's padams are always a part of a Mohiniattam dancer's repertoire.

But it was finally only in the 20th century that Mohiniattam got its fresh impetus that it actually deserved, and it has come to stay. It was when Mahakavi Vallathol set up the premiere institution for Kathakali, Kerala Kalamandalam in India that he invited three dancers practicing Mohiniattam at that time Kalpuratte Kunjukutty Amma, Tottacheri Chinnamuamma and Kalyani Kutty Amma to come and teach Mohiniattam in his institution. Till, little more than a decade ago the Mohiniattam repertoire ran almost parallel to the Bharata Natyam repertoire. But just as each region has its own individuality and identity it was natural that Mohiniattam had to find its own identity. Due to the relentless work of great researchers, scholars, performers of Mohiniattam, this dance form achieved its present classical standing.

Today, we have different schools of Mohiniattam just as you have schools for Bharata Natyam. But they all have one thing in common they all imbibe the beautiful lyrical elements of the social folk dances of the graceful women from Kerala. Every classical dance form from India has its beginnings in the local prevalent folk art forms and has also been very strongly influenced by the social, political, religious and behavioural pattern of the people of the region. The classical dance forms have imbibed these features to give them all a distinct flavour of its own, but they are still all bound by the great traditions set by the 'Natyashastra' around the 2nd century B.C.

The 'Natya Shastra' is a treatise on dance and drama and lays down rules regarding the practice and presentation of drama and dance. Each dance form adopts it to suit the regional changes in the social, religious, political and behaviour of the people. But it was around the 3rd century A.D that Nandikeshvara wrote the Abhinaya Darpanam which is very religiously followed by the practitioners of Bharata Natyam. It gives the usage of hastas (hand gestures), pada bhedas (feet positions), caris (gaits), gatis (steppings), etc.

Similarly a study of Mohiniattam wouldn't be complete without the study of Balaramabharatam. The author Maharaja Kartikatirunal Rama Varma was a descendant of the ancient Chera kings of South India who encouraged arts and literature in the 18th century.. The Maharaja was a great scholar and had an extraordinary talents not only for literature but also for music, dance and other allied arts and was also a great poet. His contribution to Kathakali (a dance drama tradition) of Kerala is incomparable. The book gives a detailed insight into the technical performing aspects for Mohiniattam. There is a mention of the use of hastas (hand gestures), angas (major limbs) upangas (minor limbs) and pratyangas (neck, wrists, knees, thighs etc.). Reading through the text and the practical details mentioned in the book leaves a student of Mohiniattam with very few doubts on the technicalities. The Balaramabharatam is an accepted text by most leading dancers, scholars of India today for Mohiniattam.

Being associated for a very long time and having the opportunity to learn under one of the pioneer's of Mohiniattam, Padmashri (Dr.) Kanak Rele who is responsible for bringing Mohiniattam into the classical map of India, I would say is a blessing. Also the privilege of working with one of the leading theater personalities, scholar, poet and a great musical composer

Shri Kavalam Narayana Panikker whose contribution to Mohiniattam also needs a special mention. Mohiniattam will flourish and go a long way. With due respect to all performers, scholars, and teachers of the art form, we shall have just one aim in mind to carry on this great art form from one century into the next. The responsibility put into us by the great performers of the last and present century to carry on this great tradition and initiate the uninitiated into another world of beauty, grace and charm.

The dance form of Mohiniattam was nurtured in the region of Kerala in southwestern India. The name Mohiniattam literally means 'Dance of the Enchantress,' and it does have a mesmerising quality. The white and gold costume, arresting hairstyle and the highly graceful movements in medium tempo, contribute to this aesthetic effect.

Mohiniattam is characterised by swaying movements of the upper body with legs placed in a stance similar to the plie position. The eyes play an important role in accenting the direction of the movement.

Mention of Mohiniattam is found in some eighteenth century texts, but the practical aspect of the style was revived in the reign of Maharaja Swati Tirunal, a 19th century ruler who was a great patron of the arts. Under Swati Tirunal, Mohiniattam crystallised as a solo dance tradition with musical compositions set to the Kamatic style of music and a distinct repertoire. Later, in the twentieth century, the great poet Vallathol established the Kerala Kalamandalam to promote the arts of Mohiniattam and Kathakali. Here, further research was done and Mohiniattam was codified and revived.

Over the past few decades, the repertoire of Mohiniattam has been developed and expanded by dedicated performers who have ensured that this beautiful dance style retains a distinct identity among the classical dance styles of India. Apart from mythology, Mohiniattam contains a range of themes from nature.

*Kalamandalam Satyabhama*

*Kalamandalam Kshemavathi*

*Kalamandalam Chandrika Menon*

*Kalamandalam Sugandhi*
*Shyamala Surendran*
*Kalamandalam Saraswati*
*Bharati Shivaji*
*Kanak Rele*
*Deepti Bhalla*
*Kalamandalam Saraswati*
*Rema Shrikant*
*Sunanda Nair*
*Shaly Vijayan*
*Pallavi Krishnan*
*Neena Prasad*
*Priyadarshini Ghosh Shome*
*Jayaprabha Menon*
*Vijayalakshmi*
*Radha Dutta*
*Sindhu Kiran*

### *Repertoirs of Mohiniattam*

The Sopanam repertoir of Mohiniattam includes the following:

***Ganapathy:*** Is customary to commence any performance with an invocation to Lord Ganesha. There are many varieties of such introductory offering to Lord Ganesha. Structured and presented from the tradition of Kerala like Marma Ganapathy from Agastia Muni's Marma Shastra. Ganapathy Tyani which is from the repertoire of the temple music.

***Mukhachalam:*** The term Mukhachalam is borrowed from Kathakali in which it is used at the opening of a performance to signify the various ragas and talas used in the repertoire. The meaning of the word itself is the movement (Chala) or the opening (Mukha). There is scope to create a garland of Kerala rhythms and ragas, which are appearing in the ensuing programme.

***Niram:*** Niram means colour or Varnam. Here Niram is an item based on the figure of Kali as drawn on the floor with five kinds of powder in five natural colours and the music sung on the side of such figure of Kali, which is traditionally called "Niram Padal".

***Padam:*** Apart from Swathi Padams we have incorporated many krities from Manipravala literature and Sangham literature like Ardhanareeshwara dance from Chilapathikaram, lyrics from Kalithokai, Dandakam from Unniyadicharitam and the like.

***Tatvam:*** Tatvam imbibes its philosophy from the circumambulation of the devotee around the temple. It also depicts the ritual offering to the sacrificial stones around the temple.

***Jeeva:*** Jeeva represents the voyage of the devotee towards the sanctum of his favourite deity climbing through the steps known as Sopanam. The progress of this slanting journey signifies a growth towards salvation-a point of union with the ultimate. It is a growth from the athivilamba (the slowest) to the athidruta (the highest) speed, which is technically called in the Kerala percussion ensemble as progression towards the needle end of rhythmic experience. The Sopanam style of Mohiniattam declares its adherence to the music of Kerala.

Contrary to the usual practice of employing the oft-repeated Kamatic rhythms, Sopanam Institute has introduced Kerala's own rhythms as defined and enumerated in the thullal works of Kunjan Nambiar, the fore runner of the aesthetic revolution in Kerala, who came out of the conventional concepts and established practices of the elitist arts and drew inspiration from the numerous folk musical and dance forms of the common people. His works are specially noted for their indigenous quality especially in the wide range of rhythms, which provide an organic vitality. Sopanam has used rhythms like Roopam, Champa, Karika, Panchari (Ayyadi), Muri Adanta, Adanta, Chempata, Kundanachi, Marmam, Lekshmi, Kumbham, etc., based on hridaya tala or the rhythm of the heart beats which gives its unique regional flavour.

### *Mohiniattam-Staging of Grace*

Indian dance styles based on legends, mythologies and devotional themes are divergent in their technique. At the same time there is a central motif running through them: the theme of devotion expressed through the heroine that is the dancer to the hero who is none other than God himself. The human soul is conceived as a female yearning for union with the male.

Mohiniattam is one of the major classical dance styles of India. This art form from Kerala is perhaps one of the most graceful dances and totally identifies with the green environment, gentle singing of the palm trees and the calm ocean waters of this state. Kerala has always preserved all traditional arts and the people of the state consider it an integral part of everyday life.

The word *Mohini* means a maiden who charms the onlooker and *attam* means dance. Usually the legends in India links the name of Mohini to that of God Vishnu who had assumed the beautiful form of Mohini to entice Demon Bhasmasura and finally destroyed him. It is said that the demon had a boon which granted him immortality. He could die only if a hand was placed on his head. Mohini danced and made Bhasmasura also dance with her and suddenly for a moment placed her hand on her head. Bhasmasura too followed without thinking and then came his end. There is a common belief that perhaps the dance form got its names from this episode.

By the 16th century, Mohiniattam seemed to have established itself as a separate classical dance form of Karla but its popularity was confined to only some regions of the state. It is only in recent times in the 20th century that Mohiniattam has spread all over India and abroad. Mohiniattam is essentially a solo form of dance.

The royal family of Travancore gave the greatest encouragement to the dances performed by *Dasis*. *Dasis* are women who used to perform in front of the deities in the temples. There were dance schools or *nataka salas* preserved by the royalty where student used to be trained. The first reference to 'Mohiniattam' in literature is to be found in *Vyanatraramala* composed by M.N. Nambuderi assigned to 1709 AD. It tells about the Guru (teacher) of the *Devdasi* and the amount to be shared in balance by the whole troupe. It was only in the 19th century AD that Maharaja Swati Thirunal the then King of Kerala encouraged and patronised Mohiniattam and thus stabilised the art form. He was a true *rasika* (connoisseur), who understood music and dance. He was a scholar, a poet and a great musician.

To make Mohiniattam a distinctive and attractive art form he composed a number of pieces called *varnams* and *padams* and made the music of this art form lyrically rich and attractive. He brought about reforms and improvements in the style and included Mohiniattam recitals in festive celebrations. He also had a dance troupe under his patronage. In his attempts to revive Mohiniattam, he took help of the famous Thanjavur quartet who were famous composers in the Bharata Natyam style of classical dance. Maharaja Swati Thirunal could undoubtedly be said to be the pioneer of Mohiniattam style.

Various teachers and Gurus kept the Mohiniattam dance tradition alive by their efforts In 1930, Mahakavi Valathol founded Kerala Kala Mandalam and along with Kathakali he included Mohiniattam so as to revive the dance form. The first dancer was Kalyaniamma. She also taught in Shantiniketan under Rabindranath Tagore's invitation. The other notable teachers in Kerala Kala Mandalam were Krishna Paniker and Madhavi Amma. In 1950 Thottasseri Chinnammu Amma Joined. It was from these Gurus that a new generation of dancers were born. These teachers maintained the classical patterns of teaching following text like *Natya Shastra* and *Abhinayya-darpana*.

As of now, Mohiniattam is a widely known and popular dance form. The contemporary well known artists, teachers and institutions are Kalamandalam Satyabhama, Ms. Kanaka Rele, Ms. Bharati Shivaji, Guru Thankamani Kutti's institution in Calcutta, Nalanda institution formed by Kanaka Rele and Nrityagram Bangalore established by Pratima Gouri provides training in Mohiniattam. The technique of Mohiniattam accentuates *lasya* and *Sringara* or romance is the prominent *rasa*. *Rasa* means the dominant emotion.

As mentioned earlier Maharaja Swati Thirunal devised a complete repertoire for Mohiniattam, and later Gurus and dancers added more items to that. The basic repertoire begins with the *Calkkettu* – which means stylised rhythm, beginning and ending with passages of invocation. It is followed by a *Jathiswaram* which is a pure dance sequence. The *Varnam* is the *piece de resistance* which has the emotive as well as the pure dance sequences. A purely emotive piece is followed by another rhythmic composition. The *Tala* or system of rhythm in Kerala is unique. Special mention can be made of *Pancha Kumbha Tala* – which are a combination of Five patterns – the five representing the five flowery arrows or *Manmatha* – the God of love. The main percussion instrument used in Mohiniatttam is *Eddaka*. The body of this drum is made of Jack wood and is about a quarter metre long. The skin of calf leather is stretched across a circular ring and placed against the mouth of the drum, one on each side.

The beauty of Indian classical dance is also its appropriate and relevant costume and jewellery. The traditional costume of Mohiniattam is white with gold. The dancer usually wears gold ornaments which symbolises, purity, truth and immortality – all these are attributed to the dance of the celestial maidens. The dancer wears a pair of large round ear studs known as Toda. The necklace is the traditional *Nagapadam* in the shape of a snake's hood, and the *powanmala* – a chain made of gold coins. The forehead is covered with an ornament called the *Nethichutti* and the nose is adorned by *Mukkuthi* or nose ring. The bangles are known as *Kappu*. The coiffure is unique as it is a gathered bun on the left side of the head. The *tilaka* or the red mark on the forehead represents conjugal fidelity of the Hindu women.

The distinctive style of Mohiniattam is the complete absence of heavy stamping and rhythmical tension. Footwork is gentle and soft and sliding. The movements are never abrupt, they are dignified, easy and natural, but the vertical line of the body is never broken. Hence, among the styles detailed by Bharata Muni in the ancient Indian treatise on dance, the *Natya Shastra*, Mohiniattam resembles the Kaisiki type meaning graceful. So, the style becomes most suitable for showing *Sringara Rasa* or the emotion of love.

***Some thoughts on Mohiniattam***

Mohiniattam is one of the most lyrical classical dance forms of India, originating from Kerala. The word *Mohini* stands for an enchantress, a beautiful woman who seduces others for a particular purpose. *Attam* means dance. So Mohiniattam is the dance of the enchantress.

The earliest known textual reference about Mohiniattam is found in a commentary on the Vyavaharamala, a Sanskrit text written by Mazhamangalam Namboodiri during the 16th century. In the commentary believed to be authored by a migrated Brahman scholar of Kerala, the word for dancers was translated as Mohiniattam artistes, etc. Another reference on Mohiniattam can be found in the Ottanthullal (a semi-classical and semi-folk dramatic art form of Kerala) script Ghoshayatra, authored by Kunchan Nambiar during the 2nd half of the 18th century.

Perhaps Mohiniattam is the only dance form of India that was subject to several revivals and renaissance. Some scholars believe that like Bharata Natyam, Mohiniattam too was associated with devadasi tradition and other scholars think Mohiniattam was a dance form performed by women but not associated with devadasi system.

Whatever it is, for several reasons the male members of the affluent and powerful Namboodiri and Nair families exploited the Mohiniattam dancers. Gradually the dance was considered inappropriate and there were few takers for it. The efforts of Maharaj Swathitirunal (1813-1846) and the attempts of Kerala poet laureate Vallathol Narayana Menon, in 1932, 1937 and in 1950, to revive Mohiniattam are important endeavors which are now considered as crucial chapters in the history of this art.

The tradition of this dance form sustained through the contributions of two veterans, Guru Kalyanikutti Amma and Guru Satyabhama. While Guru Kalyanikutty Amma's was an effort at her individual level, Guru Sathyabhama got the platform of the Kerala Kalamandalam, where since 1957, until her retirement as its Principal in 1993, she was faculty. While dance forms like Bharata Natyam and Odissi attained both national and international significance until recently Mohiniattam was sidelined. There are a few reasons behind this.

1. Kerala is a land blessed with classical arts unlike any other States of India. While Tamil Nadu is known as the land of Bharata Natyam and Orissa as the land of Odissi (Orissi), Kerala is better known as the land of Koodiyattam and Kathakali. While people and pundits of other states got either one classical form or nothing to pamper and nourish, Keralites are blessed with a few. The more stylised and classical forms got their due share. Parallel to the development of Bharata Natyam in Tamil Nadu, Kerala saw a development in sustaining Kathakali as a rich art form, followed by Koodiyattam. Hence Mohiniattam did not get much attention.
2. Mohiniattam too was revived and preserved through the efforts of Kerala poet Vallathol Narayana Menon through the institutionalisation of the art at the Kalamandalam. However, even at the Kalamandalam Kathakali enjoyed all sorts of priority, followed by Koodiyattam.
3. None took Mohiniattam seriously to the national performing scene, during the sixties and early seventies.
4. The repertoires of Mohiniattam were set similar to the Bharata Natyam. Like the Bharata Natyam, Kamatic music too was adapted for Mohiniattam. During those periods no serious research was done into the music of Kerala, the sopana sangeetam, which is most ideal for Mohiniattam.
5. Compared to Bharata Natyam, Mohiniattam is a slow, soft and graceful dance. It is basically lasya-oriented dance form. Further, no serious research was done at the esthetical appeal of the dance form and restricted to off-white dresses, though there is historical evidence that formerly Mohiniattam dancers used colored and check blouses.

6. Following or rather imitating the pattern of Bharata Natyam in terms of repertoire and music and being a slow dance form sans colorful dresses naturally pulled down Mohiniattam to treat it as a poor cousin of Bharata Natyam.
7. Mohiniattam is not yet completely free from controversy about style, excessive influence of Bharata Natyam;, etc. Certain self-adorned purists had contributed a lot of hindrances too to its development. Due to this several talented young dancers were compelled to refrain themselves from doing any serious work in Mohiniattam.
8. Generally, almost all the Kerala dancers practised three dance forms, including Mohiniattam. Their priority was Bharata Natyam, followed by Mohiniattam and Kuchipudi.

Now, slowly Mohiniattam started getting its due share in both the national and international performing scene. The identity of sopana sangeetam (Kerala music) as the music of Mohiniattam is recognised. New dancers made remarkable attempts to delineate the art from following the heels of Bharata Natyam, by choreographing new items. Jayadeb's ashtapadi got an eternally alluring charm in Mohiniattam stage.

Scholar-poet and theatre thespian Kavalam Narayana Panicker came forward with new compositions and researched theories to put Mohiniattam back to its rail, duly freeing it from imitating the Bharata Natyam repertoire, by emphasising on the aesthetics and ethnic influence of the art form. Artists like Kanak Rele and Bharati Shivaji took initiative to take it to more and more platforms. While thinking on the aesthetics of an art form, one cannot afford to overlook the ethnic or regional touches of the art form.

No doubt, the change in the coiffure of the dance form to give it more a Kerala touch was a remarkable contribution in this direction. The change in the hairstyle to give the Mohini a typical Kerala touch was done at the platform of the Kalamandalam under the initiation of Guru Kalamandalam Sathyabhama.

Kondakettal (hair being bunched upon the left side of the head with strands of jasmine flowers circling it) was accepted as the coiffure of the art form. In any old picture of traditional Kerala women one can see this coiffure, let alone the royal women in Ravi Varma paintings. Generally, for Mohiniattam off-white dresses with golden/colored borders are used. Very limited attempts are made so far to make the costume more attractive which is one of the important aspects of any dance form to satisfy the visual needs of the rasikas (audience). Even though now a day all rasas have been used for Mohiniattam items, the basic Rasa of Mohiniattam are Sringara (eroticism) Bhakti (devotion). The basic tempo is lasya, highly feminine movements. Hence, as far as the body language of the art is concerned it is equally important to consider both what should be done and what should not be done.

Now, gradually, Mohiniattam started getting its due share both at the national and international performing scene. Art lovers and connoisseurs started recognising the performance potential and significance of Mohiniattam. Mohiniattam is getting the long deserving recognition in lead festivals of the country, especially outside Kerala.

## Odissi

Odissi is an Indian classical dance style from the eastern state of Orissa in India, being apart of the ancient Odra Magadha style of dance from the eastern region. There is evidence that Odissi was danced in the temples of Orissa as far back as the 2nd Century BC. Originally performed as a sacred ritual dedicated to the Gods, Odissi is marked by sensuousness and lyricism, soft, graceful and flowing movements that reflect the divine sculptural motifs of the temples of Orissa.

Odissi owes its origin to the temple dances of the devadasis or temple dancers, whose earliest mention dates back to 10th Century AD. Female attendants of the temple, known as Maharis, danced for the Gods at various times of day to accompany various rituals of the temple deity. This dance was to the accompaniment of Mardala or the pakhawaj, small cymbals, flute and veena, a string instrument like the sitar.

Over time however, the Mahari tradition started declining and a new class of dancers was created to revive the Odissi dance tradition starting in the 17th Century. This class consisted of young boys or Gotipuas who danced in female costumes. Most of the present day Odissi gurus or teachers were Gotipuas in their youth.

These two living traditions were researched on after India's independence from colonial rule and incorporated into what is today the Odissi style. Master teachers or Gurus, such the legendary Guru Kelucharan Mohapatra, Guru Pankaj Charan Das, Guru Mayadhar Raut, Guru Deba Prasad Das, etc., scholars and performers came together for research based on these traditions and ancient texts such as the Natya Shastra and Abhinaya Darpanam, to create this style in its present form. Odissi is a graceful style of classical dance that is inspired thematically by the literature, art and spiritual movements of the Vaishnava (worshippers of Vishnu) as well as Shaiva (worshippers of Shiva) sects of Hinduism, and in technique, by the ancient Hindu temple sculptures of Orissa

What is Odissi? Orissi, or Odissi, is a classical dance form from the state of Orissa. Orissi is characterised by fluidity of the upper torso (the waves of the ocean on the shores of Puri) and gracefulness in gestures and wristwork (swaying of the palms), juxtaposed with firm footwork (heartbeat of Mother Earth). All classical Indian dance forms include both pure rhythmic dances and acting or story dances.

The rhythmic dances of Odissi are called batu/sthayi (foundation), pallavi (flowering), and moksha (liberation). The acting dances are called abhinaya. Although incorporating a range of emotions and mythologies, the eternal union of Radha and Krishna (Gita Govinda) is central to the abhinaya in Odissi Dance. Either Odissi or Orissi may be considered acceptable in writing.

Sculptures of Odissi dancers adorn many temple walls in Orissa. Carving of a dancer playing flute in the tribhangi position for a rapt listener (right) exemplifies the Odissi pose now associated with Lord Krishna. Odissi traces its origins to the ritual dances performed in the temples of ancient northern

India. Today the name Odissi refers to the dance style of the state of Orissa in eastern India. Like other classical arts of India, this ancient dance style had suffered a decline as temples and artists lost the patronage of feudal rulers and princely states, and by the 1930s and 40s, there were very few surviving practitioners of the art.

The current form of Odissi is the product of a 20th century revival. Dedicated scholars and dance enthusiasts carefully researched manuscripts and studied the sculpture, painting and poetry of the region. They also met and observed the performances of the few existing performers, in order to revive and restructure Odissi as a unique classical dance style adapted to the requirements of formal stage presentation. Over the years Odissi has become one of the most popular classical dance styles.

Like other Indian classical dance forms, Odissi has two major facets: Nritta or non-representational dance, in which ornamental patterns are created using body movements in space and time; and Abhinaya, or stylised mime in which symbolic hand gestures and facial expressions are used to interpret a story or theme. The divine love tales of Radha and the cowherd God Krishna are favourite themes for interpretation, and a typical recital of Odissi will contain at least one or two ashtapadis (poem of eight couplets) from Jayadeva's Gita Govindam, which describes in exquisite Sanskrit poetry the complex relationship between Radha and her Lord.

The technique of Odissi includes repeated use of the tribhangi, or thrice deflected posture, in which the body is bent in three places, approximating the shape of a helix. This posture and the characteristic shifting of the torso from side to side, make Odissi a difficult style to execute. When mastered, it is the epitome of fluid grace and has a distinctively lyrical quality that is very appealing.

***The Backdrop***

Like other forms of Indian classical dance, the *Odissi* style traces its origins back to antiquity. Dancers are found depicted in bas-relief in the hills of Udaygiri (near Bhubaneshwar) dating back to the 1st century BC. The *Natya Shastra* speaks of the dance from this region and refers to it as *Odra-Magadhi*. Over the centuries three schools of *Odissi* dance developed: *Mahari, Nartaki*, and *Gotipau*. The *Mahari* tradition is the *devadasi* tradition; this is the use of women who are attached to deities in the temple. The *Nartaki* tradition is the school of *Odissi* dance which developed in the royal courts. *Gotipau* is a style characterised by the use of young boys dressed up in female clothing to perform female roles.

*Odissi* dance was held in high esteem before the 17th century. Nobility were known for their patronage of the arts, and it was not unheard of for royalty of both sexes to be accomplished dancers. However, after the 17th century, the social position of dancers began to decline. Dancing girls were considered to be little more than prostitutes, and the "Anti-Nautch" movement of the British brought *Odissi* dance to near extinction.

Before Independence, the position of *Orissi* dance was very bad. The tradition of dancing girls at the temple at Puri was abolished. The royal patronage of *nartaki* had been severely eroded by the absorption of India under the crown. The only viable *Odissi* tradition was the *Gotipau*. This had weathered the British Anti-Nautch movement simply because it was danced by males. Yet even the *Gotipau* tradition was in a very bad state.

Independence brought a major change in official attitudes toward Indian Dance. Like the other classical arts, dance was seen as a way to define India's national identity. Governmental and non-governmental patronage increased. The few remaining *Odissi* dancers were given employment, and a massive job of reconstructing the *Odissi* dance began. This reconstruction involved combing through ancient texts, and more importantly, the close examination of dance posses represented in bas-relief in the various temples.

There were a number of people who were responsible for the reconstruction and popularisation of *Odissi* dance. Most notable are Guru Deba Prasad Das, Guru Mayadhar Raut,

Guru Pankaj Charan Das, Guru Mahadev Rout, Guru Raghu Dutta, and Guru Kelu Charan Mahapatra. Today *Odissi* dance is once again deemed a viable and "classical" dance.

### *Archaeological/Sculptural Evidence*

The carvings in the Rani Gumpha Caves in Orissa from the 2nd century B.C depict the first traces of dance, much earlier than the writings of Natya Shastra according to scholars. Natya Shastra mentions four types of vrittis:anti, Dakshinatya, Panchali, and Odra Magadhi. Odhra Magadhi is identified as the earliest precursor of the present Odissi.

***2nd Century B.C. to 5th Century A.D.:*** Orissa has been a home for many kingdoms, Buddhist, Jaina and Shaivite and others before the Vaishnavite cult began. Following Temples and Caves belong to the from 2nd century B.C to 5th century A.D.

***Udayagiri and the Khandagiri Caves*:** These are the first records in stone of the historic period where in full dances scenes have been found carved in the caves.

***Ratnagiri and Lalitagiri Caves:*** Later during the *Buddhism cult* we find dance figures in movement or poses which establishes a certain continuity between the dance styles seen in the Udayagiri. There are Buddhist deities such as Marichi and Aparajita.

***Tantric Temples:*** such as the Hirapur Shrine, many of the yoginis especially are depicted in poses reminiscent of present day Odissi.

***6th Century A.D. to 10th Century A.D.:*** *Shaivite Cults* took strong roots in the 7th century A.D. Although we do find some of the first dance reliefs of the Nataraja in the 4th century A.D. Like the Shiva image with 8 hands holding a veena, trishula and akshyamla, a damru with a pataka and a varda hasta. It belonged to the king of the Bhanja dynasty, Shatrubhanja, who constructed the shrines for Shiva.

### *Bhubaneshwar Temples*

From the 6th and 7th century onwards, there is a massive evidence of dance as part of worship and presumably this has inspired the sculptures of the early medieval temples of Bhubaneshwar. Within 300 years, nearly 500 temples were constructed. The temples include the Bharteshvara temple (6th Century A.D.), Parsuameshvara Temple (7th Century A.D.), Vaitan Deul, Sisiresvara, Muktesvara Temple, and Raja-Rani Temple. Each of them is a jewel of architecture in themselves built with perfect balance and proportion.

Also, the sculptors have not only carved the poses but also the execution of the dynamic movements. It includes deities like Shiva, Durga, Ganesha, Nayaka-Nayikas on the walls in beautiful dancing poses and dance compositions. By 8th century, dance had already achieved a very distinctive stylisation in Orissa. There were already the traces of the Tribhanga poses, Ardhamandali, sthanas, karanas, charis, etc.

This sculptural evidence of dance in the temples of Bhuvaneshwar belonging to the 7,8,9 and 10th centuries almost come to a close around 11th and 12th centuries when changes take place in Orissa.

***11th Century AD to 12th Century AD and Onwards:*** By the 11th Century A.D. there was the emergence of a *Vaishnavite cult* distinctive to Orissa.

***Temple of Jagannath at Puri:*** Between the rulers of Chodagandeva and Anangabhimadev, was built the Temple of Jagannath. The temple itself was outstanding in its architectural plan, its sculptural reliefs and its special hall of the dance called the *Nat Mandir*.

### *Maharis and Gotipuas*

No definite date can be conclusively ascribed regarding the practice of dance as an indispensable part of the ritual of the worship. But from chronicle records of the temple called Mandal Panji, it is clear that it was certainly co-terminus with the Jagannath cult.

The consecration of females to the service of temple dancing began in the Shaivite temples and continued in the Jagannath temple in service of the Lord Jagannath. These female attendants have been known as maharis (great women) or devadasis (servants of the lord) and have been considered the wives of Lord Jagannath. Odissi developed through their art. A class of boy dancers emerged in the 17th Century called gotipuas. Goti means single and pua means boy. They brought the dance style out of the temples and performed in public.

### *Konark*

Built round the 13th Century, Konark was a masterpiece of architectural design and an excellence in sculptural relief. Conceived as a chariot or ratha on 24 wheels dedicated to Surya (Sun), the temple reverberates with the movement of the dance whether in relief or around the main shrine or the Jagmohan or the Bhogmandap and most of all Nat Mandir. By the time of the Konark temple, the dance style had been set and a very distinctive method of body manipulation is apparent.

### *Manuscript Evidence*

From 15th century onwards, it is observed by scholars, that no architectural activity took place. But on the other hand, the artists canalised into writing of manuscripts, the illustrations of manuscripts and paitings on the walls of temples. Some of these manuscripts deal distinctively only with dance.

***Abhinaya Chandrika:*** Abhinaya Chandrika written by Maheshvara Mahapatra is a detailed study of the various movements of the feet, hands, the standing postures, the movement and the dance reperoire. It also includes illustrations of the *Karanas* mentioned in *Natya Shastra*.

***Shilpaprakasha:*** Manuscript Shilpaprakasha is among those illustrated manuscripts which deals with the Orissan architecture and sculpture as well as the figures of dance. In this one finds a elaborate analysis of the manner in which the *salabhanjikas* or the feminine figures caleed the *alasa kanyas* are carved in the temple. The illustrations of Shilpaprakãsha reinforces the evidence of sculpture in temples.

***Jain Manuscripts:*** A rather an unexpected source, the Jain Manuscripts, especially the Kalpasutra and Kalkacharya Kathãs show traces of Orissan dance style although they were being executed in Gujarat. The marginal figures of dancers show women in poses and movements similar to the distinctive style of Orissa. One of the famous illustrated Jain Manuscript called the Devasanpada Kalpasutra (1501, Jamnagar), there is depiction of the samapada, the tribhangi and the chuaka.

This shows that there was a great deal of mobility between east and west and many migrations took place. According to some historians, there were groups of dancers who were brought to Puri from Gujarat and also from Andhra.

***Textual Evidence***

The evidence of dance is further supported by the texts available on music and dance written in Orissa. Some of them include "Sangitanarayan" by Narayan Dev Gajapti (consists one section on dance called as the *Nritya Khand*), Nritya Kaumudi and Natya Manorama by Raghunath Rath (18th century), Abhinaya Darpana by Yadunath Sinha (17th-18th century), etc.

***Literary Evidence***

Many of the Orissan Literature works contain description of dance like Oriya Mahabharta by Saral Das (15th century), Dandi Ramayana by Balarama Das (16th century) and Niladri Mahodaya of Lokanath Vidyadhara (17th century).

Not many literary works survive of the Shaivite tradition of Orissa (8th to 11th century). Sanskrit Poetry, Gita Govinda by Saint Jayadev, which is an integral part of abhinaya in Odissi dance recital, was contemporary with the construction of the Jagannath temple. Some of the first commentaries on this great poem were written in Orissa and it was accepted as a text of worship in the Jagannath temple.

There were many other composers like Ramananda Rai (play-Jagannath Vallabh Nataka), Jayadeva-II (Piyush Lahari), King Kapilendra Deva (Parsuram Vijaya), the outstanding poet Upendra Bhanjadeo, Kavi Surya, Baladev Rath, Gopal Krishna Pattanayak and Banmalidas. The tradition of the compositions of the lyrical poetry and the dramatic works and the singing of the Gita Govinda both in Sanskrit as well as Oriya translations continued well into the 19th century.

***Revival:*** During the Mughal rule of India, the duties of the maharis, the temple dancers, shifted as they were also employed to entertain the royal family and courtiers in the royal courts. They became associated with concumbinage in respect to the king and ceased to be respected solely as servants to Lord Jagannath. A decline and degradation occurred in all the Indian classical dance styles during the British period, especially when a bill was passed prohibiting temple dancing.

The nationalistic leaders instigated the cultural renaissance and regeneration of India including the revival of the Indian dances as girls from respectable families learnt the almost extinct dance styles. At independence time, only Odissi had yet to be rediscovered. With the help of many, including Guru Kelucharan Mohapatra, Odissi was revived as a classical art form in 1955. Therefore, the Odissi dance recital that we see today is an attempt of reconstruction from the fragments of the Mahari tradition, Gotipua tradition, Bandhnritya tradition of martial arts, Chhau tradition known to Orissa and an ofcourse the inspiration drawn from the sculptural relief and pictorial image.

### *Style*

There are a number of characteristics of the *Odissi* dance. The style may be seen as a conglomeration of aesthetic and technical details. One of the most characteristic features of *Odissi* dance is the *Tribhangi*. The concept of *Tribhang* divides the body into three parts, head, bust, and torso. Any posture which deals with these three elements is called *tribhangi*. This concept has created the very characteristic poses which are more contorted than found in other classical Indian dances.

The *mudras* are also important. The term *mudra* means "stamp" and is a hand position which signifies things. The use of *mudras* help tell a story in a manner similar to the hula of Hawaii.

### *Themes*

The themes of *Odissi* are almost exclusively religious in nature. They most commonly revolve around Krishna. Although the worship of Krishna is found throughout India, there are local themes which are emphasised. The *Ashtapadi's* of Jayadev are a very common theme.

### *Music*

The musical accompaniment of *Odissi* dance is essentially the same as the music of *Odissa* itself. There are various views on how the music of the *Odissi* relates to the music of greater North India. It is usually considered just another flavour of *Hindustani sangeet*, however there are some who feel that *Odissi* should be considered a separate classical system.

There are a number of musical instruments used to accompany the *Odissi* dance. One of the most important is the *pakhawaj*, also known as the *madal*. This is the same *pakhawaj* that is used elsewhere in the north except for a few small changes. One difference is that the right head is a bit smaller than the usual north Indian *pakhawaj*. This necessitates a technique which in many ways is more like that of the *tabla*, or *mridangam*. Other instruments which are commonly used are the *bansuri* (bamboo flute), the *manjira* (metal cymbals), the *sitar* and the *tanpura*.

### *Movement Patterns*

The movement technique is developed from the basic position. There can be the possibility of walking in space, in different directions, in different manner and at different levels. The most characteristic amongst these is the semi-circular walk or the covering of space by one leg, more specifically the calf in semi circles, returning back to centre. The other half of the body is static. The same as the Minadandi, *i.e.* covering space like a fish. There is then the manner of covering space in circles, half circles and concentric circles. This is known as ghera.

From the tribhanga position emerge another group of movement. One half of the body is kept static along the vertical median, one knee continues to be bent and the other leg is either extended to the side or to the front or to the back. It can cross the static foot at the back or the front, it can be elevated at different levels and it can be totally extended at the back with the knee bending or calf and thigh in a straight line. Through a sitting or a kneeling position another group of movements emerge. The most characteristic amongst these is the extension of one leg to the side or to the back while one foot and knee are in contact with the ground. These movements arise out of the sitting position known by the generic term baitha. Another group of movements emerge out of basic position of the chauka or the mandalasthana. Here either movement can be in place, *i.e.* the feet can be static and only the torso can move or a complete pirouette can be executed holding the chauka position. Weight rests on the bent leg and the free leg executes a pirouette.

The Odissi technique has developed many single leg movements called the ek pada chari or using both legs or the feet called the dvipada charis and innumerable other ways of depicting the pose which can be seen in the sculptures reliefs in the Orissan temples. The dancer controls her body in the manner in which the sculpture pose is held for a spilt second only to get back into a series of movements termed. The sculpturesque quality of Odissi dance is dependent on perfect execution of these charis.

Another group of movements termed as Bhramaris are equally important. These are the spins or the pirouettes. Pirouettes can be executed in the tribhanga position or the chauka, both clockwise and anticlockwise and they can be executed in the standing position. Pirouettes also emerge from the three basic positions of the samapada, the tribhanga and the chauka. There is a simple bhramari, a bhramari with a jump therefore called an ut-pluta bhramari or an anti-clockwise pirouette called Viparita bhramari. There is also the bhramari called the antara bhramari. Here one foot touches the knee of the other leg and a pirouette is executed. The movement patterns of Odissi dance emerges from the positions, the manner of covering space and the method of executing the bhramaris.

There are then the group movements which may be called elevations, jumps or Utpluta. There is whole group of movements in Odissi dance where jumps and hopes are suggested and there is lack of contact with the ground. There are the sculptural poses which can contained within the dance techniques. From the tribhanga can emerge many sculptural poses which have been given different names some suggesting the type of heroines, *i.e.* nayikas, others suggesting the type of movement, *i.e.* half bent, full bent etc. and yet others suggesting an approach movement in Odissi dancing are called bhangis or sometimes the thais.

### *Nava Rasa (Nine Moods)*

There are 9 moods or sentiments in Indian classical dance, called rasas. They are: srngara (love), hasya (laughter), karuna (sadness), raudra (anger), vira (pride), bhayanaka (fear), bibhatsa (disgust), adbhuta (wonder), and shanta (peace). Rasa is two-fold, experienced by the dancer and the audience. Situations are depicted using the state of the rasa, called bhava.

### *More than Dance: A Feast for the Senses*

Observing Odissi awakes all the senses. Performances intertwine drama and story telling, hypnotic music, richly hued silk costumes and, of course, the intricacies of the dance itself—a panoply of hand and eye gestures, facial expressions, rhythmic footwork and soft, sensual body movements. With so much going on, how is an audience to fully absorb and appreciate the art form?

"Watch visually and on an instinctive level, without intellectualising it," Dey recommends. "The main thing is to realise that Odissi is an ancient tradition that has evolved along with the traditions of visual art, music, theatre and literature. The song lyrics are themselves great pieces of literature. The music is classical. Everything that contributes to the dance is valid and strong in its [respective] traditions. Realise the interconnectedness—that it's not just about dance, even though it is dance."

> *"The other thing to realise is that classical Indian dance works on two levels. The dances are told through stories that could be about human beings or about Gods, but its always symbolic and always about fundamental philosophical truths that come from ancient texts such*

*as the Vedas and Upanishads. We draw on sacred texts to create the basis for the dance. So, realise it's not just about what a particular choreographer or dancer feels like portraying, and usually it's not about commonplace things. There are many layers."*

To help audiences grasp all the layers, Dey provides programme notes and explanations before each piece.

*"You may not be able to appreciate all the layers at first, but it's alright because even at a basic level, there is visual beauty that gives enjoyment. As you watch more and more and get used to what it is visually, you'll be able to grasp more of the deeper layers."*

***The Discipline of Odissi***

Odissi derives from the temple sculptures and, as such, its style is sculptural in nature. Typically, the upper body is fluid and graceful, and moves in isolation to the lower body, which is strongly rooted to the earth. Because of the sophisticated array of precise techniques for virtually every part of the body, it takes years of intensive training just to learn the fundamentals.

*"Then, it all has to come together: the hands, arms, legs, head, facial expressions, torso, hips, each part of the body," Dey explains. "There are thousands of movements, each with a different name. There is a systematic learning process. We start with body conditioning exercises, everything from eyebrows to neck to lips. Each focuses on a different aspect of what is to come later—basic steps, hand gestures, eye gestures, hip positions, ways of moving the feet, using facial muscles to express different emotions. There are specific ways to learn each of these things."*

*"If you want to learn Odissi, keep in mind that it takes four to five years before you can do anything meaningful, not to say that you cannot enjoy the process and do it for pleasure. But it's not true that you can take a few classes and start performing. You have to give it time and dedication."*

As one of Dey's students, Lisa Di Gioia Nutini can attest to the level of commitment required to fully learn the art of Odissi.

> *"It's taken me two and a half years to learn the postures and build up strength to feel comfortable doing them," Di Gioia Nutini comments. "It's a lot to absorb, but for me, it has a healing aspect, whether or not I'm good at it. Odissi is not just a dance. Every movement is a sacred language unto itself."*

### *The Repertoire*

The repertoire of Odissi not only consists of dance items to present in a solo program but also represents a process in training, a process in following the spiritual path of Odissi where the Guru (teacher) is like the spiritual mentor, and a process in maturity. Today, a full traditional solo programme consists of a Mangalacharan to begin the program, possibly Batu Nritya, one or two Pallavis, one or more Abhinayas and Mokshya to conclude. Group dance dramas have gained increasing popularity in Odissi. In Odissi, as in the other Indian classical dance styles, the dances are classified as nritta (pure technical dance with no meaning), nritya (expressional dance having meaning), and natya (drama).

1. *Mangalacharan:* Mangalacharan marks the entrance of the dancer on stage in the Odissi style. The dancer invokes the blessings of the presiding deity, Lord Jagannath (the Lord of the Universe) for an auspicious beginning. The dancer offers salutations to Mother Earth, the teacher, the accompanists, and the audience. The central piece of the item is a prayer in praise of a Hindu God or Goddess. Mangalacharan begins as an invocational prayer in praise of the Hindu Lord Ganesh, the remover of all obstacles.
2. *Batu Nritya:* Batu Nritya or Batu, the second item of the Odissi repertoire, is a basic example of nritta or pure dance. In this dance, particularly, the interrelationship between temple sculptural art and Odissi dance is established with an array of

sculpturesque poses taken directly from the innumerable dancing sculptures adorning the temples of Orissa. These poses are stringed together with steps in different rhythms. The Guru and student take an oath, Batu Mantra, for the training and molding of the student's body to perform the technique in the form of the first pure dance.

3. *Pallavi:* The third item, Pallavi, is a nritta or pure dance like Batu. However, Pallavi differs from Batu in that it is more music oriented. Pallavi means elaboration. It is applicable here not only to the dance but to the music which accompanies it. Pallavi is woven with a series of lyrical movements bringing out the elaborate grace and charm of Odissi.

   In Pallavi, the technique blossoms in the dancer as he/she shows mastery and artistry in the Odissi technique.

4. *Abhinaya:* Abhinaya, the fourth item of the Odissi repertoire, is mime or nritya using a most intricate language composed of facial expressions, hand gestures, and through the use of the body. The dancer vividly depicts a song or poem. Although some Abhinayas are devotional songs, often the love theme or srngara rasa is explored between a nayaka and nayika (hero and heroine) usually Lord Krishna and Radha. For many centuries, the Odissi repertoire in the temple solely consisted of songs from the Gita Govindam, which the temple dancing girls (Maharis) would sing and dance to for the pleasure of the Lord. Gita Govindam is a famous poem, written in 12th century by poet Jayadeva, a great devotee of Lord Jagannath. Gita Govindam consists of 24 ashtapadis (8-versed songs), telling the story of Lord Krishna and Radha, showing their love in physical separation and finally in spiritual unification.

   The dancer achieves expertise in expression through the vivid portrayal of songs in Abhinaya.

5. *Mokshya:* The fifth and final item of the Odissi repertoire, Mokshya, parallels the concept of Mokshya or liberation in Hinduism, in which the dancer attempts

to attain liberation or salvation in the ultimate surrender to God through dance. Mokshya is a fast paced dance of ecstacy.

In Mokshya, the dancer uses the technique to dance with ecstatic joy, eventually to release him/her from it and unify with God.

6. *Dance Dramas:* Since the revival of Odissi dance, the dance style has seen the addition of a new form—the dance drama. The glory of the Odissi dance drama form banks upon the style's expressive and sculptural characteristics. It is particularly effective in displaying the love of a nayaka and nayika (hero and heroine).

## Sattriya

Sattriya dance is a classical dance form of India. It is devotional in character and 'Bhakti Rasa' (spiritual aspect) is predominant in this dance form. This dance form was evolved in Assam in the 15th century by the great Vaishnavite saint Shri Sankardev who was a social reformer and a great performing artist. References of this dance form are found in the ancient Indian classical texts like Natya Shastra, Kalikapurana, Yoginitantra, Abhinayadarpana and also in sculptures, historical relics, etc.

### *Purity of Form*

The efforts of Indira have helped turn Sattriya into a very aesthetic statement. Without disturbing the tradition she has introduced subtle changes that has given it an articulated strength.

*"I have always insisted that the pure form of Sattriya be retained. Only after this can one experiment with music, text or costume. For instance, the monks used only white costumes. We use a two-piece dress in Assamese silk, which is made to order. The flower prints are all traditional, like the ornaments the dancer wears. In the 'sattras', only the `taal' and `khol' were used as music accompaniments. But now we use other instruments like the harmonium, tanpura, violin and*

*flute. We have also experimented with various other texts."*

In 1982, Indira, along with her husband P.P. Bora, set up 'Kalabhumi,' a cultural organisation, in Guwahati.

"We have more than 500 students learning Bharata Natyam, Kuchipudi, Sattriya and other dance forms. Our aim is to revive and promote various traditional dance and music of the northeast, which is not very popular outside the region. Many of our students have started their own schools in different parts of the region." Carrying on the tradition is Indira's daughter Menaka.

"She is being trained at the Bharata Kalanjali, Chennai, under the Dhananjayans. She is also learning Kuchipudi," says a visibly proud mother.

***Gentle and Hypnotic; a Dream-like Effect***

Sattriya is a word derived from Sattra which means monastery. In the mid 15th century, Shankardev, a poet and religious leader united the various sects of Assam through his teachings and established a universal social brotherhood of Neo-Vaishnavism through congregational prayer. This included music, dance and drama based on the life of Lord Krishna. The monks who lived in these Sattras performed these dance dramas as a votive offering to their Lord. Shankardev composed Bargeet, Ojha Pali songs and numerous dances which were incorporated into the dance drama called Ankiya Nat.

The framework and content of these Sattriya dances were well preserved in the monasteries which were spread all across Assam. With texts like Sri Hastamuktavali which describes detailed used of hand gestures, the style has all the elements of Indian classical dance including a margam of eight sequences which encompasses the tandava and lasya elements. This eloquent ritual tradition has now been passed on to interested artistes who are vigorously engaged in performing and popularising Sattriya dance in India and elsewhere in the world. Sattras are the Vaishnava monasteries in Assam. The saint poet Shankar Deva of the 15th century AD started this institution to bring harmony to the region of Assam through religion, creating forms of dance—dramas, music, painting and collective prayer. The dance forms which have come to stay are called Sattriya dances, sharing all the characteristics of a classical dance form.

As a living tradition these dances are performed in the namghar, the prayer hall of the sattra by the celibate monks. Dressed in white costumes and turbans, head gears, they include kho lplaying, performing dance, creating soundscapes, floor patterns and choreographic designs. The numbers like "Sutradhari," "Chali," "Jhumura" partake of nritta, pure dance, nritya, expressional dance and dance-drama elements. The music is provided by khol-drum, patital, boratal-cymbals along with songs. The repertoire of Sattriya is vast. Now young female dancers also study these dances and they have come out of the sattra. They are presented on the metropolitan stages, with typical music of Assam, costumes and literary compositions viz borgeet. Both solo and group numbers enrich its presentation.

## Some Folk Dances of India

Dumhal of Kashmir is a dance performed by the menfolk of the Wattal tribe of Kashmir on specific occasions. The performers wear long colourful robes, tall conical caps which are studded with beads and shells. The party moves in a procession carrying a banner in a very ceremonial fashion. It is dug into the ground and the men begin to dance, forming a circle. The musical accompaniment comprises a drum and the vocal singing of the participants. Dumhal is performed on set occasions and at set locations.

Rouff is also a folk dance of Kashmir. It is danced solely by women on festive occasions. Rouff displays simple footwork.

Hikat is danced by women of Himachal Pradesh, and is a modification of a game played by children. Forming pairs, the participants extend their arms to the front gripping each other's wrists and with the body inclined back, go round and round at the same spot. With wide range and variety of the ethnic groups, Himachal Pradesh is blessed with natural beauty and artistic history. People living in this natural beauty, adorn themselves for the dance at all times of the year, in all regions, and continue to express themselves through music and dance.

In the Kulu valley, the festival of Dusehra is celebrated with great pomp and show. Images of Raghunathji are brought from the different shrines to a central place, and then there is singing ana dancing. Dances of the region are collectively known as Natio, though each may be meant for a different purpose. No festive occasion, including wedding and similar social ceremonies, is complete without dancing. All regions of Himachal Pradesh have their own dances. Mostly men and women dance together, close to each other in the formation. Namagen dance is performed in September to celebrate the autumnal hues. The costumes are largely woolen and richly studded ornaments of silver are worn by women. The most picturesque amongst these are dances of Gaddis. The dances of the Doms and the Bhotiyas in Uttar Pradesh range from simple performances of rejoicing to ritualistic dances. The most spectacular amongst these is the Dhurang which is connected with the death ceremonies. Its objective is to liberate the soul of the dead person from evil spirits. All the dancers hold swords and dance in a circle. The movements are virile and reminds one of the hunting dances of the Nagas on the eastern borders of India.

The Jhumeila, the Chaunfla of Garhwal and the Hurkia Baul of Kumaon, Uttaranchal, are seasonal dances. The Hurkia Baul is performed during paddy and maize cultivation. On a fixed day, after preliminary ritual, the dance is performed in different fields by turns. The name of the dance is derived from hurkia, the drum which constitutes the only musical accompaniment, and baul, the song. The singer narrates the story of battles and heroic deeds, the players enter from two opposite sides and enact the stories in a series of crisp movements. The farmers form two rows and move backwards in unison, while responding to the tunes of the song and the rhythm of the players.

A famous dance of Kumaon, Uttar Pradesh, is the Chholiya, performed during marriages. As the procession proceeds to the bride's house, men dancers, armed with swords and shields, dance spiritedly. Amongst the occupational groups, the most enthusiastic dancers are the dhobis, the chamars and the ahirs. The dhobis dance to celebrate any significant occasion. They sing and dance on the occasion of a birth or marriage, and during Holi or Dusehra. There are Rasa Dances that revolve around the early life of Krishna. The most interesting group of dances are the dances of the agricultural community which revolve round the annual seasons and which have a ritualistic and a functional dimension.

Dalkhai of Orissa is performed by women of the Sambalpur tribes at the time of seasonal festivals. The dance is quite vigorous, and is accompanied by a set of particular musical instruments, played by men, of which the drummers often join the dance. A dummy horse version is the Chaiti Ghorha, danced by a community of fisher folk. The performers are all men. Apart from dancing, the performers sing, deliver homilies of sorts, and offer brief dramatic enactments peppered with wit and humour.

Gendi or stilt dancing is fairly common among Gond children of Madhya Pradesh and Chhattisgarh. The dance is popular in the Vindhyas and the Satpura ranges. This is danced in the rainy season; from June to August. The dancer, who has the balance on the Gendi (stilts)) perform it even in water or on marshy surface. The dance is brisk, and ends with a dance in pyramid formation. This is generally confined only to children and the attraction consists in balancing and clever footwork. In the villages where the wheat seedlings festival, Bhujalia, is celebrated, children prance on their gendis, collect near the village pond or the river in which bhujalias are to be immersed. Other frolicsome children, dancing to the accompaniment of musical instrument join the group and they dance together. Sometimes, womenfolk also join them, but they do not use stilts.

The Gendi season begins on the day of Bak Bandhi festival in the month of June and concludes after the Brita or Vrita of West Bengal is one of the most important traditional folk dances of Bengal. This is an invocational dance performed by the barren woman of Bengal who worship in gratitude after their wish being fulfilled. Quite often, this dance is performed after a recovery from a contagious disease like small pox, etc. Kali Nach is a dance performed during Gajan, in honour of the Goddess Kali. Here, the performer wears a mask, purified by mantras, and dances with a sword, and when worked up can make prophetic answers.

The Bihu of Assam is the most widespread folk dance in the state and is enjoyed by all, young and old, rich and poor. The dance is part of the Bihu festival, that comes in mid-April, when harvesting is done, and continues for about a month. The participants are young men and girls, who gather in the open, in daytime. They dance together, but there is no mixing of the sexes. The dance is supported by drums and pipes. In between, the performers sometimes sing, usually of love. The most common formation is the circle or parallel rows.

The Bihu demonstrates, through song and dance, the soul of the Assamese at its richest. The sense of fun and frolic of the Nagas is seen in many of their dances. The Zemis, Zeliangs and other tribes of Assam have a series of dances. Harvesting season is naturally the time for celebrations. All the Naga tribes have their particular harvest dances. The characteristic feature of all Naga dancing is the use of the human figure in an erect posture with many movements of the legs and comparatively little use of the torso, and the shoulders.

# 2

# Indian Music

## Historical Background of Indian Music

Indus Civilization is the live evidence of Indian Music System. Two important sites of Indus Civilization *i.e.* Harappa and Mohen-Jodaro is support the presence of Indian Music. Harappa is at a distance of 100 miles to the south-west of Lahore, and Mohenjodaro is at a distance of 200 miles from Karachi. Terracotta seals, vessels, images of animals, statues, remnants of cities and forts go to prove that this was the most ancient civilization of India.

It is considered to be at least 3,500 years old. Some regard this civilization as pre-Vedic, and some as *Vedic*. Among other finds, a flute, a harp with strings, and percussion instruments have also been found. A bronze figurine of a dancing girl beating time to music with her foot has also been found. This shows that people in that remote age knew the use of harp, flute, percussion instruments, and the art of dancing. On the basis of these scanty data, we cannot say what the music of those times was like. Seals similar to those of Mohenjodaro and Harappa have also been discovered in Sumeria. There was evidently a common civilization in the Indus Valley and Syria, Assyria and Babylonia.

We have, however, a more detailed account of the music of the *Vedic* times. The date of the oldest text, *i.e.*, *Rigveda* is variously estimated by scholars from 1,500 B.C. to 1,000 B.C.

The *Vedas* were musically recited. *Udatta* (raised, Greek *oxyu,* sharp or acute), *Anudatta* (not raised, grave, Greek *baryu),* and *Svarita* (Greek *oxyubaria,* acute grave or circumflex) were the three pitches used in *Vedic* recitative. *Udatta* was an acute or sharp pitch, *Anudatta* was a grave pitch, and *Svarita* was a pitch which combined in itself the characteristics of both i.e„ it started with *Udatta* and fell down to *Anudatta.*

In *Vedic* literature, *Svarita is* called *pravana, i.e.,* it gradually descended from *Udatta* to *Anudatta.* It formed a link between *Udatta* and *Anudatta.* These three were not merely accents or stress on words; they were musical pitches used for simple recitative. Narada has mentioned seven *Grama-ragas* also, viz; *Sadava, Pancama, Madhyama-grama, Sadja-grama, Sadharita, Kaisika-madhyama* and *Kaisika.* Narada defines *grama-ragas* in the following words:

*'Svatu-raga-visesena grama-raga it ismrtah' i.e., grama-ragas* are so called because of the pleasantness of a particular note. The pleasantness of a particular note depended on its being fundamental *(amsa)* or final *(nyasa).* Sometimes the omission of a note also determined the structure of a *grama-raga* as in the case of *Sadava.*

These *grama-ragas* were not *ragas* yet in the modem sense of the term, but they contained the germ of the *raga* system. According to Sarnigadeva, they were evolved out of the *jatis* mentioned by Bharata.

Narada has also mentioned the colour of tones. He says that the colour of Sadja is that of a lotus, that of a Rishabha is grey, that of *Madhyama* is white, that of *Pancama* is dark or blackish, that of *Dhaivata* is yellow and that of *Nisada* is spotted. A Russian scientist, named Constantine Leontyv, it is reported, has succeeded in translating musical notes into colour.

The idea, therefore, of the colour of tones cannot be dismissed as entirely fanciful. Scientific research will alone show how far the colour assigned to each note by Narada can stand experimental test. Towards the end of the *Vedic* period, the solfa syllables *sa, re, go. ma, pa, dha, ni* were definitely evolved. The European solfa system *do, ri, mi, fa, sol, la, si* was evolved by Guido d'Arezzo only in 10th century A.D.

## Indian Classical Music

The Classical Music of India has its origins in the chanting of the Vedas dating back to several thousands of years ago. Since then, by oral tradition, it has been bequeathed through the generations to its present form. In the course of time, it evolved into two distinct systems, namely the Carnatic (in the South) and the Hindustani (in the North).

Indian classical music is based on melody. It can be described as contemplative and introspective. There is no intentional harmonic structure beneath the melodic lines. Such freedom permits almost unlimited melodic possibilities. Another attribute of Indian music is improvisation. Most of the classical music performed is extemporaneous. Even while playing the compositions, the performer attempts variations and embellishments which bring out a unique interpretation of the composition and the artist's individuality. This makes the ensuing music spontaneous, never ceasing to amaze the listener.

It is interesting to note that the seven notes in Indian music, Sa, Ri, Ga, Ma, Pa, Dha, Ni, correspond to Do, Re, Mi, Fa, So, La, Ti, in the West. What makes Indian classical music unique is its two important characteristics: the *raga* and the *tala*. Every piece played adheres to the confines of raga and tala. A raga defines the melodic aspects of the music. The raga is a melodic pattern defined by an ascending and a descending scale, and key notes and phrases that bring out the entire character of the raga. There are numerous ragas that span an entire spectrum of emotions, colours and characters. In fact a raga has been personified as a divine being with character and moods just like a mortal. The performer, while elaborating a raga builds up the mood(s) portrayed by the raga.

Traditionally, most performances of Hindustani music begin with alap: an extensive solo exploration of the raga by the instrumentalist. Alap is divided into three basic parts. The first section of alap begins slowly, with an invocational and meditative approach. Within this stream like, arrhythmic style the artist gradually unfolds the shape, textures, and moods of the raga. Eventually, a pulse is introduced by the soloist, and the second section known as jor has begun. In jor, there is still no specific rhythmic framework to speak of.

Moving through many variations within the jor, the musician will finally arrive at the jhalla, the culminating section of the alap. Jhalla, characterized by a faster paced and rhythmically dense exposition of the raga, is carried thought to the end of the alap. After the alap, the instrumentalist is joined by the accompanying drummer, and together they enter the section of the raga known as the gat. Here we are introduced to the rhythmic basis of Indian music: the tala. A tala is a cycle of a fixed number of beats repeated over and over again, and played as distinct patterns of strokes on the accompanying drums. There are many different talas (6 beats, 7, 10, 12, 14, etc.), and each one has a different rhythmic mood. Except for alap, every piece of Indian classical music is played within a particular tala.

The gat begins with the instrumentalist playing a rhythmic/ melodic theme within the raga. Through this theme, the soloist thus establishes the tala within which the raga will now progress. Often, the tala will not be announced prior to the performance, and is chosen on the spot by the instrumentalist. Even the accompanying drummer may not know what the rhythmic cycle will be and must infer from the first hearing of the theme what patterns to play on the drums. The gat proceeds with the drummer supporting the soloist while variations are made and the raga is further explored. The two musicians interact rhythmically throughout the performance, always meeting on the first beat of the rhythmic cycle. This dynamic interchange becomes more prevalent as the raga progresses.

Staying within the same raga, a new theme in a new tala may eventually be introduced by the soloist. This is most often a faster-paced rhythmic cycle that adds excitement to the building energy of the music. The musicians then carry the raga to its final improvised ending.

This long exposition of the raga is often followed by a performance of light-classical raga or folk melody. These pieces are usually much shorter than the opening raga, and are set in certain talas to give the music a light and lighting feel.

As regards Indian classical music in general, there are a huge number of modes (ragas). Musicians will elaborate a single mode in detail, largely through improvisation but also based on compositions and formal demands. There are also pieces (called "ragamala" or "ragamalika") in which modulations are employed. Individual pieces are shorter in Carnatic music, so recitals are constructed by selecting items in contrasting ragas. The rationale is specifically contrast (usually), as opposed to Turkish music where modes are chosen for a directed development, or Arabic music where the frequent modulations should be as unnoticed as possible, etc. A general aesthetic discussion of this type could become much more extensive; please see my regular column for a series of more speculative remarks.

In both Hindustani & Carnatic music, songs (or instrumental compositions in Hindustani music) are usually (although not always) preceded by an improvised unmeasured prelude (alap/alaapana) which is sometimes extensive. This is followed by the "composition section" in which a specific rhythmic cycle (tala) is used (ordinarily with percussion accompaniment). Although it is usually based upon a pre-existing composition, there are specific improvisational features to this section as well. This aspect earns Indian classical music comparisons with Western Jazz, with which it shares some demands.

Hindustani music is the music of North India, involving both Hindu and Muslim musicians. In this case (as opposed to every other world classical tradition, except European), there are a large number of high quality recordings. Different people will, no doubt, like different styles to varying degrees. In this case, I am only going to list some discs I particularly enjoy without any intention of coming close to encyclopedic coverage.

Dhrupad is the older style of Hindustani music, now rare. The style with which most readers will be more familiar is the more modern style, especially as represented in the Hindustani instrumental (sitar, etc.) list above. Carnatic music is the music of South India, different in many of its terms and formal demands, although similar in overall outline. The two share some common origins, but the details of these relationships can be contentious.

Indian classical music continues to gain tremendously in popularity in the West, and is now taught widely. In addition to many opportunities to learn it at universities or in specialized instruction, more general resources are appearing. The recently released "Raga Guide" on Nimbus Records is a landmark and well worth pursuing for someone interested in learning the rudiments of ragas:

## North Indian Classical Music

The subject of classical Indian music is rich, with its historical, cultural, aesthetic, theoretical, and performing facets. This discussion is limited to aspects of the North Indian instrumental genres.

The primary genres of musical composition in North Indian or Hindustani classical music are dhrupad and khayal. Dhrupad, the older of the two genres, is the ancestor to the more popular khayal that eclipses it today. The concept of the melody and rhythm, however; serves as the foundation for both khayal and dhrupad. Melody is captured in the concept of the raag (also pronounced raaga) and rhythmic foundation in the taal (alternatively pronounced as tala).

### *The Raag*

Raag, in the Sanskrit dictionary, is defined as "the act of coloring or dyeing" (the mind in this context) and "any feeling or passion especially love, affection, sympathy, vehement desire, interest, joy, or delight". In music, these descriptions apply to the impressions of melodic sounds on both the artist(s) and listener(s). A raag consists of required and optional rules governing the melodic movements of notes within a performance.

The rules of a raag can be defined by:

- The list of specific notes that can be used during playing of the raag

- The manner in which the notes are used, *i.e.* specific ways of ornamenting notes or emphasizing/de-emphasizing them
- Manner in which the scale is ascended or descended
- Optional or required musical phrases, the way in which to reveal these phrases, and/or combine them
- The octave or frequency range to emphasize
- The relative pacing between the notes
- The time of day and/or season when the raag may be performed so as to invoke the emotions of the raag for maximum impact on the mental and emotional state of the performer and listener

Observance of these rules during the performance of a raag does not aspire to be purely a technical or intellectual exercise, but also to evoke the rasa or bhava (the experience, mood, emotion, or feeling) of the raag in both the artist and the listener. A raag is best experienced rather than analyzed. Theoretically, there is no limit to the number of raags, but only a few hundred are documented, and designated by specific names. Of these, only a small percentage are usually performed in concerts.

The melodic performer utilizes a raag as the foundation for improvisation. A recital explores a raag in an non-metered form and/or within the confines of a cyclical rhythmic structure, using intricate ornamentation of notes. First the raag is introduced with a note or group of notes, and then the improvisation progresses to a more melodically and rhythmically complex form.

The manner in which raags originate is a fascinating subject. Many raags are polished forms of a family of regional folk melodies while others have been created through the imagination of musicians. Some of the latter are raags with their own distinct characteristics whereas other creations are a combination of one or more existing raags. The names of some established raags have changed with time and the characteristics/ definitions of raags also are not as rigid as claimed in theory.

### *The Taal*

Just as the "note" is the basis of the melodic component of music, the bol (pronounced bowl) is the foundation for taal. Bol literally means speech or syllables. The vocal bols sound very similar to bols played on the percussive instrument. The most common tabla bols are Dha, Dhi/Dhin, Ti/Tin, Ra, Ki, Ta, Na, Tin, and Te. Different schools of percussion may pronounce the same bol differently. Several bols structured in a specific manner and arranged in sub-divisions are called thekas.

Each bol usually takes up one, halt or quarter of a beat (matra) in a theka. The first beat of a theka is called the sam (pronounced sum). It plays a crucial role in the improvisation structure during a recital—since it becomes a point of convergence for both the melodic and percussive improvisation. A theka also consists of layers of accents or voids in the first beat of a sub-division. A degree of symmetry, with an elegant manner of the theka leading to the sam, is quite common in the arrangement of the bols in a theka. A theka (also referred to as tool) can theoretically contain between two and 108 beats, although in reality there is no limit. While bols have existed in the percussion repertoire for a long time, thekas are probably a recent phenomenon (perhaps only around 600 years old ) The commonly heard thekas are dadra (6 beats), roopak (7 beats), keherwa (8 beats), jhaptaal (10 beats), ektaal (12 beats), chautal (12 beats), dhamar, deepchandi, jhumra (all 14 beats but with different bols and sub-divisions), and teentaal (16 beats). Although thekas are usually standard, bols of thekas can vary slightly, depending on the musical school or individual style of the tabla player.

### *A Brief History of Dhrupad and Khayal*

Dhrupad derives from the word dhruv, which literally means fixed, and pada literally verse/text. Dhrupad refers to both a type of composition (hence the name) (in chautaal or sooltaal) as well as a genre in North Indian classical music. The discussion here focuses on the genre.

Dhrupad probably evolved from a family of musical styles called prabhand that flourished during the twelfth and thirteenth centuries. The bhakti (devotional) movement of the Vaishnavas and Shivites also substantially contributed to the format and composition styles of dhrupad performed in the courts of Raja Man Singh Tomar of Gwalior and other courts in Delhi, Rajasthan, Punjab, and Gujarat in the fifteenth century. The popularity of dhrupad arose when it entered the court of Emperor Akbar's court in the sixteenth century. Tansen, a legendary musician in Akbar's court, is considered to be the father of the current form of classical dhrupad and most classical performers trace their tradition to him.

In his book "Sitar Technique in Nibbadh Forms", Dr. Stephen Slawek summarizes the history of the Seni gharana (Tansen's lineage): "The Seni gharana consisted of two schools: (1) descendants of Tansen's son, Bilas Khan, who were known as rababiyas (rabab players), and (2) descendants of Tansen's son-in-law, Misri Singh, who were known as binkars (bin players). The rababiyas branch gradually lost favor because of limitations inherent in the instrument.

The binkar gharana, however, incorporated many of the techniques of the rababiyas and flourished. The binkars, a tightly knit family taking pride in their ancestry, were very reluctant to pass the technique of their instrument on to anyone other than blood relatives. According to most Indian scholars, the binkars began to use the sitar and surbahar (an instrument similar to kachua sitar in shape but larger) to teach music to students not belonging to their family. On surbahar, they taught anibaddh sangit (music not bound to tal) such as alap and jor-alap. On sitar, they taught compositions that were based on popular vocal genres of the time."

Dhrupad itself has evolved considerably since Tansen's time. Since North Indian classical tradition is transmitted orally, the music heard today is probably different from what listeners experienced five centuries ago. Khayal is a more recent style of music that evolved from dhrupad and crystallized in the seventeenth century. Khayal, (literally meaning imagination) combines facets of dhrupad styles, techniques, and structure. A wider variety of ornamentation is used in khayal, and the improvisation takes place within the confines of a taal. The structure of a performance is less restricted and the artist has a wider latitude in structuring and improvising the performance. Due to its open nature, khayal has become far more popular than dhrupad ever was and has eclipsed its predecessor.

### *Dhrupad*

Dhrupad is essentially a poetic form incorporated into an extended presentation style marked by precise and orderly elaboration of a raga. The exposition preceding the composed verses is called *alap*, and is usually the longest portion of the performance. This aspect of dhrupad has been the most influential, and is reflected in other North Indian musical formats, especially in instrumental music and even khayal singing.

The term dhrupad itself means "the literal rendering of verse into music" and so the songs have a particularly potent impact. The actual *dhrupad* song-form is set in the rhythm *chautal* (4+4+2+2), and rendered in steady declaration in an austere style. Some performances in this idiom include related songs, especially the called *dhamar*, in *dhamar tala* (5+5+4 beats), but there are also other rhythmic forms which sometimes appear. These are usually somewhat lighter in content than the dhrupad proper. The rhythmic sections are generally accompanied by the two-head drum *pakhawaj* (similar to the *mridangam* of Carnatic music).

Dhrupad is often presented as the oldest Indian music, with an explicit continuity to ancient times. In this respect, it is perhaps the most direct development of Vedic chanting, and the literal respect for text in dhrupad is representative of those scriptural ideas. However many of the codifications of dhrupad are dated more specifically to the same period as the origin of khayal, and the two might be viewed more accurately as parallel developments, although dhrupad is certainly more austere in its formalism.

This music provides a wealth of depth in melodic nuance, with the smallest motion elaborated for minutes in a variety of time-tested techniques. The sophistication of the unmeasured exposition is nearly impossible to match in the world's music, and is buoyed by a variety of patterns derived from the original melody of the *raga*. Today the Dagar family dominates the scene of dhrupad vocal performance due to their dedication and world-wide prominence, but there are other styles remaining.

At this point, this list represents only a third of the available dhrupad vocal recordings. I have heard most of the others, and they are generally good or at least interesting, but I have decided to remain selective here. There are still not too many recordings available, although there are still some significant older recordings which have not reappeared on CD. The recorded sound quality is excellent for all citations.

### *Structure of a Modern Instrumental Recital*

Indians consider the voice as the supreme medium for performing music. Therefore all instruments attempt to imitate the vocal nuances. Audiences attending an instrumental recital hear facets of both dhrupad and khayal styles since instrumentalists are expected to be proficient and perform both genres.

Dhrupad approaches a performance very systematically—taking a raag from its abstract to a more concrete form, from un-metered to metered to a cyclically-metered arrangement, from simple to complex melodic and rhythmic structures. It is marked by a lengthy and structured exploration of a raag, followed by the presentation of a short fixed composition (dhruvpad). Austere ornamentation of notes is a characteristic of dhrupad. Emphasis is laid on resting a long time on single notes as well as slow and smooth glides between notes.

The quality of a performance is judged by the artist's interpretation of a raag, the technical and aesthetic control they have over laya (rhythm), and the mastery over their performance medium. Of these, the raag interpretation is perhaps the most important. Considering that raag structures seem extremely rigid, it is quite interesting how different the same raag can sound by different artists or by the same artist at different recitals. The reasons for the variation are improvisation and the personal interpretation of the raag by the performer. Most of a North Indian classical music performance is usually improvised spontaneously, making every recital a very unique experience.

A performance usually begins with the artiste selecting a raag that fits the situation (their mood, time of day/season, and audience). The raag is gradually revealed to the listener in a form of improvisation called the alap (literally introduction)- a meditative exploration of the raag. It is considered to be the ideal (and difficult) manner of presenting the raag. The artist is expected to adhere strictly to the rules of the raag in this phase.

First the tonic is established and the detailed introduction of the raag begins. The melodic features of the raag are exposed in an unmetered form, elaborately and systematically, gently unveiling the beauty of the raag's scale, its definitive phrases, as well as notes and their transition. Ideally, the scale is traversed slowly starting at the tonic (note Sa), followed by exploration of the lower octave ranges, one note at a time. When the embellishment of a note or phrase has been completed, the artist returns to the tonic and emphasizes it with a characteristic pattern called the mohra. This phrase helps provide a sense of temporal variation in an otherwise free and un-metered melody.

The performer then continues to unfold the raag, returning to the mohra after each phase of the exposition. The exposition continues in a gradual methodical manner until the upper tonic is reached. Usually, performers tend to spend a longer time emphasizing the approach to the upper tonic, since this usually marks the end of the alap. It is not uncommon for an artist to spend some additional time on notes higher than the tonic before ending the unmetered section and progressing to the next phase of the performance.

The alap is followed by the second section, called jor (literally to join). Jor (also referred to as alap-jor), a transition from the free melodic form of the alap, injects a more purposeful rhythm by introducing a pulse. The general structure conforms to an expanding of the range of the notes with the mohra used as a transitional point. The melodic patterns and rhythm become more ornate and complex respectively as jor proceeds. The tempo is also gradually increased as the performance progresses. The jor climaxes when the exposition reaches the tonic on the higher octave.

The final section is called nom-tom (transformed to a technique called jhala in the instrumental repertoire) in which the tempo escalates further and the rhythmic structure usually becomes a multiple of four. Shorter melodic phrasings are employed and more notes are compressed into a beat. The solo performance of presenting the raag in its alap form ends with nom-tom. Most of the performance is spent on the alap, jor, and nom-tom. It is unclear when and how alap became the primary part of a dhrupad recital, since the name of the genre implies a fixed composition.

Generally, an instrumental performer continues with a khayal styled composition (called gat-pronounced guth) in a particular taal and repeats it several times, varying the gat slightly each time. At this point, the tabla player joins the instrumentalist and improvises for several cycles of theka, synchronizing at a same after a tihai (a pattern repeated three times). The elaborate exploration of the raag is dispensed with, since the alap performed earlier has built the foundation. Therefore, the instrumentalist alternates between the gat and improvisation, with the latter progressing from simpler to more complex patterns, both rhythmically and melodically. The number of notes per beat also increases progressively. Usually the tempo speeds up in a quantified manner as well.

The artist may then switch to a different gat, perhaps in a different taal and continue to improvise further with even more intricate and sophisticated patterns at faster speeds. The time comes when the gat is no longer played and a smooth transition to the jhala may take place, within the confines of the taal. The jhala may end with a elaborate tihai (melodic/rhythmic pattern repeated three times) after which the performance of the raag ends. The artist usually performs two or more raags in a recital. The first raag is usually in dhrupad (alap)-khayal style as described above. The next few raags are normally presented in a more elaborate khayal style. The unmetered alap is very short and is followed by a gat in a slower tempo. The raag elaboration/exposition (badhat/vistar) takes place between repetition of the gat. The vistar is followed by the antara (a pre-composed section that introduces the upper tonic), after which more rhythmically complex improvisations are presented. The performance usually climaxes with thejhala described earlier.

The final pieces are performed in "lighter" genres such as bhajans (spiritual songs), thumris (romantic or sensual themes), dhuns (folk tunes), tappa, dadra, hori chaiti, or kajri. The rules of the raags are not adhered to as strictly in these renderings and may even flow from one raag to another in a form called raag-malika (garland of raags) in which the listener should be able to easily identify the shifts in rasas (moods).

It is worth noting that the descriptions above are general and not absolutes. One has to study music, listen to numerous recordings, and attend recitals to experience the broad spectrum of Indian classical music and thus appreciate its finer nuances. The University of Texas at Austin has an excellent collection of books, recordings, and courses available to those interested in further investigating the subject.

Reproduced by kind permission of author and Sitarji Amitava Sarkar and ICMCA.

If you live in or near Austin and are interested in Indian Music, ICMCA is a valuable resource for you as they have many resources not least of which are a series of Indian Music concerts throughout the year.

### *Hindustani Khayal Singing*

Khayal (literally "imagination") is the standard classical vocal form in Hindustani music. Its development is more recent than dhrupad, and it generally eschews the long alaps, but has a larger degree of improvisation (analogous to an instrumental gat) in the metrical singing. It does have its own long history, and has a very wide variety of performance styles (gharanas). Standard accompaniment is the tabla for rhythm, as well as a melodic accompaniment (sarangi, giving way to harmonium).

Khayal tends to be less well-received in the West than instrumental music or even dhrupad, but this is partly coincidental. Although the raga bhava of dhrupad is extremely impressive, the typical khayal recital will contain more suprises and personal touches.

In addition, while there is a certain "universal" feel to instrumental music, khayal is based largely on nonsense phrases, making an understanding of the language not especially important (although it can help).

As with the other lists, this one could obviously be much larger. I am highlighting only a few styles and recitals I particularly like. In the present case, the choices are also mediated by the fact that relatively much less khayal is available in top-quality widely-available production. Nonetheless, the present list is varied enough to allow some range of styles and consequently to build a broader interest in the listener.

## Carnatic Music

Nature has endowed this universe with many beautiful life forms, of so many different shapes, sizes and abilities. Most animal forms have the ability to produce sounds and some of them even have the capability to communicate using varied sounds. Man is unique in that he can express his thoughts using sound." This is how Swami Jayendra Saraswathy, the Sankaracharya of Kanchipuram, introduces the Kamalaambaa Navaavarna Kritis of Muthuswamy Dikshithar. The ability to express thoughts through sounds has evolved into an art which we call music.

Music can thus be defined as an art form that arranges sounds in a fashion that follows certain natural principles and provides that special inner feeling of happiness and contentment. It is important to note that the basic principles are natural and thus the theory of music is only an attempt by man to rationally explain what is already beautiful. As a fringe benefit, this rationalization helps in understanding the inherent beauty of music and creates increasingly higher levels of appreciation in the listener.

The most basic unit of music is the swara (or note) which simply indicates the position in the audible spectrum occupied by a particular sound or the pitch of the sound. Actually, the spectral position is better described as swara sthana. Inherently, certain sounds 'go together' and certain others do not. This property was realized by man thousands of years ago and is indicated by the term harmony; lack of harmony is called disharmony. Before going any further, let me introduce, as a practical tool, a keyboard, that will help us immensely as we go along deeper into the fundamentals of Carnatic music. Purists may frown at this, but as long as we realize the limitations of the keyboard and why the purists frown, we are committing no sin.

At first glance, a keyboard is simply an assortment of black and white keys of two different lengths, usually the black keys being the short ones. A closer examination shows a pattern of keys repeating a few times to produce the full keyboard. The repeating pattern is shown in the following figure. Many keyboards indicate the location of the 'C' key as shown in the figure. In any case, a C key can be identified as the white (or long) key immediately to the left of a group of two black keys or the first key in the above figure. Evidently, there is more than one C key (perhaps 4 or even more) on the keyboard.

The C key is so called due to the notation used in western music for the notes. The successive white keys to the right of C are labeled D, E, F, G, A and B. As a first example of harmony, play a C key and the next C key simultaneously and listen carefully (It is assumed here that the keyboard is polyphonic *i.e.*, has the ability to produce more than one tone at a time. Many inexpensive keyboards lack this ability and are not suitable for this demonstration). The combined sound has an oneness. Playing a C key and the white key next to it (the D key) does not produce a similar effect and the two tones stand out separately.

Changes in raga or tala designation are regarded as a natural part of the evolution of Carnatic music, whether as clarifications of structural concepts or as simple improvements to the fit between words and music. There may or may not be a danger to the idea of evolution in music, but from a purely scholarly perspective, there is an inherent interest in knowing how something was done at an earlier time in history. Some of these details are recoverable in Carnatic music, but there is consequently an implied question regarding the guru-shishya system and its ability to reproduce music exactly.

Already many prominent performers will train with multiple teachers from different lineages and that is a clear indication that no style will be preserved exactly. In the past, the same must have been said for those artistes sophisticated enough to forge their own new style.

It would certainly be pointless to suggest that the talented musician of today should not develop his or her own gifts and ideas or that the opportunity to travel and study on friendly terms with many prominent teachers should not be taken. It is a philosophical truth that isolation undertaken as a choice is not the same as that enforced by circumstances, and so there is not even the possibility of a return to other methods. What I am suggesting is that we will see a natural bifurcation between the continuing development of "mainstream" Carnatic music and an increasing number of scholar-performers who will recreate historical and regional styles. Given the ubiquity of the Western university tenure system, one cannot underestimate the motivation provided by mandatory publication and thesis in developing these ideas, for better or worse.

Dynamic and invigorating interaction between tradition and innovation has been a hallmark of Carnatic music, and even an increased polarization between the two does not need to damage the overall balance. If anything, it will broaden the scope of performance opportunities and the range of available ideas. It is precisely the dual richness of a long-standing tradition together with ample opportunities for modern virtuoso treatments which serve to place Carnatic music among the world's greatest musical styles. As the divergence increases, as long as one aspect keeps respectful sight of the other, the available scope for interaction increases as well. An analogy may be drawn between the manifest and unmanifest instantiations of Brahma, and indeed I view the duality between tradition and innovation in a similar way, dependent on each other. After all, a stagnant tradition is not true to its origins either, because its origins are in the crucible of creativity.

The success of music is ultimately in the mind of the listener, and specifically in the physical and emotional changes which can be provoked. It is a simple fact that Carnatic music has only a positive effect in this way, while the same cannot be said for various forms of popular music. Both the ability of music to build and release tension, as well as its potential to unlock latent energies in the mind are respected and developed. When discussing lofty ideas with people, there are often various mental blocks which must be overcome, and knowing the way around them gracefully is a large part of the art of teaching. With its rich variety of ragas, Carnatic music provides a nearly limitless array of melodic patterns which can be used to effect this navigation under a variety of circumstances. Together with a system for organizing them, these melodies make it possible to clear the mind of obstacles. It is no coincidence that the kucheri traditionally begins with a song on Ganesha, and the same concept may be extended to include the audience's apprehension in general.

To return decisively to the opening question, I value Carnatic music first for the effectiveness with which it can build positive mental discipline. It helps me to focus and organize my thoughts, and it helps to eliminate negative mental habits. How does it do this? Of course, I do not really know. However, I do claim that music naturally illustrates patterns of thought, and in the case of the great composers of Carnatic music, these mental patterns have been effectively conveyed at the highest level. I am personally attracted to Mutthuswamy Dikshitar more than the others. One challenge for Carnatic music is to continue to meet the demands of modern times, especially as the basis for communication with the audience changes. Modern composers have continued admirably in this regard, although the pace of change for the younger audience will be much faster, and the act of composition may need to adapt accordingly.

Even as its range expands, Carnatic music will continue to communicate the highest ideals, and many people around the world will be listening. There will be more interaction with other traditions, but there is also an audience for the strictest styles in the West. Carnatic music is one of the world's great treasures. I am honored to have been associated with it in some small way, and to have had the opportunity to write this article.

### *Swaras and Swarasthanas*

There are seven swaras in Carnatic music, namely, Shadjam (Sa), Rishabam (Ri), Gandharam (Ga), Madhyamam (Ma), Panchamam (Pa), Dhaivatham (Da) and Nishadam (Ni). There is some theoretical basis for why there is an odd number (seven) of swaras and we will deal with this subsequently. For simplicity, let us fix the Sa at one kattai and place the remaining swaras at the successive white keys. This provides us with a scale or a raga (in this case, containing all the seven swaras).

As mentioned previously, ancient Vedic chants have but three swaras and somewhat later forms of music (Indian as well as other forms, eg. Chinese) use five swaras-eg. the Sa, Ri, Ga, Pa and Da of the scale we just created. Our present system is based on seven swaras, and perhaps, a few thousand years from now, the human race will advance to a point of discriminating scales of more swaras (unlikely). The seven swaras are mythologically associated with the sounds produced by certain animals and the names of the swaras are related to the names of these animals. The name Madhyamam appears to be related to the central or madhya location in the seven notes and Panchamam is most probably derived from the number five, denoting the position of the note. We observed earlier that doubling the pitch of a swara by a factor of two results in going up in pitch by one octave.

Thus, doubling the pitch of Sa (say Sa1) results in another Sa (Sa2) which is one octave higher than our original Sa. A further doubling produces Sa3 which is one octave higher than Sa2 and two octaves above Sa1. Three times the original Sa produces the Pa located between Sa2 and Sa3. In other words, the pitch of the swara Pa is one and half times the pitch of the Sa below it (and three-fourths the pitch of the Sa above it). Now we come to an important limitation of the keyboard-the way the octave is divided into the twelve swara sthanas. Since it is based on current western music norms, the division is done on a logarithmic basis (which is just a more technical way of saying that the pitch values of the successive swara sthanas form a geometric progression).

An octave is a factor of two and there are twelve intervals in it. If we make all the intervals equal to a multiplicative factor x, then the pitch corresponding to any key will be x times the pitch of the key (white or black) immediately to the left of it. Extending the procedure we arrive at what the value of x should be. The thirteenth swara sthana results in an octave, or, stated mathematically, x12=2. Then, we have x to be the twelfth root of two or a factor of approximately 1.06. Using this logarithmic division procedure, Pa (the 8th swara sthana) corresponds not to a ratio of 1.5 but 1.498. Though the discrepancy is very small, a well trained ear (eg. professional musician) can pick out this difference.

Carnatic music is based not on logarithmic division but on rational division. An octave is based on the ratio 1:2; Pa is located through the ratio 2:3; similar definitions exist for all the twelve swara sthanas. A few centuries ago, Western classical music too was based on rational division (the resulting scale was called as the natural scale), but this has given way to the equally tempered (also called chromatic) scale produced by logarithmic division. The difference is subtle, but quite important.

The rational division claim is supported by the fact that tuning of instruments (for example, in setting the frets of veena) is performed mostly by the ear and not by reference to standards. Further, the swara sthanas of Carnatic music define only nominal locations for the swaras. Depending on the raga in which the swara is used, it manifests a deviation from the nominal sthana. Actually, the deviation from the nominal sthana depends on the swara phrase in which the swara occurs; thus, a single swara in a given raga can appear at different deviations from its nominal sthana when occurring along with various other swaras of the same raga. In a general sense, this deviation is called gamaka. Gamaka can refer to a constant deviation from the nominal swara sthana or a time dependent deviation or the path taken in reaching the nominal swara etc.

Truly, gamaka is the life blood of Carnatic music and the raga system. Ragas are defined more by the gamakas and the way in which certain swara phrases (chain of swaras) are used than by the mere presence or absence of certain swaras. Thus, playing the keys corresponding to the swara sthanas of a certain raga will not reproduce the true character of the raga but only provide a general idea of what it sounds like. This is the reason why purists object to the use of keyboard instruments in Carnatic music-the lack of gamaka, which leads to a mutilation of the raga swaroopa. The use of gamaka also implies that the method used for defining nominal swara sthanas (rational or logarithmic division) is not too critical as long the correct raga swaroopam can be accommodated.

## *Ragas*

Ragas are sometimes defined as melody types. The raga system is a method of organizing tunes based on certain natural principles. Tunes in the same raga use the same (nominal) swaras in various combinations and with practice, the listener can pick up the similarity. Each raga has a swaroopam (a musical form or image) that is defined by the swaras used, the gamakas given to these swaras, the sequence in which the swaras occur etc. This definition is termed as the raga lakshanam. (The magazine Sruthi usually contains a discussion of ragalakshanam of one or two ragas in each issue). Raga lakshanam usually contains the arohanam, avarohanam, details of raga chaya swaras (the swaras which are chiefly responsible for the characteristic melody of the raga), gamakas, characteristic swara phrases and general usage notes.

It is intended more for the performer than for the listener. We shall first define arohanam and avarohanam. Arohanam is the sequence of swaras used in a raga in the ascending passages *i.e.* as the pitch goes up. Avarohanam is the sequence of swaras to be used in descent. The arohanam and avarohanam (or the scale) of a raga provide only a skeletal outline upon which the rest of the raga is formed.

### *The Melakarta Scheme*

Contemporary Carnatic music is based on a system of 72 melakarta ragas. These 'creator' ragas are also called janaka ragas and thai (mother) ragas. The current system can be traced to the works of Venkatamakhi who appears to be the first to use 72 melakartas. Earlier works generally contain fewer melakartas and most have flaws in organization. At that time, (16th century) many of Venkatamakhi's melakartas were unknown and were not assigned names. Later, all 72 were given names and this system is sometimes referred to as the Kanakaambari-Phenadhyuthi system after the names of the first two melakartas in it. Muthuswamy Dikshithar's compositions are generally based on the raga names and lakshanams (definitions) in this system while Thyagaraja used a later scheme devised by Govindacharya in the late 18th century. Venkatamakhi did not believe that melakartas must be of simple sampoorna arohanam-avarohanam but favored the idea of calling a raga as a melakarta if all the seven swaras occurred in either the arohanam or the avarohanam.

Thus a raga which went Sa-Ri-Ma-Pa-Ni-Sa, Sa-Da-Pa-Ga-Ri-Sa could be a melakarta under this scheme. Govindacharya's insistence on sampoorna arohanam-avarohanam leads to a system which is more elegant from a mathematical viewpoint. In this scheme, the melakartas arise out of systematic permutation of the seven swaras into the twelve swara sthanas. Seen this way, the melakarta scheme is a product of mathematical abstraction and the naming of swaras (and the introduction of vivadi swaras) is of no consequence as far as the organization of the melakartas is concerned. No wonder, Venkatamakhi is reputed to have said that even Lord Maheswara could not create more melakartas!

### *Melakarta Ragas*

Many of the melakartas have alternate names like in the example just cited and some of these are listed in the Appendix. In addition, some of the common ones (like Thodi) are listed with prefixes (Hanumathodi). This is in accordance with the so called 'Katapayaathi' formula. Using this formula, numerical values are assigned to consonants as listed in the following table (the devanagari script is the basis upon which this assignment is done). To find out what is the location of a melakarta in the table, the first two consonants are deciphered using the numerical assignment table and the resulting number is inverted left to right. For example, consider Hanumathodi-the first two consonants being Ha and Na. Ha is assigned 8 and Na is zero.

### *Janya Ragas*

Janya ragas, as we have seen before, are derived from the melakarta ragas. The simplest way to generate a janya raga is to leave out one or more of the swaras in the arohanam and/or avarohanam. For example, if we drop out the Ma and Ni in the arohanam of Dheerasankaraabharanam, we end up with Sa-Ri-Ga-Pa-Da-Sa for the arohanam and a sampoorna avarohanam. The resulting raga is called Bilahari. Thus, Bilahari is described as a janya raga of the 29th melakarta Dheerasankaraabharanam with an arohanam-avarohanam of Sa-Ri-Ga-Pa-Da-Sa, Sa-Ni-Da-Pa-Ma-Ga-Ri-Sa. This means that when going up the scale, one may use only the notes of the arohanam, namely, Sa, Ri, Ga, Pa, Da and Sa whereas, all seven notes can be used in descent. Thus, when a Ma or Ni is used, one has to necessarily descend (using notes from the avarohanam).

### *Elements of a Recital*

The exact form of a concert or recital changes with time, adapting to the perceived needs of the listener and the performer. Much of the form as described here is generally attributed to the tradition established by Sri Ariyakkudi Ramanuja Iyengar. There are two essential portions in any Carnatic Music Recital-a composed portion and an extempore portion. The composed portion is fixed (more or less) while the extempore or improvisational portion is heavily dependent on the skills and imagination of the performer. This extempore portion is thus governed by the mind and is hence referred to as manodharma sangeetham. Recitals often start with a Varnam. A Varnam is a composed piece of fairly short duration usually set to Aadi or Ata taalam. It is usually performed at the start of a recital as a warm up piece.

The lyrics are simple and consist mostly of long syllables and swara phrases of various lengths which bring out the essential features of the raga. There is usually a Pallavi and an Anupallavi, followed by a Mukthaayiswaram and repetitions of a Charanam with various Chittaswarams. The Pallavi establishes a characteristic theme of the raga, typically in the lower portion or purvangam of the raga, while the Anupallavi provides a parallel or contrasting theme in the upper portions (uttarangam). The Mukthaayiswaram and Chittaswarams both consist of chains of swaras rendered using the swara syllables themselves (Sa, Ri, etc.). The Charanam is often composed on a raga theme related to the Pallavi and the Anupallavi.

### *Grahabedam and Symmetries*

The topics of this section are of fairly advanced nature and somewhat abstract and mathematical. Readers who are not mathematically oriented may skip this section. The basic principles behind Grahabedam and symmetry are rooted in mathematics. Thus, a certain amount of mathematical notation is almost unavoidable in any explanation of these concepts. Grahabedam is the process of modifying ragas by shifting the base note Sa or the sruthi to various swara sthanas.

## Gharana and Schools

Indian classical music is defined by two basic elements: it must follow a classical mode, the raga, and a specific rhythm or tal. A music which follows the characteristics of this tradition is called classical—in opposition to Western classical music, where classical means belonging to a period of time (approximatively from 16th to 17th century). This concept of classical music is, in that way, very open. A musician can "invent" new classical forms, new poetical forms, new modes, new rhythms and Indian instrument makers can produce new instruments.

All Indian classical music follows this rule even if some completely different styles exists side by side. To develop precisely a raga, the musician needs the presence of a drone, whatever the music: singers are always accompanied with the tambura or the harmonium, that produce the singer's tonic and dominant (SA and PA). Classical Indian music is mainly divided into two branches, North and South. The South Indian music is called Carnatic, in reference of the Southern State of Karnataka, and the northern branch, Hindustani, in reference of the Hindi speaking region going to North-West Frontier and to Poorab, the East. Carnatic music is nearly totally unified and the different schools are based on the same ragas (about 300 different ragas), same solo instruments, mainly the veena, flute, violin and same rhythm instrument, the mridangam and the ghatam.

The actual development of a concert has been codified recently, around 1920 by an eminent singer, Ariyakudi Ramanuja Iyer: a dozen of short pieces are enclosing a long "alapam, tanam, pallavi, or improvisation on notes, on rhythm and poem, a classical scheme you will find also in North Indian music, except for the short piece of music at the start. On the contrary, Hindustani Music has never been really unified, many styles and genres have been developed and encouraged by a family system now called gharana. Those numerous gharanas all over North India have developed very different styles of music, genres and instruments. The patronage of royal families (India has been a set of feudal states for all its history before 1948) has given those gharanas the "peace of mind" necessary to create, preserve and nourish an incredible amount of genres.

Today those are:

*Dhrupad, the 15th century temple and court genre.*

*Qawwali, a 14th century Muslim fusion with Persian music.*

*Khayal, the 18th century most fashionable court music.*

Thumri, the old dance oriented music, and Ghazal, the Panjabi love song, in vogue from 19th century till now. Each one of these names covers an incredible amount of different styles, and a layman will not make any connection between the music of instrumental court Dhrupad of the Dagar and a singer of Darbhanga Temple dhrupad. Those genres are focusing more on a poetical form: Dhrupad, on strangely complex verse with no rime, Qawwali, on Persian couplet versification etc. Originality comes from the fact that all those musics are inseparable of the poetry they are structured on. So even strings and percussion instruments always try to reproduce vocal music and its poems: the instrument talks, its speaks with words. Inside each genre (including Carnatic music), many ways of singing, or vanis (same roots as "voices") have been developed. In khayal, those vanis have disappeared and dozens of schools have emerged.

As we said earlier, musicians are not obliged to play a specific instrument on a style but the musicians and their family instrument makers have invented instruments suited to each style: Rudraveena, surshringar and pakhawaj for Dhrupad. Those are fantastic, tune oriented instruments that fit dhrupad's precise tuning obligations. Sitar, sarod, sarangi, vichitraveena, flute, shehenai, santoor and tabla are suited to the fast playing speed of Khayal, Thumri and Tappa.

| *Musician* | *Genre* | *Instrument* |
|---|---|---|
| Pandit Chandrashekar | Dhrupad (Dagarvani) | surbahar |
| Pandit Vidur Mallik | Dhrupad (Darbhanga) | vocal |
| Ustad Iqbal Ahmad Khan | Khayal (Delhi Gharana) | vocal |
| Purnima Sen | Khayal (Agra Gharana) | vocal |
| Sulochana Brahaspati | Khayal (Rampur Gharana) | vocal |
| Bahauddin Dagar | Dhrupad (Dagarvani) | Rudraveena |
| Partho Sarathy | Khayal (Maihar Gharana) | sarod |
| Uday Bhawalkar | Dhrupad (Dagarvani) | vocal |
| Indira Misra | Ghazal (Delhi Gharana) | vocal |
| Ustad Hameed & Chhote Rahimat Khan | Khayal (Gwalior Gharana) | Sitar |
| Ustad Sabri Khan | Khayal (Moradabad Gharana) | Sarangi |
| Pandit Jal K. Balaporia | Khayal (Gwalior Gharana) | vocal |
| Aruna Sayeeram | Carnatic (Veena Dhanamal) | vocal |
| Pandit Indra Kishore Mishra | Dhrupad (Khandarvani) | vocal |
| Pandit Ritwik Sanyal | Dhrupad (Dagarvani) | vocal |
| Ustad Shujaat Khan | Khayal (Imdadkhani Gharana) | Sitar |
| Padmavati Shaligram | Khayal (Jaipur Gharana) | vocal |

*Contd...*

| Musician | Genre | Instrument |
|---|---|---|
| Meraj Nizami Qawwal | Qawwali (Qawwal Bacche) | vocal |
| Sunil Kant Gupta | Khayal (Gwalior Gharana) | Flute |
| Purnima Chaudhury | Thumri (Benares) | vocal |
| Dr Mustafa Raza Vichitraveena | Khayal (Patiala Gharana) | |
| Pandit TD Janorikar | Khayal (Bhindi Bazar Gharana) | vocal |
| Pandit VR Kadnekar | Khayal (Jaipur Gharana) | vocal |
| Shree Pichumani Iyer | Carnatic (Tanjore vani) | Sarasvati veena |
| Pandit Shrikant Mishra | Dhrupad | Packawaj |
| Raga Bhairavi | 16 different Makar Musicians | vocal/ instrumantal |
| Pandit Channulal Mishra | Khayal (Kirana Gharana) | vocal |
| Girish Karya | Dhrupad (Nathdwara) | vocal |
| Ranganayaki Rajagopalam | Carnatic (Karaikudi vani) | Saraswati veena |
| Begum Akhtar | Ghazals (Pachahin) | vocal |
| Uday Bhawalkar | Dhrupad (Dagarvani) | vocal |
| Suhasini Koratkar | Khayal (Bhendi Bazar Gharana) | vocal |
| Bahauddin Dagar | Dhrupad (Dagarvani) | Rudraveena |
| Kishore Kumar Mishra and Ram Kumar Mishra | Khayal (Benares and Delhi Gharana) | Tabla |
| Rajesh Vaidhya Hori | Carnatic (Yemani vani) Dhrupad | Saraswati veena vocal |
| Ustad Nasiruddin Saami | Khayal (Delhi Gharana) | vocal |
| Ashoka Dhar | Dhrupad (Dagar vani) | vocal |
| Ustad Z. Fariduddin Dagar | Dhrupad (Dagar vani) | vocal |
| Ustad Shamsuddin Faridi | Dhrupad (Khandar vani) | Been |
| Pandit Shivshankar Mukherjee | Dhrupad (Gohar vani) | vocal |

## *The Bhendibazar Gharana*

The Bhendibazar gharana is a branch of the Gwalior gharana founded by the illustrious Ustad Aman Ali Khan. If the aspect of the compositions and presentation of the rag does not really differ from the Gwalior school, the singing techniques used in their development are very original (some are borrowed from the techniques of the been, the main instrument of dhrupad). An exceptional musician, Aman Ali Khan was one of the most celebrated musicians in the 1940's Bombay.

The concert is generally divided in two parts: the khayal features a presentation of the poem, without accompaniment, then one, two or three poems developed on improvised phrases. The last student of Aman Ali Khan still alive: Pandit TD Janorikar, and the great lady singer, student of Pandit TD Janorikar, Suhasini Koratkar Lata Mangeshkar was from this school before to change to film music.

***The Agra Gharana***

The Agra gharana derived from the dhrupad tradition of the Nauhar Bani and was founded by Saras Khuda during the reign of Emperor Aurangzeb. Thereafter, his grandson Ghagge Khudabaksh received rigorous training from Natthan Khan of the Gwalior gharana in khayal gayaki and thus developed a happy synthesis of the majestic dhrupad tradition and the melodious khayal gayaki. Apart from this, a series of alliances between the houses (gharanas) of the original Agra gharana and the Atrauli gharana have further brought together these two great tradition and it would be more correct to describe the gharana as the Agra-Atrauli gharana.

***Banis:*** The Gobarhar Bani or the Gwalior gharana as derived from Mehboob Khan alias Daas Piya the Dagur Bani of the original Atrauli Dhrupad gharana which underwent a transformation when Ustad Alladiya Khan took to khayal gayaki from Mubarak Ali of Jaipur (since then called Jaipur-Atrauli gharana) and finally the inflow of the Nauhar Bani of the third Atrauli offshoot as derived through Puttan Khan, maternal uncle of Ustad Mushtaq Husain of the Rampur Sahaswan gharana. Probably this is what accounts for the many splendoured appeal of this 'Rangeeli' gayaki as it came to be known, particularly since the advent of Aftab-e-mousiqi Ustad Faiyaz Khan whom many regard as the fountainhead of Agra-Atrauli gharana.

The Agra gharana was founded by a Rajput family of Dhrupad musician who were singing in the Nauhar bani style. Settled in Agra in the 16th century, they converted to Islam and were allowed to sing in the court of Akbar. Through marriage they associated with Mian Tansen, a famous court singer from Gwalior.

The gharana started singing khayal at the end of the 18th century. The distinctive features of the style are the melodic fluidity and complexity of the compositions associated to simple and sober poems. The compositions sung here are signed by Muslim artists with a devotion to Krishna. The concert is generally divided in three parts: the "great" khayal which contains a short alap presenting rapidly the notes of the raga and then a poem sung and developed with improvised phrases; the "small" khayal following on a rapid tempo; a thumri which closes the concert. One of the only singers still singing pure Agra style is Purnima Sen.

### *The Dagar Style*

Originally composed of an alap (an improvised form of progression), then of a long poem sung to the accompaniment of the pakhawaj drum, Dagarvani dhrupad has progressively come to particularly stress the alap rather than the poetical composition. The alap starts on a very slow tempo, nearly one beat a minute, and increases its speed step by step. The medium fast part is called Jor, the fast one, Jhala. In this Dagar style, a whole alap may last more than one hour. At the end of the alap the poems are sung. They are based on a rhythm (tal) of 12 beat for vilambit (slow) dhrupad, 10 or 7 beat for the madhyalay and drut (medium and fast tempi) dhrupad.

Soloist and drummer develop the composition, playing with rhythm and note, in simultaneous and different ways. They both improvise on the poem and on the meter of the composition. Two main branches of the Dagar vani exist now: the lineage of Ziauddin Dagar with Ustad Fariduddin Dagar, Pandit Chandrashekar, Bahauddin Dagar, Uday Bhawalkar and Ritwik Sanyal and the Nasiruddin Dagar branch with Ashoka Dhar.

### *The Darbhanga Style*

The Darbhanga school, according to legend, was born in the 18th century when two brothers (whose pious occupation was to sing in a temple) made the rains pour down when asked to do so by the Maharaja of Darbangha: for that miracle the maharaja rewarded them with land and the title of Mallick (land owner). Consisting of an alap (first improvised movement) followed by one or several compositions (accompanied by the pakhawaj drum), dhrupad pours out precisely the notes and intervals that shape the raga. Compositions are set on a fixed rhythm structure (tal) of 12, 14, or 10 beats.

Soloist and drummer develop the composition, playing with rhythm and note, in simultaneous and different ways. They both end on a musical phrase typical of the composition. A lively style using also fast tempo, Darbhanga has preserved a light and happy style of dhrupad, especially in the Dhamar exposition. The members of the Mallick family are the Darbhanga's style masters and Pandit Vidur Mallik is the senior most musician.

### *The Delhi Gharana*

The Delhi gharana was founded in the 14th century by Amir Kushrau, famous musician and poet in Persia, whose descendants were court musicians of the Great Mughal until the end of the empire in the 19th century. There are many different influences on the style of this gharana: Qawwali, as the Delhi gharana invented it, dhrupad, which is part of the training there, vocal khayal, ghazals and sarangi (this difficult instrument has been taken up by this family). Just as in dhrupad, the rules of the raga are very well respected in the Delhi gharana, and there is a wealth of beautiful compositions from previous masters.

From this school comes the Patiala gharana. Tanras Khan the khalifa of the Delhi gharana during the XIXth century gave his vast poem and composition patrimony to the young virtuosos Ali Baksh et Fateh Ali. Those singers, known later under the common name of "Aliya-Fattu" became a famous duo in their time and settled as court musicians to the very rich Patiala Maharaja. Two branches of this school are existing today, one in India, the other in Afghanistan. The concert generally consists of a first khayal called "great" khayal, including a long alap (improvisation without tabla), a poem sung slowly and developed, and a second shorter poem.

The second khayal or "small" khayal, starts on a shorter alap, followed by a composition on a fast and accelerating tempo. In Pakistan, the Delhi Gharana is represented by Ustad Nasiruddin Saami. The actual Khalifa of the Khayal Delhi gharana is Ustad Iqbal Ahmad Khan. His student is the excellent ghazal singer Indira Misra The actual Khalifa of the Qawwal bacche of the Delhi gharana is Meraj Nizami Qawwal.

### *Hori Dhamar*

Hori Dhamar is a very ancient form. Hori is sung during Holi, the festival of spring and colours, which takes place after the first full moon of the month of Phalgun in the Indian calendar (generally beginning of March). For hundreds of years, Dhrupad singers have composed these songs that hail the arrival of spring, love and pleasure and describe the amourous play of Krishna. This particularly happy music follows a 14 beats rhythm (taal) called Dhamar, which is very helpful for rhythmical improvisation Dhamar and Hori are so closely linked that they have become synonymous. Hori is now sung in all seasons, and belongs to the repertoire of nearly all Dhrupad concerts. It has also always been associated to other classical genres such as Khayal or Thumri.

### *Dhrupad*

Dhrupad and dhamar belong to the North Indian classical tradition of Hindu religious music, and take very sophisticated musical and poetical forms. A favourite of the Great Mughals, this music has spread all over North India from the 15th to the 17th century. At first mainly vocal, dhrupad can also be played on string instruments which allow an important sustain of the note (Been, Rudraveena). Consisting of an alap (first improvised or composed movement) followed by one or several compositions (played with the accompaniment of the pakhawaj drum), dhrupad slowly pours out the notes and intervals that shape the raga. Compositions are set on a fixed rhythm (metre) structure (tal) of 12, 14, or 10 beats. Soloist and drummer develop the composition, playing with rhythm and note, in simultaneous and differents ways. They both end on a musical phrase typical of the composition There are many different Dhrupad schools in India:

*Dagar vani*

*Khandar vani*

*Gohar vani*

*Haveli dhrupad*

*Darbhanga vani*

### *The Gwalior Gharana*

The rise of the Gwalior gharana started with the reign of the great Mughal emperor Akbar (1542-1605). The favourite singers of this patron of the arts, such as Miyan Tansen, first amongst the vocalists at the court, came from the town of Gwalior. This Indian classical music school has counted numerous dhrupad poets and musicians, who have invented a great number of poetic styles and ragas.

Born in the XVIIIth century the khayal of the Gwalior school has flourished on such an inheritance: Dhrupad has nearly vanished, leaving the front to a new and fashionable style: khayal. In this gharana a large number of poems have been composed on each raga.

Those poems are structured by different tals such as Ektal, Tilvara, Jhumra, Adachautal and Saveri. The concert is composed of an alap followed by the presentation of numerous poems with melodic et rhythmic improvisations, on a tabla accompaniment. One of the seniormost singers of the Gwalior gharana is Pandit Jal K. Balaporia.

### *Haveli Dhrupad*

Haveli dhrupad is an Indian classical music mainly sung in the Pushtimargi's temples, a Hindu khrisnaite religion founded by Vallabhacharya, adoring Krishna as Shri Nathji. Their main temple is situated in Nathdwara (Rajasthan).

Composed of a short alap (an improvised form of progression), then of a long poem sung to the idol, with the accompaniment of the pakhawaj drum, Haveli dhrupads are particularly short and intense. They are made for a very short session during which the idol is shown to the public, the darshan.

The choice of raga depends on the time of the day, and the season. The poems are based on a rhythm (tal) of 12 beat for vilambit (slow) dhrupad, 10 or 7 beat for the madhyalay and drut (medium and fast tempi) dhrupad. Soloist and drummer develop the composition, playing with the subdivision of rhythm, and improvise on the notes of the raga, in simultaneous and different ways. Only one recording of haveli dhrupad is available worldwide, the one of: Girish Karya.

### *The Atrauli Jaipur Gharana*

The Atrauli Jaipur gharana is a dissident branch of the Agra Atrauli gharana, founded by the illustrious Ustad Alladiya Khan. Born in 1840 in Baroda, Alladiya Khan learnt his music for 35 years under his uncle Jehangir Khan a student of his own father, Khawaja Ahmed Khan Settled in Bombay. He was invited in Kholapur to be the court singer of a very modern and rich Maharaja.

Alladiya Khan Saheb knew and wrote down almost 5,000 compositions, distroyed later by his suns. The concert is generally divided in two parts: the khayal features a short alap, a quick presentation of the raga, then one or two poems developed on composed and improvised phrases of a very rich and virtuous rendition then a thumri ends the concert. Still alive and preserving the real style of Alladya Khan is a lady singer Padmavati Shaligram. Another master of the Jaipur Gharana is Pandit VR Kadnekar.

### *The Khandar Vani*

The Khandar vani is one of the most ancient schools of Dhrupad. This style was at first instrumental, founded by the descendants of the famous Mian Tan Sen, who was, during the 16th century, the favourite singer of India's greatest emperor Akbar. The shape of the improvisations, the specific gamaks and the origins of the poem are a way to indentify this school. The Khandarvani Dhrupad singer on our record is Indra Kishore Mishra. The Best Khandarvani Instrumentist is Ustad

Shamsuddin Faridi, on been. Some khayal musicians has maintained a vani, like Ustad Nasiruddin Saami who sings a in perfect Khandarvani.

***The Kirana Gharana***

The Kirana gharana is a very old school from a village near Delhi which style has been completely renovated by Ustad Bande Ali Khan, a dhrupada from the Indore gharana The Ustad taught his own style when he was living in Kirana and his students spread all around India: a branch came to the South, attracted by the generosity of the Bangalore and Mysore royals patrons. His most famous khayal student, Abdul Karim Khan, founded a school in Dharwar, Karnataka: Bhimsen Joshi, Gangubai Hangal and Kumar Gandharwa all came from that school.Dhrupad from the Kirana gharana is represented by the dagar family.

It is the North Branch that we are presenting here, which has not much differed from the original style. The khayal concert is generally divided into three parts: the great khayal features a presentation of the poem with improvisation, accompanied with tabla, followed by a small khayal, sung on a fastest tempo, and at last a series of thumri, hori, etc. A great musician of the Kirana: Pandit Channulal Mishra.

***Rampur Gharana***

The Sahaswan gharana (affiliated to the Gwalior gharana, and having links with Mian Tansen) is a Indian classical school of music, khayal, settled in Rampur in the second part of the XIXth century. For a century, Rampur was for musicians a very welcoming place. They led a good life under the patronage of a maharaja who was himself an excellent musician. Most of Bhatkande's (the famous musicologist) work is based on the Rampur School heritage. The alap is sober and not improvised, it is a presentation of the distinctive features of the raga.

Then the musician performs on a poem on a very slow lay (tempo), then two other poems, one on a medium lay and one on a fast lay, and this is where improvised phrases come in. A great singer of this great school: Sulochana Brahaspati.

### *The Gohar Vani*

The Gohar or Gouhar or Gouri vani is one of the most ancient school of Dhrupad. During the 16th century, Myan Tansen, the favourite singer of India's greatest Emperor Akbar, founded this school of dhrupad and transformed dhrupad into the most famous music in India. With a slow and forcefully exposed improvisations, heavy gamaks this vani enhances the religious and devotional aspect of its music. This school has influenced the Dagar vani school. The name comes from the Town of Gwalior, corrupted into Gohar, but it may come also from the caste name of Myan Tansen, who was a Gaura Brahman. The exponent of gohar vani is Pandit Shivshankar Mukherjee.

## Modern Instruments

### *Harmonium*

Peti or baja are the Indian names for the harmonium. This instrument has its origin in Europe, and ever since it came to India in the $19^{th}$ century it has become an essential part of Indian musical compositions. This musical instrument is a blend of the east and west. Its keyboard is similar to that of the piano and the body with its other parts creates sounds for Indian classical compositions.

The harmonium is a portable instrument in the shape of a rectangular box. The musician can sit comfortably on the floor playing it, using both his hands. One hand dances along the keyboard and the other is engaged in pumping the instrument.

The body of the harmonium houses bellows that are the pumps, which push the air through the instrument. There are external bellows that are pumped manually and the internal ones that are reservoirs for the air pumped by the external ones. This instrument has stops, which are a series of valves that controls the way in which air flows. There are also drone stops that determine the flow of air over the reeds that do not have keys. The keys, called *chabi* in Hindi, are controls made from wood. The keyboard, as mentioned earlier, is like that of the piano, minus the chords. When the harmonium is not in use it is protected by a cover either made from wood, cloth or glass. The harmonium is most commonly played while sitting. However, one could also sling this instrument across their shoulder and play it as they walk.

The following are the various Indian music genres that require this instrument:

- Bhajan
- Folk Music
- Ghazal and qawwali
- Hindustani music variations

***Sitar***

Sitar is said to be one of the prime musical instruments of Indian music and the most used of all the stringed instruments. It has been almost 700 years since this music instrument was introduced to India. The word sitar originates from the Persian term sehtar, which is broken into si meaning three and tar meaning strings. According to historians, the famed musician of the 13th century, Amir Khusrao, reversed the strings of the veena, thereby inventing this instrument. Further modifications to the sitar were made in the eighteenth century with the addition of three strings. This popular stringed instrument of Indian classical music consists of various parts, which are:

- *Tumba:* This is the lower hemispherical, hollow gourd
- *Dandi:* This is the stem of the sitar
- *Gulu:* This is the upper gourd that is used as a balance for the musician as he or she plays the instrument
- *Kunti:* These are the tuning pegs. They are of two sizes. The larger ones are used to tune the main strings and the smaller ones for the sympathetic strings
- *Tar:* This is the string of the sitar. The sitar has three types of strings, which are the drone strings, sympathetic strings and the playing stings
- *Parda* are frets that are metal rods tied to the stem or

neck of the sitar. They are adjusted by the musician for the required pitch

Basically there are two types of sitars, which are distinguished on the basis of the number of strings they have:

- The sitar with 13 sympathetic strings. This is tuned to the notes of the raga. It has 3 playing strings to cover three octaves; a fourth one reaching the bass octave and 3 rhythm strings
- The sitar with 11 sympathetic strings. This smaller instrument is specifically designed high speed playing

Generally sitar is rested on the right shoulder with the right hand plucking the strings. The index finger of the left hand travels up and down the neck of the sitar. Playing the sitar may seem like an easy task to on lookers, but it does require a high degree of concentration and co-ordination. Even one string plucked out of sync will take the entire composition to a different tune.

***Sarod***

The sarod is a stringed instrument that is generally carved out of a single piece of teakwood. Its belly is covered with goatskin. This instrument is played with plectrum made from coconut shell. This is probably one of the oldest instruments of Indian music. Carvings of it have been found in the Champa temple that was constructed in the 1st century. One also comes across paintings and carvings of this stringed musical instrument in the Ajanta caves. The history of Indian classical music claims that the famous musician of the 13th century, Amir Khusrao had modified the sarod, creating the sitar; and later Ustad Ali Akbar Khan modified the shape of the original instrument thereby improvising the tonal quality.

The sarod has a number of strings that are fixed onto the instrument in accordance to the roles they have to play. There are basically three types of strings:

- Four main strings
- Six rhythm and drone strings
- Fifteen sympathetic strings

All the strings are made from metal. This instrument has gone through several modifications to suit the needs of the varied musicians. Being one the prime instruments of Hindustani music, the various gharanas added or reduced the number of strings according to their musical needs. For instance the maihar gharana sarod had a larger number of strings being strung at three levels, which were the upper, middle and lower. Whereas, the traditional sarod commonly had only two levels

***Sarangi***

The name derives from *Sau Rangi* meaning 100 colours. Sarangi is played with a bow and has four main strings and as many as forty resonant strings. It is generally used to accompany singers but can also be a solo instrument. A number of bowed instruments across the country base their name on this instrument. It was commonly by musicians who created folk compositions. The following are some of the varied sarangis found across the country:

- Sarinda
- Chikara
- Sindhi sarangi
- Gujrtan sarangi
- Dhadya sarangi
- Dedh pasli sarangi

The instruments *dilruba* and *esraj* have common physical characteristics that make them resemble the classical sarangi. This instrument was played to the tunes of the khayal, dhrupad and thumri vocals. However, as time went by this instrument gained prominence amongst courtesans and musicians began to look towards other musical instruments. However, this instrument has not lost complete existence because of prominent musicians like Gopal Misra, Pandit Ram Narayan, and Ustad Sabri Khan, who are regarded as sarangi maestros.

This bowed instrument is not too large as far as size is concerned. It is carved from a single piece of wood. Its body is hollow. At the top and bottom end it is one-inch thick. The sides are barely half-an-inch in thickness. The sarangi has a metal bar placed along it. There are three main strings and one brass sympathetic string tuned by four pegs in the lower part of the instrument. The upper part has eleven pegs that tune the thirty-five to forty sympathetic strings fixed there.

### *Tanpura*

The tanpura is a stringed Indian musical instrument that produces the drone, which is an essential background, required for all Indian music genres. This instrument is believed to have been invented either in the sixteenth or seventeenth century. The basic structure of a tanpura consists of:

- Tumba, which is the hemispherical base that functions as a resonance chamber
- Tabli, which is resonating plate covering the opening in the tumba
- Dandi is the stem that has a fingerboard
- Gulu is the neck of the tanpura that connects the tumba and dandi
- Four tuning pegs of which two are placed on either side of the top end and the other two at the forefront.
- Two bridges over which the strings are suspended. The one on top is called meru or ara. The bridge at the lower end is called ghodi or ghodaj.
- Silk or cotton pieces of thread which cushion the strings
- Four metal strings of which one is tuned to the lower pitch and the other three are meant for the higher pitch.

In north India this instrument is known by its actual name being tanpura; however in the south it is also called:

- Ttambura
- Tthamboora
- Thambura
- Tamboora

It is also available in three distinct styles being:

- *The Miraj Style:* This is the typical north Indian version of the instrument as discussed above

- *The Tanjore Style:* This is mainly found in the southern parts of India and a favorite amongst the Carnatic musicians
- *Tamburi:* This is the smallest type of tanpura and is popular amongst musicians who travel

***Santoor***

The santoor is a musical instrument that originated in the beautiful lands of Kashmir, also known as heaven on earth. The ancient or rather original santoor had over a hundred strings and was considered the forerunner of the piano. This instrument was formerly known as the Shatatantri Veena since it had a hundred strings.

The modern day instrument has eighty-seven metal strings that are strung across a hollow trapezoidal box carved either from walnut or maple wood. The top and bottom of the instrument's framework is covered by either veneer or plywood. The strings are clubbed together in sets of three, thus there are 29 sets of strings. Steel tuning pegs are fixed on the right side of the instrument.

While playing the santoor the musician is required to keep the instrument in a particular manner. He or she has to bear in mind that the wide side should be facing them and the narrow end should be towards the audience or listeners. Also, the musician could either place this musical instrument on their lap or on a stand, which is of comfortable length.

The Indian Santoor has counterparts that are played in various parts of the world. These are:

- Yang qin (China)
- Zymbalon (Romania)
- Cimbalon (Hungary)
- Santoori (Greece)
- Santoo (Iran)
- Kanteli (Finland)

This instrument can be played solo or then can be accompanied with other instruments. Initially it was played as an accompaniment for Sufi hymns. According to archeological and historical findings this instrument was made from dried grass during the Vedic period.

### *Veena*

The veena is probably the most ancient of all the Indian stringed instruments. It basically has a large body with a hollow belly; a stem; and the neck, which is generally carved into a strange figure that resembles the head of a dragon. This instrument has seven strings. Four of them are the main strings that are attached to the pegs, which are fixed on the neck. The other three are attached to the side. They are used as rhythmic accompaniments. The musician plays this instrument by being seated on the ground. They then place the instrument in front of them resting the neck on one of their shoulders. The right hand is generally used for plucking the main strings and the left hand for tuning the pegs as per requirement. Above is the description of the veena in general. However, this instrument is available in a variety of modified versions, each been given a title. These are as follows:

- *Saraswati Veena:* This probably the oldest of all the veena types and has been given an important stature in Indian society. This is said to have been the divine musical instrument of Saraswati, the goddess of music. Its body is generally carved from jack wood. Saraswati veena has four playing strings and three drone strings.
- The Rudra Veena is commonly associated with the Dhrupad type of Hindustani music. The body of this instrument is basically a hollow tube carved out of teakwood.
- The Vichitra Veena is a modified version of the rudra veena. It has a broad stem with six main strings attached to the wooden tuning pegs. A plectrum is used to string this instrument.

The veena has been mentioned in most of the Hindu scriptures, especially in the Vedas. The cave paintings of Ajanta and temple art of the sixth and seventh centuries have depictions of this archaic stringed musical instrument.

### *Tabla*

The tabla though in the singular is the name given to the two drums that are either played as an accompaniment to other instruments or vocalists; or as a solo performance. This is one of the essential instruments of the Hindustani music forms and is also regarded as the principal percussion instrument of Hindustani music. One of the drums is made to create high-pitched sounds and the other one is used for low pitch sounds. Generally, the one with high pitch is played by the right hand and the low-pitched is played by the left hand. The right hand drum is also known as dahina and then left one is known as bayan. One can make out the difference between the two, as the dahina gives rise to a number of resonant ringing and clicking sounds. Whereas the bayan produces swooping bass sounds.

Both the drums have a large black spot their playing surfaces. These spots are made from a mixture of gum, soot and iron filings. Their primary function is to bring about a bell-like resonance, which is one of the outstanding characteristics of this percussion instrument. After the initial days of the tabla being invented, various musicians created their own schools of playing thereby bringing into being a number of tabla gharanas. Each one had a peculiar style and form, which was carried forward for generations. These include:

- Delhi gharana
- Agara gharana
- Benares gharana
- Farukhabad gharana
- Lucknow gharana
- Punjab

In general a tabla solo performance is divided into 5 stages, which are:

- *Uthan or Mohra:* This is the prelude or introductory piece. It usually begins slowly and flows into a crescendo to lay the ground for the next stage of performance
- Peshkar is the first performance of the concert. In this

stage the musician is given an opportunity to warm up for the rest of the show.

- Kaida is the central section or the part where the theme is elaborated. This word actually means 'rule'. The musician generally begins this section with a preconceived composition and as he or she goes through it they add improvisations
- Tukda are the small short compositions that follow the kaida
- Gat actually means gait and this stage marks the steady movement of the rhythms emanated by the tabla player

Rela means rushing or flooding. In this section the tabla player plays rapidly non-stop till he or she reaches the finally beat. This is like the grand finale of every stage performance.

***Indian Percussion Instruments***

There are a large number of Indian percussion instruments. Some of them are known around the world such as the tabla, while a large number of them have never been heard about either in India or abroad. Here is a an exhaustive list of almost all Indian percussion instruments that has existed in the past or continues to exist even today:

- Pakhawaj is the traditional north Indian wooden drum that is played horizontally. It has a long body and both sides are covered with skin having a long body.
- Mridangam is mainly used as an accompaniment for Carnatic music. It looks like the pakhawaj, with the actual difference being the coverings of the ends
- Dholak is a cylindrical side drum, which is one of the basic accompaniments for north Indian folk music.
- Nagara is a percussion instrument made out of clay and played with mallets
- Ghatam is a clay pot with metal shavings that create a resonance when being played. The pot's opening is held against the musician's body while the broad round end is being tunefully tapped upon.

- Bhangam is a percussion instrument made from clay and has been mentioned in various Tamil texts
- Mondai is a south Indian clay percussion instrument
- Ubhangam is an archaic clay instrument that was used in South India
- Bheri is a drum in a conical shape
- Damaru is a drum in the shape of an hourglass. It has a string tied in the center and the ends knotted. When this drum is shaken the knotted ends strike the ends of the drum. It is also known as Lord Shiva's instrument.
- Dholki is a horizontal drum in the shape of a barrel
- Gummati is a pot drum that was used by the rural inhabitants of Andhra Pradesh

***Bansuri***

Bansuri is a type of flute that is carved from bamboo. It is generally played in the vertical position. It has six to seven finger holes, and some of them have additional one or two holes for tuning. Apart from being one the oldest Indian musical instruments, it is presently used in the west too. A large number of fusion bands as well as musicians belonging to other genres of music use this variation of the flute.

The music from this instrument is soothing and relaxing. The bansuri is mainly played in north India. Venu is a south Indian variation of this flute and has eight holes. This Indian music instrument is known by varied names such as algoza, bansi, kolalu, kolavi, kukhi, murali, nar, pava, pillankuzhal, pillangrovi, pulangoil and vamsi.

According to Hindu mythological texts and certain scriptures Lord Shiva chose the bansuri to play the role of goddess of destruction. Apart from that is was the musical instrument of Lord Krishna. Radha and the gopis are known to have danced to Lord Krishna's tunes.

There are basically two types of bansuris:

- The vertical type is only popular as a folk instrument in the northern parts of India

- The horizontal type is used in varied genres of music such as folk, classical and devotional

The parts of a typical bansuri include:

- The dandi, which is its body. It is generally made from reed, cane or bamboo. They are made in a design to taper at the mouth end
- The mukha randhra is the blowing hole, which technically known as the embouchure
- Swar randhra are the finger holes, which produce the tunes in accordance to the dance of the fingers on them.
- Garbha randhra is the opening at the other end of the flute from where the tunes flow out.
- Rassi is the twine that is wound around the bansuri to prevent it from cracking.

The technique for playing this musical instrument is basic, however you would require training in creating tunes and compositions. Basically the opening of the flute is placed on the lower lip so that you can blow through it. You hold the flute horizontally with your thumbs and three fingers of the left hand, and four of the right hand directs the sound. This is done by opening or closing the holes on the body of the flute.

### *Shennai*

The shennai is an Indian wind instrument. This quadruple-reed instrument has a tube that widens towards the lower end. This instrument has either eight or nine holes of which the lower two are used for tuning and the upper ones are meant for playing. This instrument is considered a symbol of festivity and celebration. For centuries the shennai has held an important position in Indian culture. Since time immemorial every auspicious function commenced to the sounds of this wind instrument. Those this maybe a traditional custom, even today, many temples begin the day by playing this instrument. It is considered an auspicious way of waking up the gods.

Though there are not to many renowned exponents in the musical field of shennai playing, going down into the deeper regions of north India, you will come across innumerable budding talents. Unfortunately they have not been given adequate formal training and minimal exposure. They are just known locally and asked to play at weddings and other festive occasions. Playing this instrument is not very simple. You are required to learn the basic technique in terms of the notes that emanate as you move your fingers. Apart from this breath control is an important aspect in creating tuneful compositions. Though this instrument is played solo during auspicious functions and occasions, it is also used as an accompaniment either with other instruments or a vocalist.

Few in Western countries had ever heard the Indian stringed instrument, called the sitar, before Ravi Shankar began playing in Europe and the United States in the 1950s and xs. It was a time when India was reasserting itself culturally following independence from British rule, and the West was open to influences from "the mystic East." Young Westerners were seeking new experiences, and the haunting and intricate melodies of Ravi Shankar's Hindustani style of music gave them what they wanted.

Deepak Raja, a well-known music writer in India, said Ravi Shankar soon rode a wave of popularity, successfully straddling the classical music worlds of both the East and the West. "He built bridges of understanding and cooperation with Western composers, with Western popular musicians, with modern composers and conductors," said Mr. Raja, "and that itself is an immense contribution to ensure that internationally the Hindustani music tradition was recognized as one of the world's great classical traditions." Ravi Shankar has always been an innovator.

He wrote compositions using the violin and sitar, starting an era of fusion music. He made classical music more appealing to modern audiences and his influence on the Beatles led to them incorporating Indian elements into their songs. Soon the sitar and other Indian instruments such as the tabla were familiar to many Western ears. In fact, some music critics say Ravi Shankar has done more for Indian classical music in the West than in his own country. Others disagree, saying the sitarist helped bridge the vacuum that existed between the

North Indian and South Indian classical traditions. They say his enduring contribution is to have moved classical music from the confines of a tiny elite to a wider audience. K.V. Ramanathan, editor of the Indian dance and music magazine Sruti, says the musician's charisma played a vital role in the shift. "His competence, his popularity and if I may say so his personality attracted more people, got more people to listen to him, which meant more and more people got drawn into the sphere of appreciators of classical music," said the editor.

Ravi Shankar continues to perform in both East and West, and many say age has not dimmed the appeal of his music. "I am sure his music is as good as it used to be," noted Deepak Raja. "OK, it may not have the sparkling dexterity it had, but the soulful quality will never go." Accolades have been heaped on him. George Harrison called him the "Godfather of World Music." He has received honours and awards from all over the world, including three Grammy awards in the United States. But for many he simply remains India's greatest musical ambassador.

Sri Tyagaraja, the most celebrated Carnatic Music saint was a great devotee of Lord Sri Rama. Tyagaraja lived to the full extent that God realization is best achieved through *Nadopasana* (music with devotion). His songs are filled with an intimate devotion to Rama, all through revealing his deep understanding of the tenets of the Vedas and Upanishads.

Saint Purandaradas is considered as the grandfather of Carnatic Music. Sri Tyagaraja, along with Muthuswami Dikshitar and Syama Sastri are considered as the "Trinity of Carnatic Music." Sri Tyagaraja has composed more than 800 songs in his long devoted life to Lord Rama, most of them written in his Mother tongue Telugu, but a few in Sanskrit, including the masterpiece *"Jagadanandakaraka"* composed of 108 names describing Lord Rama's attributes. But, his songs are well loved in Tamil Nadu, the seat of South Indian (Carnatic) Music scholarship and performance.

# 3

# Theatre and Cinema of India

## Indian Theatre

Indian tradition of theatre is rich and evolved with the ancient rituals and seasons of the country. It is believed that Lord Brahma created Natyaveda, the fifth Veda on Natya (action) as a mode of recreation for all class of the society by incorporating words from Rig Veda, music from Sama Veda, action from Yajur Veda and emotion from Adharva Veda. Sage Bharata who perfected the dramatic art and wrote Natya Shastra, a great comprehensive work on the science and technique of Indian drama, dance and music enacted the first drama to the audience of 'Devas'. Through the medium of drama, common man was presented with the Ithihasas, Puranas, and Mythology.

Dance has played an important role in the birth of theatre. According to Natya Shastra, dancing and dramatic representation has an intimate relationship. Drama gradually moved from deficting mythological themes to social issues of today. Cinema and serials on the mini screen are nothing but offshoots of this age old culture.

### *Inheritance, Transitions and Future*

The Indian theatre has a tradition going back to at least 5000 years. The earliest book on dramaturgy anywhere in the world was written in India. It was called *Natya Shastra, i.e.*, the grammar or the holy book of theatre by Bharat Muni. Its time has been placed between 2000 B.C. to 4th Century A.D.

A long span of time and practice is needed for any art or activity to form its rules and notifications. Therefore, it can be said with assurance that to have a book like *Natya Shastra*, the Indian theatre must have begun long, long before that if we go back to historical records, excavations and references available in the two great epics *The Ramayana* and *The Mahabharata*.

Theatre in India started as a narrative form, *i.e.*, reciting, singing and dancing becoming integral elements of the theatre. This emphasis on narrative elements made our theatre essentially theatrical right from the beginning. That is why the theatre in India has encompassed all the other forms of literature and fine arts into its physical presentation: Literature, Mime, Music, Dance, Movement, Painting, Sculpture and Architecture-all mixed into one and being called 'Natya' or Theatre in English.

Here it can be said that all the ancient traditions in the world-whether Eastern or Western-present almost the same picture of the theatre. On a superficial overview of both the traditions, they may sound similar in their exterior or physical manifestations but if we go deeper into the philosophy and outlook of both the worlds, it will be easier to understand that both of them are poles apart in their basic nature. The western philosophy of life is deep-rooted in the belief that there is no life after death whereas the Indian philosophy, especially the Hindu doctrine, sees life in a continuity, *i.e.*, there is no end even after death.

Life keeps on moving as a circular activity. Theatre in the West presents life as it is whereas in India it presents life as it should be. In other words, this can be explained like this: Life in the West has been portrayed nearer to realism whether in theatre or other arts but in India it has been illustrated more in idealistic terms. This has been so right from the beginnings of the theatre in both the hemispheres.

### *Phases*

After understanding this basic nature of Indian theatre, we can elaborate further on its development in India. Roughly it can be divided into three distinctive phases: the classical period; the traditional period and the modern period.

Phase I includes the writing and practice of theatre up to about 1000 A.D., almost based on rules, regulations and modifications handed by *Natya Shastra*. They apply to the writing of plays, performance spaces and conventions of staging plays. Playwrights such as Bhasa, Kalidasa, Shudraka, Vishakhadatta and Bhavabhuti contributed in a great measure through their dramatic pieces in Sanskrit. They based their plots on sources like the epics, history, folk tales and legends. The audience was already familiar with the story. Therefore, a theatre language required a visual presentation through gestures, mime and movement. The actor was supposed to be well-versed in all the fine arts. In a way, it was a picture of total theatre. The noted German playwright and director, Brecht, evolved his theory of 'Epic Theatre' and concept of 'Aliegnation' precisely from these sources.

Phase II involves that practice of theatre which was based on oral traditions. It was being performed from about 1000 A.D. onwards upto 1700 A.D. Even today it continues almost in every part of India. Emergence of this kind of theatre is linked with the change of political set up in India as well as the coming into existence of different regional languages in all parts of the country. As the languages themselves were taking their birth around 1000 A.D. it was too early to expect any writing in those languages. That is why this whole period is known as folk or traditional, *i.e.*, theatre being handed over from generation to generation through an oral tradition. Another major change also took place with this kind of traditional theatre.

The classical theatre which is based on *Natya Shastra* was much more sophisticated in its form and nature and totally urban-oriented whereas this traditional theatre evolved out of rural roots. Though other elements of theatre remained almost the same, *i.e.*, use of music, mime, movement, dance and narrative elements. This later theatre was more simple, immediate and improvisational even to the extent of being contemporary. Morever, whereas the classical theatre was almost similar in its presentation in all parts of India at a particular time, the traditional theatre took to two different kinds of presentational methods-all the folk and traditional forms in northern India are mainly vocal, *i.e.*, singing and recitation-based like Ramlila, Rasleela, Bhand Nautanki and Wang without any complicated gestures or movements and elements of dance.

Phase III is again linked with a change in the political set up in India—this time an outside force coming from the West. The time span of about 200 years under the British rule brings the Indian theatre into direct contact with the western theatre. For the first time in India, the writing and practice of theatre is geared fully towards realistic or naturalistic presentation. It is not as if realism or naturalism was totally absent in our tradition. It was always present as also envisaged in *Natya Shastra* through concepts of Lokdharmi, *i.e.*, a style of presentation connected with day-to-day gestures and behaviour and Natyadharami,-*i.e.*, a style more and more presentational and theatrical in nature. But the stories used were invariably from the same sources. In the modern theatre the story also changed its nature. Now it is no more woven around big heroes and gods, but has become a picture of common man.

In a way this is the complete picture of the Indian theatre from the ancient time up to the present. As we have already seen, the theatre in contemporary India is a combination of the three different phases of its evolution illustrated in its historical perspective. But it has never been professional in the true sense of the world, *i.e.*, people have not been entirely dependant on the theatre for their livelihood right from the beginning. Though it seems that the theatre in India has been a continuous activity,yet in reality it has not been so. It has always been a part of festivals or such other occasions which are related to entertainment. At the most, theatre used to be performed between October and March-only for six months even by the so-called commercial or professional companies.

In the rest of the year, the people remained engaged either in agriculture or other vocations. This kind of set up creates a big problem for the Indian theatre. It has not yet become a part and practice of our life as in the West. Even in States like West Bengal and Maharashtra, where theatre is very prolific, none of the performers is totally devoted to the theatre. They are involved in some job or the other during daytime and only in the evenings they come to rehearse or perform. The concept of professional repertory companies in India is a recent one. How can theatre become a profession for an Indian actor and theatre worker? This is the biggest question. How can it provide him his bread and butter as well as opportunities to practise his art?

***Identity***

Another question relates to the identity of Indian theatre today. When the theatre was being performed in one single language like Sanskrit, it had a national identity of its own. But today the picture is completely changed. India is a vast country with 22 languages and as many different cultures. It is not like any Western country where the language are culture are one and, therefore, the theatre can be identified immediately with these elements. In India, the concept of National Theatre has to be seen purely in regional terms.

All the regions have their own language,history and culture and their theatre is also deeply rooted in those circumstances. Therefore, sometimes it becomes a problem of choosing any particular form or region. Does it give a complete picture of Indian character, culture and civilization? That is why over the last 30 to 40 years, there has been a search for its true and authentic form which may represent the aspirations of Modern India as well as a continuity of its traditions.

***Changes***

The exodus from the theatre to films is not a new phenomenon. But of late, television, video, film and the satellite channels have attracted the maximum number of people from the theatre to these options because of more money, glamour and market opportunities. As a result, theatre activities have suffered a severe setback in the last 15 years or so. The situation, however, has started changing slowly again. The audience appears to be fed up with the small screen. Theatre being a live and direct medium and always operating on human level with its audience, can never die. Even after innumerable obstacles and upheavals in history, it has always emerged a winner in the end.

## Indian Cinema

### *Pre-cinema Age*

Telling stories from the epics using hand-drawn tableaux images in scroll paintings, with accompanying live sounds have been an age old Indian tradition. These tales, mostly the familiar stories of gods and goddesses, are revealed slowly through choreographic movements of painted glass slides in a lantern, which create illusions of movements. And so when the Lumire brothers' representatives held the first public showing at Mumbai's (Bombay) Watson's Hotel on July 7, 1896, the new phenomenon did not create much of a stir here and no one in the audience ran out at the image of the train speeding towards them, as it did elsewhere. The Indian viewer took the new experience as something already familiar to him.

Harischandra Sakharam Bhatwadekar, who happened to be present for the Lumiere presentation, was keen on getting hold of the Lumiere Cinematograph and trying it out himself rather than show the Lumiere films to a wider audience. The public reception accorded to Wrangler Paranjpye at Chowapatty on his return from England with the coveted distinction he got at Cambridge was covered by Bhatwadekar in December 1901- the first Indian topical or actuality film was born.

In Calcutta, Hiralal Sen photographed scenes from some of the plays at the Classic Theatre. Such films were shown as added attractions after the stage performances or taken to distant venue where the stage performers could not reach. The possibility of reaching a large audience through recorded images which could be projected several times through mechanical gadgets caught the fancy of people in the performing arts and the stage and entertainment business. The first decade of the 20th century saw live and recorded performances being clubbed together in the same programme.

The strong influence of its traditional arts, music, dance and popular theatre on the cinema movement in India in its early days, is probable responsible for its characteristic enthusiasm for inserting song and dance sequences in Indian cinema, even till today.

***History***

*Raja Harishchandra* (1913) was the first silent feature film made in India. It was made by Dadasaheb Phalke. By the 1930s, the industry was producing over 200 films per annum. The first Indian sound film, Ardeshir Irani's *Alam Ara* (1931), was a super hit. There was clearly a huge market for talkies and musicals; Bollywood and all the regional film industries quickly switched to sound filming. The 1930s and 1940s were tumultuous times: India was buffeted by the Great Depression, World War II, the Indian independence movement, and the violence of the Partition. Most Bollywood films were unabashedly escapist, but there were also a number of filmmakers who tackled tough social issues, or used the struggle for Indian independence as a backdrop for their plots.

In the late 1950s, Bollywood films moved from black-and-white to colour. Lavish romantic musicals and melodramas were the staple fare at the cinema. Successful actors included Dev Anand, Dilip Kumar and Raj Kapoor. In late 1960s and mid 1970s, violent movies's era was started but romantic movies also co-existed and Dharmendra was a major star. In the late 1970s and 1980s, romantic confections made way for gritty, violent, films about gangsters and bandits. Amitabh Bachchan, the star known for his "angry young man" roles, rode the crest of this trend. In the early 1990s, the pendulum swung back towards family-centric romantic musicals with the success of such films as *Hum Aapke Hain Koun* (1994) and *Dilwale Dulhania Le Jayenge* (1995).

The Indian film industry has preferred films that appeal to all segments of the audience, and has resisted making films that target narrow audiences. It was believed that aiming for a broad spectrum would maximize box office receipts. However, filmmakers may be moving towards accepting some box-office segmentation, between films that appeal to rural Indians, and films that appeal to urban and overseas audiences.

***Regional Cinema***

The first film in Southern India was made in 1916 by R Nataraja Mudaliar-*Keechaka Vadham*. As the title indicates the subject is again a mythological from the Mahabharata. Another film made in Madras-*Valli Thiru-Manam* (1921) by Whittaker drew critical acclaim and box office success. Hollywood returned Ananthanarayanan Narayanan founded General Pictures Corporation in 1929 and established filmmaking as an industry in South India and became the single largest producer of silent films. Kolhapur in Western Maharashtra was another centre of active film production in the twenties.

In 1919 Baburao K Mistry-popularly known as Baburao Painter formed the Maharashtra Film Co. with the blessings of the Maharaja of Kolhapur and released the first significant historical-*Sairandhari* (1920) with Balasheb Pawar, Kamala Devi and Zunzarrao Pawar in stellar roles. Because of his special interest in sets, costumes, design and painting, he chose episodes from Maratha history for interpreting in the new medium and specialised in the historical genre. The exploits of Shivaji and his contemporaries and their patriotic encounters with their opponents formed the recurring themes of his 'historicals' which invariably had a contemporary relevance to the people of a nation, who were fighting for liberation from a colonial oppressor.

The attack against the false values associated with the Western way of life and their blind imitation by some Indians was humorously brought out by Dhiren Ganguly in his brilliant satirical comedy-*England Returned* (1921)-presumably the first 'social satire' on Indians obsessed with Western values. And with that another genre of Indian cinema known as 'the contemporary social' slowly emerged. Baburao Painter followed it up with another significant film in 1925-*Savkari Pash* (The Indian Shylock)-an attempt at realistic treatment of the Indian peasant exploited by the greedy moneylender.

In Bengal, a region rich in culture and intellectual activity, the first Bengali feature film in 1917, was remake of Phalke's

*Raja Harishchandra*. Titled *Satyawadi Raja Harishchandra*, it was directed by Rustomjee Dotiwala. Less prolific than Bombay based film industry, around 122 feature films were made in Calcutta in the Silent Era.

The first feature film in Tamil, also the first in entire South India, *Keechakavatham* was made during 1916-17, directed by Nataraja Mudaliar.

*Marthandavarma* (1931) produced by R Sunder Raj, under Shri.Rajeswari Film, Nagercoil, directed by P V Rao, got into a legal tangle and was withdrawn after its premiere. Based on a celebrated novel by C V Raman Pillai, the film recounts the adventures of the crown prince and how he eliminates the arch-villains to become the unquestioned ruler of the Travancore State. The film has title cards in English and Malayalam, some of which are taken from the original text. A few of the title cards and action make obvious reference to the Swadeshi Movement of the time. Had it not been for the legal embargo, the film would have had a great impact on the regional cinema of the South.

### *Indian Cinema Starts Talking*

In the early thirties, the silent Indian cinema began to talk, sing and dance. *Alam Ara* produced by Ardeshir Irani (Imperial Film Company), released on March 14, 1931 was the first Indian cinema with a sound track. Mumbai became the hub of the Indian film industry having a number of self-contained production units. The thirties saw hits like *Madhuri* (1932), *Indira,M A* (1934), *Anarkali* (1935), *Miss Frontier Mail* (1936), and *Punjab Mail* (1939).

### *Calcutta Film Industry*

Madan Theatres of Calcutta produced *Shirin Farhad* and *Laila Majnu* (1931) well composed and recorded musicals. Both films replete with songs had a tremendous impact on the audience and can be said to have established the unshakeable hold of songs on our films. *Chandidas* (1932, Bengali), the story of a Vaishnavite poet-priest who falls in love with a low caste washerwoman and defies convention, was a super-hit. P C

Barua produced *Devdas* (1935) based on Saratchandra Chatterjee's famous story about frustrated love, influenced a generation of viewers and filmmakers.

### *The South Indian Cinema*

Tamil cinema emerged as a veritable entertainment industry in 1929 with the creation of General Picture Corporation in Madras (Chennai). Most of the Tamil films produced were multilingual productions, with versions in Telugu, Malayalam and Kannada until film production units were established in Hyderabad, Trivandrum and Bangalore. The first talkie of South India, *Srinivas Kalyanam* was made by A Narayanan in 1934.

### *The Golden Fifties*

Fifties saw the rise of great directors like Mehboob, Bimal Roy, Guru Dutt and Raj Kapoor who changed the fate of Indian cinema. These directors entered the film industry during the 1930s and '40s, which were traumatic years for the Indian people. The fight for independence, famines, changing social mores, global fight against fascism all contributed to the ethos in which the directors grew up.

### *Bollywood*

Bollywood is the informal name given to the popular Mumbai-based Hindi language film industry in India. The term is sometimes used incorrectly to refer to the whole of Indian cinema. The name is a combination of *Bombay*, the old name of Mumbai, and *Hollywood*, the center of the American film industry. Though some purists deplore the name, arguing that it makes the industry look like a poor cousin to Hollywood, it seems likely to persist and now has its own entry in the Oxford English Dictionary.

Bollywood and the other major cinematic hubs (Tamil, Bengali, Telugu, and Malayalam) constitute the broader Indian film industry, whose output is the largest in the world in terms of number of films produced and in number of tickets sold. Bollywood is a strong part of popular culture of not only India and the rest of the Indian subcontinent, but also of the Middle

East, parts of Africa, parts of Southeast Asia, and among the South Asian diaspora worldwide. Bollywood has its largest diasporic audiences in the UK, Canada, Australia and the U.S., all of which have large Indian immigrant populations.

Bollywood is also commonly referred to as "Hindi cinema", even though use of poetic Urdu words is fairly common. There has been a growing presence of English in dialogues and songs as well. It is not uncommon to see movies which feature dialogues with English words and phrases, even whole sentences. A few movies are also made in two or even three languages (either using subtitles, or several soundtracks).

### *Genre Conventions*

Westerners would tend to classify most Bollywood films as musicals, because few movies are made without at least one song-and-dance number. However, such labelling fails to recognise the unique nature of the genre. In the Western tradition, a "standard" movie has no songs, at least none that are sung by the protagonists. A movie with such songs is therefore a "musical". To understand the Bollywood genre, it is necessary to unlearn this straightforward concept.

The standard Bollywood movie is *expected* to contain a number of elements, and one of the essentials is catchy music in the form of song-and-dance numbers woven into the script. Indeed, a movie's music often sells the film through advance release — a populace that is already humming the songs from a movie is far more likely to troop into theatres to see the movie when it is finally released. A Bollywood movie *without* songs and dances would need to be particularly strong in other departments to avoid being considered a rip-off.

Indian audiences expect full value for their money, with a good entertainer generally referred to as *paisa vasool*, (literally, "money's worth"). Songs and dances, love triangles, comedy and dare-devil thrills— all are mixed up in a three-hour-long extravaganza with an intermission. Such movies are called *masala* movies, after the Hindi word for a spice mixture, *masala*. Like *masalas*, these movies are a mixture of many things. If a movie lacks an ingredient (such as songs), the audience has not received its full money's worth. Bollywood plots have tended to be melodramatic. They frequently employ formulaic ingredients such as star-crossed lovers and angry parents, love triangles, family ties, sacrifice, corrupt politicians, kidnappers, conniving villains, courtesans with hearts of gold, long-lost relatives and siblings separated by fate, dramatic reversals of fortune, and convenient coincidences.

There have always been Indian films with more "artistic" aims and more sophisticated stories, both inside and outside the Bollywood tradition. They often lost out at the box office to movies with more mass appeal. Bollywood conventions are changing, however. A large Indian diaspora in English speaking countries, and increased Western influence at home, have nudged Bollywood films closer to Hollywood models. Film kisses are no longer banned. Plots now tend to feature Westernized urbanites dating and dancing in discos rather than arranged marriages. Plots can be less melodramatic, more sophisticated.

### *Bollywood Song and Dance*

Songs from Bollywood movies are generally pre-recorded by professional playback singers, with the actors then lip synching the words to the song on-screen, often while dancing. While most actors, especially today, are excellent dancers, few are also singers. One notable exception was Kishore Kumar, who starred in several major films in the 1950s while also having a stellar career as a playback singer. K. L. Saigal, Suraiyya and Noor Jehan were also known as both singers and actors.

Playback singers are prominently featured in the opening credits and have their own fans who will go to an otherwise lackluster movie just to hear their favourites. One of the most recorded of these playback singers is Lata Mangeshkar who, through the course of a career spanning over six decades, has recorded thousands of songs for Indian movies. Many of the female songs in films from the 1950s, 1960s, and 1970s were sung by Lata or by her sister Asha Bhosle. Some of the famous male playback singers were Mohammed Rafi, Mukesh, and Kishore Kumar. The composers of film music, known as music directors, are also well-known. Their songs can make or break a film and usually do. Remixing of filmi songs with modern beats and rhythms is a common occurrence today, and producers may even release remixed versions of some of their films' songs along with the films' regular soundtrack albums.

The dancing in Bollywood films, especially older ones, is primarily modeled on Indian dance: classical dance styles, dances of historic northern Indian courtesans (tawaif), or folk dances. In modern films, Indian dance elements often blend with Western dance styles, though it is not unusual to see Western pop *and* pure classical dance numbers side by side in the same film. The hero or heroine will often perform with a troupe of supporting dancers, usually of the same sex. Many song-and-dance routines in Indian films feature unrealistically instantaneous shifts of location and/or changes of costume between verses of a song.

If the hero and heroine dance and sing a pas-de-deux (a dance and ballet term, meaning "dance of two"), it is often staged in beautiful natural surroundings or architecturally grand settings. This staging is referred to as a "picturisation." Switzerland has become a popular setting for these picturisations, largely because its Alpine valleys are reminiscent of Kashmir. Though considered by many to be one of India's most beautiful regions, Kashmir has been generally off-limits for quite some time due to armed conflict and terrorism.

Songs typically comment on the action taking place in the movie, in several ways. Sometimes, a song is worked into the plot, so that a character has a reason to sing; other times, a song is an externalization of a character's thoughts, or presages an event that has not occurred yet in the plot of the movie. In this case, the event is almost always two characters falling in love.

Bollywood films have always used what are now called "item numbers". A physically attractive female character (the "item girl"), often completely unrelated to the main cast and plot of the film, performs a catchy song and dance number in the film. In older films, the "item number" may be performed by a courtesan (tawaif) dancing for a rich client or as part of a cabaret show. The dancer Helen was famous for her cabaret numbers. In modern films, item numbers may be inserted as discotheque sequences, dancing at celebrations, or as stage shows.

For the last few decades Bollywood producers have been releasing the film's soundtrack, as tapes or CDs, before the main movie release, hoping that the music will pull audiences into the movie theater later. In the last few years some producers have also been releasing music videos, usually featuring a song from the film. However, some promotional videos feature a song which is not included in the movie.

### *"Dialogues" and Lyrics*

The film script or lines of dialogue (called "dialogues" in Indian English) and the song lyrics are often written by different people. The lines of dialogue are mostly written in Hindi, with use of Urdu in situations which require poetic speech. Contemporary mainstream movies also make great use of English. The language is often melodramatic and invokes God, family, mother, duty, and self-sacrifice liberally. Music directors often prefer working with certain lyricists, to the point that the lyricist and composer are seen as a team. This phenomenon is not unlike the pairings of American composers and songwriters that created old-time Broadway musicals. Song lyrics are usually about love. Bollywood song lyrics, especially in the old movies, frequently use Urdu or Hindustani vocabulary.

### *Cast and Crew*

Bollywood employs people from all parts of India. It attracts thousands of aspiring actors and actresses, all hoping for a break in the industry. Models and beauty contestants, television actors, theatre actors and even common people come to Mumbai with the hope and dream of becoming a star. Just as in Hollywood, very few succeed.

Stardom in the entertainment industry is very fickle, and Bollywood is no exception. The popularity of the stars can rise and fall rapidly, even based on a single movie. Very few people become national icons, who are unaffected by success or failure of their movies, like Amitabh Bachchan and now recently Shahrukh Khan. Directors compete to hire the most popular stars of the day, who are believed to guarantee the success of a movie (though this belief is not always supported by box-office results). Hence many stars make the most of their fame, once they become popular, by making several movies simultaneously.

Only a very few non-Indian actors are able to make a mark in Bollywood, though many have tried from time to time. There have been some exceptions, one recent example is the hit film *Rang de Basanti*, where the lead actress is an Englishwoman. *Kisna* and *Lagaan* also featured foreign actors. Bollywood can be very clannish, and the relatives of film-industry insiders have an edge in getting coveted roles in films and/or being part of a film's crew. However, industry connections are no guarantee of a long career: competition is brutal and if film industry scions don't succeed at the box office, their careers will falter. Some of the biggest stars, such as Dharmendra, Amitabh Bachchan, and Shah Rukh Khan have succeeded despite total lack of show biz connections.

### *Bollywood Awards*

The Indian screen magazine Filmfare started the first Filmfare Awards in 1953. Modeled after the poll-based merit format of the Academy of Motion Picture Arts and Sciences, individuals may submit their votes in separate categories; The awards are presented at a glamorous, star-studded ceremony. However, unlike the Oscars, voting is not restricted to members of a specific club or academy, but is open to all people. Like the Oscars, they are frequently accused of bias towards commercial success, rather than artistic merit.

Lately, other companies, such as Stardust Magazine, Zee TV, etc have joined the movie award bandwagon. Some of the other popular awards are:

- Zee Cine Awards
- Star Screen Awards
- Stardust Awards
- IIFA Awards

Most of these award ceremonies are lavishly staged spectacles, featuring singing, dancing, and lots of stars and starlets.

Since 1973, the Indian government has sponsored the National Film Awards, awarded by the government run Directorate of Film Festivals (DFF). The DFF screens not only Bollywood films, but films from all the other regional movie industries and independent/art films. These awards are handed out at an annual ceremony presided over by the President of India.

## Indian Parallel Cinema

Through his first film *Pather Panchali* (1955) Satyajit Ray became the pioneer of a genre of films latter known as the 'Indian Parallel Cinema'. Even though Ritwik Ghatak made his first film *Nagarik* in 1952, he became well known by his film *Ajantrik* (1958) and became a strong presence in parallel cinema. Mrinal Sen made his first film *Raatbhor* in 1955.

The first film society was founded in Bombay in 1943 and Satyajit Ray founded a film society in Calcutta in 1947. By the beginning of 1970s there existed above 150 film societies all over India. Through these societies people could see the best of Indian cinema and also they got access to the best of foreign cinema. The first International Film Festival of India was held in Bombay, Madras and Calcutta by the Films Division in 1952. Western classics like De Sica's *Bicycle Thieves* shown in the film festival created waves among young filmmakers who were frustrated with the mindless song-dance dramas made in India. The Film Training Institute of India (FTII-presently Film and Television Institute of India) was set up in Pune in 1961 and the National Film Archives of India (NFAI) was established in 1964. The Film Finance Corporation (FFC) was set up by the Government in 1960, with the objective of giving loans to directors who wanted to make feature films outside the commercial circuit. All these factors lead Indian Cinema to a revolutionary change, a new genre of Indian films arrived, which are often termed as the 'New Wave Indian Cinema' or the 'New Indian Cinema'.

Mrinal Sen's *Bhuvan Shome* (1969) and Mani Kaul's *Uski Roti* (1969), both sponsored by State owned Film Finance Corporation (FFC), inspired by the French nouvelle vague, set new film sensibility and cinematic language in India. This movement was labelled as the 'New Indian Cinema' or the 'New Wave Indian Cinema'. FTII graduates Kumar Shahani, Mani Kaul, Saeed Mirza, Shyam Benegal and Ketan Mehta were the important names of New Wave Indian Cinema in Hindi. Mani Kaul's *Ashad Ka Ek Din* (1971) and *Duvidha* (1973), Kumar Shahni's *Maya Darpan* (1972) and Shyam Benegal's *Ankur* (1973) played important role in this new movement in Hindi during the 1970s. M S Sathyu's *Garam Hawa* (1973) Govind Nihilani who entered film industry as Shyam Benegal's cameraman made his directorial debut through *Aakrosh* (1980) he continued making socio-political films like *Party* (1984), *Tamas* (1987) and *Drishti* (1990). Saeed Mizra made notable political films like *Arvind Desai ki Ajeeb Dastan* (1978), *Albert Pinto ko Gussa Kyon Aata Hai* (1980), *Mohan Joshi Haazir Ho!* (1984) and *Salim Langde Pe Mat Ro* (1989).

Adoor Gopalakrishnan through his first film *Swayamvaram* (1972) extended the New Wave Cinema to Malayalam cinema. Aravindan through his first film *Uttarayanam* (1974) strengthened the movement. John Abraham, K R Mohanan and P A Backer were strong presence of the new Malayalam cinema. Kannada was the other film industry in South India, which took over the cinema movement in South India. B V Karanth, Girish Karnad and Girish Kasaravalli spearheaded the Kannada parallel cinema. Girish Kasaravalli, graduated from the Pune Film Institute, directed his first film, *Ghata Shradha* in 1977, which won the National award for best film. In Assamise, Janu Barua made his first film *Aparoopa* (1982). His *Halodhia Choraye Baodhan Kali* (1987), which achieved international recognition, dealt with social problems of rural Assam. Bhubendra Nath Sikia made his first film *Sandhyarag* (1977) followed by *Agnisnaan* (1985), *Kolahal* (1988), *Sarothi* (1991) and *Abarthan* (1993).

# 4

# Indian Paintings

Indian paintings traditions go back to antiquity, as is evident from the murals of Ajanta, Ellora and other frescoes, the Buddhist palm leaf manuscripts, the Jain texts and the Deccan, Mughal and Kangra schools of miniature Indian painting. Indian Painting is an old tradition, with ancient texts outlining theories of Colour and anecdotal accounts suggesting that it was common for households to paint their doorways or indoor rooms where guests resided. Cave paintings from Ajanta, Bagh and Sittanvasal and temple paintings testify to a love of naturalism.

Indian paintings provide an aesthetic continuum that extends from the early civilization to the presentday. This form of art in India is vivid and lively, refined and sophisticated and bold and vigorous at the same time. From being essentially religious in purpose in the beginning, Indian paintings have evolved over the years to become a fusion of various traditions which influenced them.

At first glance, an Indian miniature painting, to the uninitiated, appears nothing more than a clutter and tangle of pastoral settings, dominated by masculine and feminine figures. Yet these scenes are not detached visions of artistic expression but provide the basis of Indian music and art forms. Most of these masterly works are visual creations of emotional and perceptive concepts that depict the *ragas* or musical modes of Indian classical music. Miniature painters employed at various medival courts, discovered the potential of limitless self-expression in their depiction, and today there are 130 known sets of such miniatures. The Indian paintings have now acquired a stature of their own. They use materials and techniques from all over the world but express Indian realities and Indian experiences.

The respect for tradition and the ability to transcend it at the same time is clearly evident in Indian art of today. This is the essence of what has been described as the eclecticism of the Indian contemporary expression. Starting with the Bengal school, many contemporary painters have been influenced by modern styles.

***Prelude:*** The earliest Indian paintings were the rock paintings of pre-historic times, the petroglyphs as found in places like Bhimbetka, and some of them are older than 5500 BC. Such works continued and after several millennia, in the 7th century, carved pillars of Ellora, Maharashtra state present a fine example of Indian paintings, and the Colours, mostly various shades of red and orange, were derived from minerals. Thereafter, frescoes of Ajanta and Ellora caves appeared. India's Buddhist literature is replete with examples of texts which describe that palaces of kings and aristocratic class were embellished with paintings, but they have largely not survived. But, it is believed that some form of art painting was practised during that time.

India has one of the greatest traditions of painting of the ancient world. A high degree of technical excellence was achieved even in very early times, and the art, born out of the deep philosophy of the land, was graceful and sublime.

The earliest surviving paintings in the Indian subcontinent are those of Ajanta. The paintings here were made in two phases. The oldest date to around the 2nd century BC. The marvellous latter phase was around the 5th century AD, under the patronage of the Vakatakas who ruled the Deccan.

The subjects are scenes from the life of the Buddha and the Jatakas, stories of his previous births. These paintings bring to us great beauty of form, with extremely fine rendering which imparts a sense of volume and roundedness. Yet, amidst the tender and elegant beauty of the world, these paintings constantly take us to that which is within.

The great Bodhisattvas (seekers of truth) who are painted upon the walls of Ajanta, always look within. It is this life of the spirit which pervades the entire world of these paintings.

Ajanta is known to be the fountainhead and inspiration of Buddhist paintings across the whole of Asia.

The sophisticated ancient tradition of painting, which was inherited by the artists of Ajanta, was documented as the *Chitrasutra* of the *Vishnudharmottara Purana*. This was a verbal tradition, which would have come over many centuries, passed on through guilds of painters. It was penned on paper by perhaps the 5th or 6th century AD. This ancient treatise places a sophisticated grammar in the hands of the painter. However, he is informed that rules do not make the painting. It has to be given a life of its own by the painter.

Contrary to what is generally known, there are several remnants of ancient paintings found in all corners of the subcontinent, belonging to practically every century of the last 1,500 years and more. These display the fact of a great and unified tradition of painting in ancient India.

There are fragments of paintings of the time of Ajanta which survive at many Buddhist cave sites, including Pitalkhora near Ellora, in Maharashtra.

Nine caves were excavated on the slopes of the Vindhya hills above the Bagh river during the reign of the Guptas, between the 4th and 6th centuries AD. Unfortunately the paintings on the walls of these caves have been practically lost to the ravages of time. Reproductions of earlier times show that, as at Ajanta, the Buddhist paintings of Bagh present a sense of stillness. There is all the activity of life and yet a profound sense of peace upon the faces of the painted figures.

Very little of the paintings survive in the 6th century Hindu caves of Badami in Karnataka. As at Bagh, what remains evokes the magic of a world of painted splendour when all the walls and ceilings were covered with murals.

In the meantime, in the 7th century, the Pallava kings of what is now Tamil Nadu gave exuberant and glorious expression to themes relating to Shiva in the paintings in the temples of Panamalai and Kailashanatar in Kancheepuram.

Worshipper gathering lotuses, Sittannavasal, Tamil Nadu, 9th century: The figure is made with a lilting grace, like the stalks of the lotuses he gathers. The flowers are painted with a great sense of tenderness and beauty and are as large as the humans and animals in the painting.

The niches in the outer ambulatory path of the Kailashanatar temple were once covered with paintings in brilliant colours. Traces of these are still discernible. In these paintings, we see the beginnings of a sense of imperial grandeur represented through art, in the emphasis on the depiction of lavish crowns and jewellery.

In the 9th century Jain cave of Sittannavasal in Tamil Nadu, there is a marvellous lotus pond painted on the ceiling. It is a scene of the faithful gathering lotuses to place upon the resting place of a Tirthankara, a Jain saint. Elephants, buffalos, geese and fish frolic in the water, which is overflowing with beautiful lotuses. The painter has used the occasion to present a joyous world. He brings to us a sense of sublime happiness; as fish swim in the waters, an elephant appears to smile, and gentle men gather lotuses larger than themselves.

In the meantime, the magnificent Kailashnath temple had been hewn out of a mountain at Ellora in the 8th century. The walls and ceilings of this temple were once covered with murals. Fragments of these, which remain, show the beauty and quality of the art.

There are also paintings of the late 9th century in the Jain caves at Ellora. The painters here continue the older tradition but with contributions of their own. Besides the naturalism and grace inherited from Ajanta, the figures painted here are stylised and elongated. These are significant changes, which, in later years, are reflected in paintings over the whole of India.

In the heart of the Brihadeeswara temple in Thanjavur in Tamil Nadu, protected by massive walls of stone, are the finest paintings of the theme of Shiva ever painted. Towards the end of the 10th century, King Rajaraja Chola expressed his devotion and also his power and grandeur by commissioning murals on a spectacular scale.

The colours in the paintings are soft and subdued, the lines firm and sinuous and the expressions true to life. More than ever before, we see the artists' lavish use of embellishments of crowns and jewellery, portraying the royal splendour of the times.

King Rajaraja Chola and Guru Karuvurar Brihadeeswara temple, Tamil Nadu, 11th century: This is the earliest royal portrait in Indian painting. In keeping with ancient traditions, the guru is given importance and the king is shown standing behind him.

At an altitude of over 3,000 metres, the barren desert plateau of Laddakh is a fascinating crucible of cultures. In days gone by, this was not an isolated place; it was an active centre of trade.

In the 11th century, King Yeshe Od of Guge built 108 monasteries across his kingdom in Laddakh, western Tibet, Kinnaur and Lahaul-Spiti. Craftsmen and artists from Kashmir were invited by Yeshe Od and they constructed and painted these monasteries, which were to become the backbone of trans-Himalayan Buddhism.

The philosophy of Vajrayana Buddhism offers a new path towards attaining enlightenment. The worshipper meditates upon images of the deity and, by absorbing the qualities personified in the image, he becomes the deity himself. Thus, paintings are very important for Vajrayana Buddhists as an essential part of religious practice.

The monastery of Alchi is an oasis of beauty and colour in the midst of the vast and barren landscape of Laddakh. The dhoti of an Avalokitesvara statue in the three-storeyed temple of Alchi has some of the most gorgeous paintings. These are the only surviving visual representations of the culture and architecture of ancient Kashmir.

One of the masterpieces of the Alchi paintings is the Green Tara. We see here the marvellous shaping of the form with skilful shading. There is also the depiction of the protruding eye which extends beyond the line of the face. This is a convention in Indian painting, which was first seen in the murals of Ellora.

The Kashmiri artists present a lively world, with the grace and beauty of form coming to them from the classical Indian tradition. The rich textiles and decorative elements of these paintings are remarkable and they show that the artists had assimilated the traditions coming to them from Gandhara and Central Asia.

Goddess Tara, Alchi, Laddakh, 11th century. This is a depiction of the Goddess as a saviour. She is surrounded by representations of many fears and the figures turn to her for protection. There is a sense of animated movement caught in these tiny figures, as the goddess stands in dignified majesty.

The Kashmiri style was mainly responsible for the lovely wall paintings still seen in the beautiful monasteries at Alchi, Mangyu and Sumda in Laddakh, in the Tabo monastery in the Spiti valley and in the Nako monastery in Kinnaur district, Himachal Pradesh.

On the western edge of the trans-Himalayan plateau in Spiti is the monastery complex of Tabo. This appears to be one of the first among the 108 monasteries built by Yeshe Od. It is dated around AD 996. The paintings here show close similarity to Alchi. The sinuous and even exaggerated body forms and the supple lines show a form of painting which is uniquely Kashmiri.

The monastery of Nako, in Kinnaur district of Himachal Pradesh, comprises four temples within an enclosure of mud walls. The wall paintings at Nako display a considerable delicacy of execution and an inner grace.

The traditions of Vajrayana Buddhist paintings, which were laid at the time of the grand conception of King Yeshe Od's 108 monasteries, continued in the centuries to come. From Laddakh in the west to Arunachal Pradesh in the east, across the highest mountains of the world, is the one region which has an unbroken tradition of Indian mural painting.

Parvati with her companions, Lepakshi, Andhra Pradesh, 16th century. This lively paintings reflects the cosmopolitan culture of the Vijayanagar empire. The rich and varied textiles are remarkable. The angular features and protruding eye exhibit the pan-Indian medival traditions of painting.

Deep in the heart of the plains, in the Lalitpur district of Uttar Pradesh, stand the Shiva and Vishnu temples, which are known as the Kacheris. The Choti Kacheri has on the ceiling the remains of exquisite paintings of the 13th century. These are extremely valuable as, after the fragmentary remains at Nalanda and Satdhara, these are the oldest surviving paintings of the northern plains in India.

After the 11th century, the art of painting came to prominence again during the rule of the Vijayanagar kings from the 14th century onwards. In the cosmopolitan atmosphere of Hampi and other sites, we see fine examples of mural paintings.

The ceiling of the Virupaksha temple in Hampi is covered with paintings of the 15th century. There is simplicity and vigour in the style of the paintings. A sense of movement and energy is caught in the painted figures.

In these paintings, there is a deep intertwining of the story of the Vijayanagar empire and its kings with the stories of the gods they believed in. There is also a painting of the procession of the revered sage Vidyaranya, who was the spiritual mentor of the founders of the Empire.

The temple at Lepakshi was built in the 16th century by the Nayaka brothers, Virupanna and Viranna, at a centre of trade and pilgrimage in the Vijayanagar empire. The paintings on the ceiling of the mandapa here are some of the finest mural paintings of the medival period in India.

Lepakshi presents the richness and colour of a great cosmopolitan society. It presents one of the great moments in Indian painting. There is a sense of liveliness here, which is enhanced by the depiction of the protruding eye. The liveliness is also conveyed by angular features and by the peaked corners of clothes. Flautist, Fatephur Sikri, 16th century: Though Mughal miniatures are well known and celebrated, few know that murals were also commissioned by the Mughal emperors.

This painting is in the interior of Mariam's Palace and depicts a Western lady playing the flute.Legends associated with Shiva and Parvati, Krishna and Rama were painted on the walls of palaces and temples in Kerala from the 16th to the 19th century.

There is a new sense of power and majesty which one sees in the painted gods of Kerala. The manner of shading to depict volume reminds us of Ajanta and Alchi. Each figure here is larger than life. Their limbs are strong and their bodies are full and firm. The gods painted are proud, vigorous and protective. The idiom of Kerala is unique. Its close relationship to the ancient dance dramas of the land are seen in the elaborate headgear and the heavy forms.

In the 16th century, under the Mughal emperor Akbar, the art of painting was revived in northern India after many centuries. The finest miniatures were made in the court of Akbar and the emperors who succeeded him. At Fatehpur Sikri, the capital city built by Akbar, we have the remnants of mural paintings. These are fine paintings and are very similar to the miniatures of that period. There are representations of busy marketplaces, elephants and horse riders and a depiction of a flautist.

The Bundelas, who were powerful in central India, founded the city of Orccha in 1531. Mural paintings were made on the walls of all the palaces within the magnificent Orccha fort. The Raj Mahal was completely adorned with mural paintings of the 17th century. What remains of these exhibits a blend of the two most significant styles of painting in India at that time—the Mughal and the Rajput. The expressions are often gentle. Exposure to the Mughal court has also led to a sense of courtly sophistication.

There are surviving mural paintings from the 17th century onwards in Rajasthan. They present a varied tapestry, with the constant interaction of the indigenous idiom of mural painting and the influences coming from the imperial Mughal court.

Krishna with a Gaja, Bhojanshala, Amer Palace, Rajasthan, c. 17th century: These simple yet sophisticated drawings have an easy natural sense, which is reminiscent of ancient Indian art. The twinkle in the eye of the elephant is in keeping with the Indian artist's sensitivity towards all forms of life.

The finest wall paintings of Rajasthan are found in the Bhojanshala of the Amer Palace near Jaipur. These are exquisite drawings of the 17th century, on Vaishnava themes. In depicting the divine images, the artist appears to transcend himself. The drawings are made in panels upon the wall and are small in scale for murals. However, the painter's sensitivity and honest depiction creates an intimacy between the viewer and the painting.

Rajasthan was on the major trade routes of days gone by. The area of Shekhawati has a concentration of 19th and 20th century *havelis* which are profusely painted. The paintings here reflect the opulence of the flourishing trading community, the Marwaris.

The cultural impact of the sudden exposure to European influences is reflected in the varied and indiscriminate depiction of a wide array of subjects. These range from the eternal religious themes to the new inventions which the traders would have seen in their visits to the major port cities.

The verdant Pahari hills saw the finest continuation of the tradition of murals in India. The 18th and 19th century paintings on the walls of the Rang Mahal in Chamba are among the best surviving examples of Pahari murals.

The themes are mostly religious and the styles are closely related to those of the miniature paintings of the region. We see fine expressions, the refinement of Pahari miniatures, and an exuberant and joyous sense of life.

Shiva, Shivdwala temple, Chamba, Himachal Pradesh, c. 18th century. The paintings of the temple reveal a world of beauty and innocence. Shiva is depicted with great tenderness as a gentle and loving god. Orissa, in the eastern plains of India, is a land of the rich continuation of ancient culture. The 18th century paintings on the walls of the Viranchinarayan Temple at Buguda are some of the finest surviving murals of that period in India.

These are a rare instance of the continuation of the ancient Indian mural tradition. These are not like miniatures made upon the walls. The themes are from the Ramayana. The sense of humanity and humility in these paintings remind one of the finest of ancient Indian paintings.

The murals of Punjab perhaps represent the last phase of wall paintings in India. We see here shades of realism from the tradition of Mughal miniatures and yet faces that are distinctly of the Punjab. The themes and the manner are deeply rooted in the local culture.

There is a quiet sense of dignity, which emerges in the best of these paintings. Mural paintings are found hidden away in temples in the midst of busy market places in Amritsar, in temples in villages such as Kishankot, and in Qila Mubarak and Qila Androon in the Patiala fort.

In ancient times, the philosophical ideas of Hinduism and Buddhism spread from India to practically every corner of Asia. As art was an integral part of life and religion, the concepts of Indian art spread far and wide, along with philosophy.

Lakshmana, Viranchinarayan temple, Orissa, 18th century. While Lakshmana sharpens his arrow, monkeys and other animals are engaged in playful activity. The angular and stylised idiom of painting, seen here and in the manuscripts of Orissa, travelled to Bali in Indonesia where it is seen till today.

In 1930, Laurence Binyon, Director of the British Museum, wrote: "Whoever studies the art of China and Japan, at whatever point he begins, starts on a long road which will lead him ultimately to Ajanta." Scholars in all Asian countries trace the roots of their classic paintings to the murals of India.

The paintings of the 5th century of Sigiriya and of the 12th century of Polonnaruva in Sri Lanka; mural paintings of the 12th-13th century pagodas of Bagan in Myanmar and the classic paintings of the Horyuji temple in Japan closely reflect the traditions of Indian paintings.

The art of Asia has been informed by a deep vision of the eternal harmony of the world. It is this vision of life which shaped the grace and forms of the paintings of Ajanta. The art travelled with its philosophy of compassion across Asia to create a vision that shaped the culture of a whole continent.

### *Wall Paintings*

The art of painting in India goes back to pre-historic times. The pre-historic paintings in the cave shelters of Bhimbetka and Pachmarhi are simple designs showing scenes of hunting, farming and dancing against mottled rock and were initially done in black or earth colours. The palette soon expanded to include white, red, yellow, blue and green. This progression can clearly be seen in the wall art of Bhimbetka. Drawings on walls of caves and rock shelters served a twofold purpose: decorating homes and appeasing deities. While the adivasis (tribals) of yore traced simple, very basic forms to ward off evil spirits and disease, more sophisticated art survives in the Buddhist rock-carved monasteries of the middle of the first millennium AD, such as Ajanta in Maharashtra and Bagh in MP.

The Rathwa Bhils of MP and eastern Gujarat commonly install a deity in the form of a ritual wall painting within the home. Outside the sacred enclosure other paintings depict incidents from daily life, usually featuring horses. The Bhils and Bhilala tribes of Madhya Pradesh paint myths related to creation called pithora paintings. Horses, elephants, tigers, birds, gods, men and objects of daily life are painted in bright multi-coloured hues. Mughal miniature paintings also figure as a footnote in MP because the Persians of the court of Malwa were enthusiastic patrons.

### *Early Painting Traditions*

From the ninth century, important schools of manuscript illumination flourished in the Buddhist monasteries of eastern India and in the Jain temples of western India. The subjects were religious and scriptural. Paintings were inscribed on palm leaves until the introduction of paper in the fourteenth century. The oldest known Hindu texts date from the second half of the fifteenth century and relate to the Jain manuscript tradition. Hindu myths and epics were the subjects of these early works, produced in north India. By the early sixteenth century, a new style had arisen that illustrated secular as well as religious themes. In the courts of the pre-Mughal Muslim sultanates, both the styles and the themes of painting began to combine the traditions of Persian painting and an indigenous sensibility.

### *Mughal Painting*

When Humayun (reigned 1530-1540 and 1555-1556) took refuge in Tabriz at the Safavid court of Shah Tahmasp II, he was exposed to the Persian painting and manuscript tradition. Humayun returned to India with two noted painters, sowing the seeds of the development of a distinctive Mughal style. It was Humayun's son Akbar who became a great patron of the arts. In Akbar's atelier, approximately one hundred artists recruited from the pre-Mughal centres of painting were trained under the Persian masters. Eventually a new painting style, called Mughal, emerged.

European prints and paintings that came to the court gave artists the opportunity to study and incorporate Western artistic techniques. Another significant contribution to Indian art at the time was the development of portraiture as a genre. Akbar's son and grandson continued to patronise court painting, but his grandson Aurangzeb chose to enforce his version of Muslim orthodoxy, which showed disdain for the visual arts. Artists left to find new sources of support in the Rajput courts of what are now Rajasthan and Himachal Pradesh (the Punjab Hills).

Perhaps no event would prove more important to the history of painting in India than the Mughal conquest of 1526. An Islamic dynasty of Mughalian and Turkish descent, the Mughals claimed direct ancestry to Genghis Khan (1162-1227) and Timur (1336?-1405).

### *Mughal Empire Timeline*

Early Mughal rulers brought with them a passionate love and demand for illustrated books and manuscripts. The founder of the Mughal empire in India, the emperor Babur (reigned 1526-1530), was not only a courageous warrior but also a connoisseur of poetry. While his son and successor Humayun (reigned 1530-1540; 1555-1556) did not inherit his father's military capabilities (his reign was interrupted by a period of exile in Persia during which the empire was ruled by the Afghan leader, Sher Shah), he did share Babur's love of literature and art. When Humayun returned to power in India in 1555, he included master artists from the Persian courts in his entourage and charged them with establishing royal ateliers, or studios.

Dynamic, brilliant, and tolerant, Humayun's son Akbar (reigned 1556-1605) became one of the world's greatest rulers. During the early years of his reign, he established a workshop of artists drawn from all parts of India and representing a variety of indigenous styles. To the vibrant colours and lively forms of traditional Indian painting was added the Persian love of pattern, blended colours, and sophisticated finishes. European prints and paintings imported into the cosmopolitan Mughal court during Akbar's reign encouraged experimentation with the use of atmospheric perspective; space and form began to be defined by use of light and shading. This cross-fertilization created an astonishing new style of painting that documented the intellectual curiosity and opulent lifestyles of the Mughal court.

### *Rajput Painting*

Although pre-Mughal artistic traditions continued, painting was affected in both style and content by artistic developments at the Mughal court. Rajput rules fought in Mughal military campaigns and spent time at the Mughal court, where they absorbed the ethos of the court, adopted its way of dressing, and became patrons of the arts. Each Rajput kingdom evolved its own distinctive style. The decline of Mughal power in the eighteenth century and the dispersal of artists from the imperial atelier ushered in a period of florescence for the court painting of the Rajput courts.

### *How Paintings were Viewed?*

Many Mughal paintings were parts of bound manuscripts and albums. Most of the Rajput paintings were not bound, but were collected and stored like books, until they were brought out to be examined, as you would a book.

India is the seventh-largest country in the world (1,269,340 square miles), so large, in fact, that it is often referred to as a subcontinent. From the tall, snow-capped mountains of the north to the lush, tropical forests of the south, India's landscape in between ranges from fertile plains to barren deserts. It is a country of contrasts in ways other than geography: there are huge, modern cities in India and there are small villages that in many ways retain centuries old traditions and lifestyles.

A large section of India juts out into the Indian Ocean, forming a peninsula. India's neighboring countries are Pakistan, China, Tibet, Nepal, Bhutan, Myanmar (Burma), and Bangladesh. Off the tip of the Indian peninsula is the small island nation of Sri Lanka. The nation of India itself is divided into 28 states, and within those states reside more than one billion people. India's population is the second-largest in the world (China's population is the largest).

India's history is an ancient one dating back thousands of years. Like other early civilizations in Egypt, China, and Mesopotamia, Indian civilization began along a river, the Indus. The people who first settled there were the Dravidians; later, nomadic people from the Northwest, the Aryans, invaded the Indus Valley and eventually settled throughout the country. Over the centuries, these two groups combined to form a unique culture with a flourishing religion, Hinduism. Over the course of India's long history, however, many other peoples would enter the country, some peacefully and some with an eye to conquest. As a result, India has evolved into a country shaped by many different faiths, languages, and traditions that today constitutes a vital presence and power in the global community. As in every culture, art has been a mirror of India's fascinating history from the beginning, reflecting religious beliefs, political events, and social customs. Especially in Indian miniature painting do we find a compelling and beautiful record of centuries of Indian culture.

### *Indian Miniature Painting*

Entering the world of Indian miniature painting may require a slight shift of focus for the modern viewer. To begin with, these intimate works were rarely framed and hung on walls. Viewing them was an infinitely more personal, even tactile, experience: one sat, held each delicate painting in hand, and lingered over its content. The extraordinary richness of detail and wealth of narrative invited careful and thoughtful exploration. Not intended for today's quick glance or cursory appraisal, the works were visually tuned, almost like a passage of music. They resonated in the receptive viewer's mind and provided for the sheer physical and intellectual delights of looking, seeing, and imagining.

### *Early Indian Painting*

Indian miniature painting is one of the world's great artistic traditions. While scholars are not able to pinpoint its first appearance in India, miniature painting probably began with illustrations of religious texts written on palm leaves and then blossomed with the import of paper and papermaking technology during the 14th century. Other painting formats were established earlier on in the subcontinent: wall paintings adorned palaces, aristocratic homes, and religious buildings; paintings on cloth were used for devotional purposes and storytelling; illustrated manuscripts gave visual punctuation to sacred religious texts.

The earliest examples of India's long tradition of painting are the first century BC wall paintings in Buddhist caves at Ajanta. Exemplifying what is known as the "Classical Indian style," these lyrical and naturalistic works depict fully modelled figures and elaborate compositions. A second, slightly later, school of early painting, the "Western Indian style" features religious subjects that are rendered more abstractly, with wiry, angular figures and a limited palette. The Western Indian style was used to illustrate both Hindu and Jain subjects (by the end of the 13th century, Buddhism had virtually disappeared from India), finding full expression in manuscripts for meditation, worship, and instruction.

Resourceful artists utilised leaves from the talipot palm for early illuminated manuscripts; the leaves were boiled, dried, and rubbed to produce a flexible writing support. These palm-leaf paintings were stacked and strung on one or two cords through pre-bored holes. A pair of covers, usually wooden, protected the final compilation. Interestingly, the illumination on these pages rarely illustrated the texts; instead, the deities depicted were meant to protect the manuscript and the devotee who commissioned it to earn spiritual merit.

By the late twelfth and early thirteenth century, paper began to replace palm leaf as the preferred support. In addition to the Western Indian style, other modes of painting were also practiced during the fifteenth and early sixteenth centuries in North and West India.

The "Caurapancashika" or "Caura" style, with its vibrant colours and flat pictorial space, was primarily used to depict Hindu subjects. Influenced by Persian painting traditions, the "Indo-Persian" or "Sultanate" style was employed by artists who worked for Muslim rulers and noblemen of North India.

Indo-Persian calligraphers and artists produced elaborate copies of the *Quran* embellished with beautiful, abstract designs; secular texts and poems were also colourfully illustrated and, though unlike the *Quran*, often employed the human figure. These and other early styles would prove critical to the development of one of South Asia's greatest artistic achievements: imperial Mughal painting.

### *Subimperial, Popular and Bazaar Painting*

Prevailing Mughal court fashions invariably set the artistic standards throughout North India, and noblemen, affluent merchants, and others sought to emulate imperial tastes. Styles of painting thus emerged based in varying degrees on Mughal standards: "subimperial" paintings for the aristocracy closely imitated court images; "Popular" Mughal paintings contained some elements of court styles but were less naturalistic, with bolder colours and more abstract compositions. "Bazaar" paintings were further removed from court aesthetics: quickly produced, these inexpensive works were purchased by a more general audience to decorate homes or serve as gifts or mementos. At their best, they possess a vigorous charm.

Successors to the Mughal empire, Jehangir (meaning "World Seizer," reigned 1605-1627) and Shahjehan (meaning "King of the World," reigned 1628-1658) further refined the imperial style initiated by Akbar. To the keen observation and depiction of the physical world, i artists added a psychological dimension, attempting to capture the inner reality of outward appearances. Shahjehan's painters sought to portray the world not as it was, but as it should be: idealised, perfected, and sublime.

In the later years of Shah Jahan's reign such works stood in poignant contrast to an empire torn by a devastating war for the throne. Under Shah Jahan's least-favored son and successor, Aurangzeb (who referred to himself as "Seizer of the Universe" and reigned 1658-1707), interest in the arts as a valued component of life at court faded. Reduced patronage under Aurangzeb forced imperial artists to seek work elsewhere. Many migrated to the Hindu courts of Rajasthan and the Punjab Hills where they forged dynamic new additions to the history of Indian painting.

## Rock Paintings

Somewhat surprisingly for such a wide continent, Indian rock art has often been considered as pertaining to a "cultural unity", as is the case for Upper Palaeolithic cave art in Europe. Disparities do exist according to the areas, so that regional groups have been and will no doubt be defined (see for example Chandramouli 2002 for the rock art of Andhra Pradesh in the south of India, or Mathpal 1985 for that of Kumaon in the north). However, "in spite of the great distances of the different regions Indian rock paintings bear surprising affinity in forms, subject matters and design elements to their contemporaries".

The only petroglyphs (*i.e.* rock engravings) we have mentioned are cupules, because we hardly saw any other engraved motifs during our trip. Still, it is necessary to recall their existence and their importance in many parts of India, even if we are here focusing on pictographs (*i.e.* rock paintings).

Among the colours used red is overwhelmingly dominant, at all periods. It comes from iron oxides such as haematite.

White (from a white clay like kaolin) has also been widely used. Other colours are scarcer, like "green and yellow derived from copper minerals" or "blue or coal black obtained from manganese or charcoal" (Chakravarty & Bednarik 1997: 46). Painting was carried out "by rubbing the colour nodule dry, or with water, without any visible use of organic binding material, using finger tips, twigs, hair brush or by spraying with the mouth".

The subjects represented are quite varied and numerous. Depending on the periods and the areas, their relative proportions may change hugely. For example, animals, as we have seen, are less abundant at some Bhimbetka sites than in the Chambal valley and humans are central to Historic paintings.

The diversity of the animals and of the ways to represent them is much greater than what is found in European cave art. Nearly thirty different species were for example identified in the rock art of the Upper Chambal valley (Badam & Prakash 1992).

The techniques used to render them are also far from stereotyped: for the simplest figures, only the outlines may be drawn or they may be in flat tint with the whole body coloured. A great many animals, however, have a body infilling with sometimes very intricate motifs in the form of parallel lines, grids and all sorts of geometric patterns which make the art distinctive. They may be sexed or not. Sometimes pregnant females have been painted with the foetus showing in a sort of X-ray style. Two (generally red and white) or more colours may be used for the same subject. The animals may be represented in isolation or in herds or in conjunction with humans.

Humans may sometimes be dominant but in any case they are nearly always present even among the earliest paintings. In their case too, variety is the main characteristic, even if they seem to have been given less details than the animals, except for the horse riders and fighters of the later ages (Chakravarty & Bednarik 1997: 69). They may be stick figures and be stiff or, on the contrary, quite dynamic, seeming to be running, dancing, hunting or fighting. Others have double lines for the body and arms and sometimes inner decoration, though far less than is the case with animals.

Their heads are rarely detailed, even if they may occasionally sport some headgear. They often wield weapons, such as bows and arrows, variously tipped spears or axes. They are often engaged in activities with other humans (dancing, fighting, having sex, curing the sick, carrying loads, eating, sometimes inside a house or a tent...) or with animals (hunting, fishing, riding horses, elephants or oxen, driving carts or chariots, drawing ploughs). The abundance of scenes of all sorts in Indian rock art is one of its major and most appealing characteristics.

Various objects, as well as geometric signs, can be represented independently of humans and animals. In Historical times, inscriptions have been used to help establish a chronology. Superimpositions are frequent. "The particular portions of rock were probably sacred parts of shelters or the artists painted upon the old drawings simply to enhance the power of his new pictures. It might be a taboo to erase the old drawings" (Mathpal 1998: 9). Establishing a succession of styles from superimpositions has often been attempted.

As always, dating the art is a thorny problem which has been tackled in various ways, with not completely satisfying results, right from the first discoveries in the 19th century until now. In general, Indian rock art has been divided into three main periods each with (or without) a number of phases. Leaving apart the possibility of Palaeolithic art, which until recently was discarded by a number of scholars and is still being discussed, the "traditional" chronology distinguished the Mesolithic art of the hunter-gatherers, with naturalistic animals, from the Chalcolithic art of the agriculturalists, with the appearance of cattle and chariots, and finally the Historical periods, with an emphasis on fighting (Neumayer 1992).

Pandey (1992: 25) brought in the weathering of the art, as, according to him, Mesolithic paintings were invariably patinated, whereas those of the Chalcolithic sometimes were while it was never the case with Historic art. The latest attempt is due to Dr. Giriraj Kumar, who, after establishing the presence of rock art in thirteen of the Indian states, in nearly 700 "complexes"—which means in fact many thousands of indvidual sites-, has most clearly stated the methods which have been used by him and others to provide a chronological classification of Indian rock art: "Using archaeological evidence obtained from rock shelters, comparison of animal drawings in rock art with that on Chalcolithic pottery, superimpositions and stylistic developments in rock art, observation of the mode of human life, wild and domestic fauna apparently depicted, etc." (Kumar 2000/2001: 8). These methods, pending systematic radiocarbon datings which sooner or later will bring new data, have been the time-honoured ones to assign a chronology to rock art the world over.

In addition, Kumar's "fresh attempt" "involves three approaches (...): 1. Classification of rock art on the basis of evolutionary traits visible in the development of forms, motifs, styles, inventions, technology, fauna, and human cognitive and creative abilities. 2. Periodisation on the basis of internal evidence from the rock art and rock art sites, and external evidence provided by other scientific disciplines. 3. Establishing antiquity of the rock art by (a) indirect dating methods, and (b) direct dating methods" (Kumar 2000/2001: 9).

## Cave Paintings

### *Ajanta and Ellora*

***Ajanta:*** The Ajanta Caves carved out of volcanic rock in the Maharashtra Plateau was not far off from the ancient trade routes and attracted traders and pilgrims through whom the Ajanta art style diffused as far as China and Japan. The Buddhist Monks employed artists who turned the stone walls into picture books of Buddha's life and teachings. These artists have portrayed the costumes, ornaments and styles of the court life of their times.

The artists applied mud plaster in two coats—the first was rough to fill in the pores of the rocks and then a final coat of lime plaster over it. The painting was done in stages. They drew the outline in red ochre, then applied the colours and renewed the contours in brown, deep red or black. The attenuated poses, supple limbs, artistic features, a great variety of hair styles, all kinds of ornaments and jewellery indicate skilled artisans.

In a mural in Cave 10, some 50 elephants are painted in different poses bringing out the skill of the artist in handling these bulky forms in all perspective views, with erected tails and raised trunks, depicting sensed danger. The styles of the later murals reveals a merging of two streams of art, Satavahana of Andhra and Gupta art of North India. This resulted in the classical style which had a far reaching influence on all the paintings of the country for centuries to come.

A high degree of craftsmanship incorporating all the rules laid down by ancient Indian treatises on painting and aesthetics are evident. One cannot but notice the fluid, yet firm lines, long sweeping brush strokes, outlining graceful contours, subtle gradation of the same colour, highlighting nose, eyelids, lips and chin making the figures emerge from the flat wall surface. Animals, birds, trees, flowers, architecture are pictured with an eye to their beauty of form. Human emotions and character are depicted with great understanding and skill—indignation, greed, love and compassion.

***Ellora:*** Mural paintings in Ellora are found in 5 caves, but only in the Kailasha temple, they are somewhat preserved. The paintings were done in two series—the first, at the time of carving the caves and the subsequent series was done several centuries later. The earlier paintings show Vishnu and Lakshmi borne through the clouds by Garuda, with clouds in the background.

The sinewy figures have sharp features and pointed noses. The protruding eye typical of the later Gujarati style appears for the first time in Ellora. In the subsequent series, the main composition is that of a procession of Saiva holy men. The flying Apsaras are graceful. Very few murals in the Jain temples are well preserved. Painting as an art form has flourished in

India from very early periods as is evident from literary sources and also from the remnants that have been discovered. Indian Paintings can be broadly classified as the murals and miniatures. Murals are huge works executed on the walls of solid structures. Classic examples are the paintings in Ajanta and Kailasantaha temple.

Miniature paintings are those executed on a very small scale on perishable material such as paper, cloth, etc., Though this style had been perfected by artisans under the various rules, not many remain today. Prime examples are the Rajasthani and Mughal miniatures. Contemporary artists have kept up to the times and excel in their modern works, giving free expression to their imagination and artistic liberty.

Ajanta murals

Miniature Paintings

Tanjore Painting—Tamilnadu

Madhubani Painting—Bihar
Madhubani paintings

Kalamkari Painting—Kalahasti, Masulipatnam, Andhra Pradesh

Kalamkari Unit in Kalakshetra
Pithoro Painting—Gujarat

Raja Ravi Varma's paintings

## Miniature Paintings

The miniatures, as the name indicates were small works, which were made on perishable material and hence no definite proof of their birth and development can be traced.

In Bengal, Bihar and Orissa, Buddhist manuscripts were illustrated, mostly paintings of Buddha on palm leaves. They resemble the Ajanta style but on a miniature scale.

In Gujarat, illustrations in Jaina manuscripts can be seen. The style of the Jaina caves at Ellora was followed. Some illustrations were done on paper. In the later stages the fine application of colour diminished. There was also some Persian influence which spread from here to other places such as Mandu and Jaunpur.

The Mughal emperors introduced their own style of miniature paintings with Persian inspiration. Court scenes were depicted in grandeur. The background was usually hilly landscapes. Flowers and animals were also vastly depicted and in these the Indian artists applied their own skill to develop on the Persian ideas. The Rajput paintings can be put under two broad groups, the Rajasthani style and the Pahari style. The subject matter of the paintings was mostly religious and love subjects, based on Lord Rama and Lord Krishna. Court scenes were depicted as also royal portraits. Bold outlines and brilliant colours are characteristic of Rajasthani paintings.

Indian Miniatures are intricate hand-made illuminations executed flawlessly with subtle brushwork. Miniature painting derived its name from its diminutive size and intricate designs.

These beautiful miniatures had emerged in the middle ages. The colours used in the miniatures were derived from minerals, vegetables, precious stones, indigo, conch shells, pure gold and silver. The illustrated manuscripts of Jains and Buddhists, and the Mughal, Rajput, and Deccan Miniatures are noted for their meticulous execution and artistic skills.

The fine stroke of brushes conveyed the themes from the Ramayana, Mahabharata, Bhagvata Purana, Rasikpriya, Rasamanjiri, etc. These masterpieces of yore have a universal appeal which still touch the right chord of the audience

Miniatures paintings are intricate, colourful hand-made illuminations or paintings, small in size, executed meticulously with delicate brushwork. The colours used in the miniature paintings were derived from minerals, vegetables, precious stones, indigo, conch shells, pure gold and silver. Many of the miniature paintings are based on 'Ragas' or musical codes of Indian classical music. Some of the noted miniature schools were those of Mughals, Rajputs and Deccan. You can browse though our collection of miniature paintings belonging to different Indian Schools of Miniatures, explore them and buy them at your wish.

The tradition of Indian miniature paintings goes back to the ancient times. Miniatures are small, colourful pictures painted in glowing mineral and vegetable colours. The exclusive illustration in the Indian miniature paintings gives a visual image to the literary plot, making it more enjoyable and easier to understand. The world of miniature paintings is perhaps the most fascinating in Rajasthan, India, with exclusive and distinctive schools of painting—Mewar, Marwar, Bundi-Kota and Amber-Jaipur.

Highly talented and skilled artists produce the ostentatious paintings on paper as well as on ivory panels, wooden tablets, leather, marble and fabric. Multi-painting sets of Ramayana, Gita-Govinda, Sur-Sagar, Arsh Ramayana, Rasikapriya etc., were prepared in an unmistakably bold, colourful and well defined styles. A series of portraits, sets of Ragamala paintings, divinities and scenes of folk legends are also produced.

In western India from the 16th to 18th century miniature painting developed. These small paintings were part of manuscripts written at the time and illustrate the subjects of the manuscripts.

Manjun stroking a dog because it has come from near his beloved LEILA

Due to its rich subject matter, longevity, and freshness Turkish miniature painting of the Ottoman period occupies a special place in the history of Islamic painting. This form of art continued without interruption for nearly four centuries. There are examples of miniature painting which date from the middle of the fifteenth to the beginning of the nineteenth centuries. Artistic trends and tastes are also evident throughout this period.

Ottoman miniatures and illuminated manuscripts were prepared mostly for sultans but also for important and powerful figures in their retinues. The most important of these works are still preserved in the place in which they were produced, for example, Topkapl Palace in Istanbul, and other palaces of the Ottoman sultans. Other museums and libraries in Istanbul also house rare manuscripts containing outstanding examples of Turkish miniature painting. In addition, Ottoman miniatures can be found in museums, private collections, and libraries around the world, most notably the Chester Beatty Library in Dublin.

A distinctive feature of Ottoman miniature art is that it portrays actual events realistically yet adheres to the traditional canons of Islamic art, with its abstract formal expression. Nearly all these paintings are concerned with important events of the day, such as Turkish victories, the conquest of fortresses, state affairs, festivals, formal processions, and circumcision feasts.

. The nakka's (designer-painters), of the Ottoman court were required to illustrate daily events. To preserve the freshness of the works they prepared and to ensure that the orders of the Sultan were carried out, they worked very rapidly, with the result that the Turkish miniature is devoid of fine and elaborate ornamentation. The Ottoman painter arrived at a spare mode of expression, free of superfluous detail and focused on the essence of its subject. Ottoman miniatures are also records of contemporary events, filtered through the artists' own concepts of reality.

The fact that Ottoman art fostered more portraiture than the art of any other Islamic culture, with the exception of Mughal India, is another indication of this trend towards realism. From the fifteenth to the twentieth centuries, royal portraits formed an integral part of the art of the book. Ottoman miniature painting, which was periodically affected by different artistic influences, was essentially a form of what can be called "historical painting". The bulk of Turkish miniatures comprise works of documentary value deriving from the depiction of actual events.

## Mughal Paintings

Mughal painting is a particular style of Indian painting, generally confined to illustrations on the book and done in miniatures, and which emerged, developed and took shape during the period of the Mughal Empire (16th-19th centuries).

Mughal paintings were a unique blend of Indian, Persian and Islamic styles that flourished in India during the reign of the Mughal emperors from the 16th to 18th centuries. It was exclusively a court art and its developments depended to a large extent on the patron and his enthusiasm. Traditional Persian themes—battles, court scenes, receptions and legendary stories were richly captured with infinite detail by a team of artists.

Mughal painting began during the reign of emperor Humayun (1530-40). Returning from exile, Humayun brought with him two Persian artists to India, Mir-Sayyid Ali and Abd-us-samad. The earliest work that comes under the category of mughal painting is "The princess of the house of Timur". A painting that has been repainted throughout the Mughal era at the command of various emperors.

The greatest of the Mughal emperors, Akbar (1556-1605), ruled over a vast Indian empire and was its greatest patron of arts. He encouraged poets, scholars, and painters, making his court a centre of culture. During his reign, about a hundred artists worked under the guidance of the two Persian artists. Akbar had a childlike love for tales and this is reflected in what he commissioned his artists to paint. The Mahabaratha, Ramayana and other Persian epics were illustrated. Mughal paintings were lively and realistic and showed increasing naturalism with illustrated animal fables, detailed landscape backgrounds and elements of individual portraiture.

The emperor Jehangir (1605-27) showed a strong patronage for paintings. During his reign, Mughal art became more refined with finer brushwork and lighter colours. He favoured paintings of events from his own life, and encouraged portraits and studies of birds, flowers and animals. "Jehangirnama"—illustrated biography—contains among other pictorial idiosyncrasies paintings depicting the copulation of a saint and a tigress, the fight between spiders on the road which the emperor happened to see and the beheading of his rebellious son's supporters.

The elegance and richness of the Jehangir period style continued during the reign of Shah Jahan (1628-58) but with an increasing tendency to become cold and rigid. Genre scenes—such as musical parties, lovers on a terrace, or ascetics gathered around a fire—became frequent, and the trend continued in the reign of Aurangzeb (1658-1707). Despite a brief revival during the reign of Muhammad Shah (1719-48), Mughal painting continued to decline, and the creative activity ceased during the reign of Shah Alam II (1759-1806).

Mughal painting is a particular style of Indian painting, generally confined to illustrations on the book and done in miniatures, and which emerged, developed and took shape during the period of the Mughal Empire (16th-19th centuries).

### *Genesis*

When the second Mughal emperor, Humayun (reigned 1530-1540 and 1555-1556) was in Tabriz in the Safavid court of Shah Tahmasp II, he was exposed to Persian painting. When Humayun returned to India, he brought with him two artists well accomplished in the Persian style of painting. Their works, and during succeeding decades, assimilation of local styles, gave shape to a distinct style, which became known as Mughal painting. The Tutinama (literal meaning "Tales of a Parrot"), now in the Cleveland Museum of Art, is among the earliest examples of Mughal painting. The manuscript was made in the reign of Humayun's son, Akbar.

### *Themes*

Mughal painting was rich in variety which included portraits, events and scenes from the court life, wild life and hunting scenes, and illustrations of battle fronts. The Victoria and Albert museum in London have a large and remarkable collection of Mughal paintings.

### *Development*

The Mughal painting developed and flourished during the reigns of Akbar, Jehangir and Shahjehan. During the reign of Akbar (1556-1605), the imperial court, apart from being the apex nerve centre and administrative authority to manage and rule the vast Mughal empire, also emerged as a centre of cultural excellence. In this background, Mughal painting also thrived and hundreds of painters created innumerable paintings depicting scenes from various Hindu epics including the

Ramayana and the Mahabharata; themes with animal fables; individual portraits; and paintings on scores of different themes. The Mughal paintings during this period continued to get refined with elements of realism and naturalism coming to the fore.

During the reign of Emperor Akbar, a host of local artists worked under the direct supervision of Seyed Ali and Adus Samad. This system of production, seems almost to suggest that the painting of Mughal miniatures was more craft than fine art, at first. Painters were assembled in a hall or workshop, and there, under a headman, each was employed in executing those parts of picture with which he was almost familiar. The actual composition or layout of miniature would be sketched in by the chief artist, which, when approved, would be passed from hand to hand, one artist drawing the figures, another painting background, a third putting in the features and so on, until each had completed the portion of the work allotted to him and the whole was finished. Thus, under such system, it was extremely difficult to attribute painting to a single artist.

Fortunately, this "division of labour" system did not last long and, in the course of time, the school evolved vision of reality all its own. Mughal miniatures present unique blending of styles, especially in some early works, such as illustrations found in "Dastan Amir Hamzeh", where Persian style and conventions are quite in the composition, architecture, ornamentation and colour scheme.

In fact, everything points to the painter (or painters) of these illustrations as having been trained in Deccan School. Yet, design and layout rigidly to Mughal conventions and the delicacy of detail owes a great deal to Persian painting.

Gradually, Mughal School, absorbing multitude of influences, developed individuality which is easy to recognise and even easier to appreciate. Mughal miniatures are primary different from Persian ones, because they are more realistic, pulsating with life and vigour.

The most formative phase in the development of Mughal miniature painting was during the reign of Akbar, real founder of Mughal School of Art. During his reign, many famous works were produced, such as "Hamzeh-nameh", "Shah-nameh', "Tarikh Khandani" Teinourian and "Akbar-nameh". Among the local artists the most prominent were Daswanth, Basawan and Mansour, whose best works are to be found in paintings of animals and flowers, hunting scenes, portraits and paintings concerning court life. But even these artists owe a lot to Persian masters, as far as their basic style is concerned.

It is only during the reign of Emperor Jehangir that we see greater contacts being made with Western world, that the naturalistic tendency comes to the forefront. This tendency is revealed quite clearly in many paintings animals, birds, flowers and trees executed during this period.

All that was Persian in Mughal Miniature seems to steady, but surely disappear. The style predominant at Jehangir's time was continued and slowly perfected during the reign of Shahjehan. The most popular themes in both these reigns seem to be Royal Court in all its glory, and portraits of courtiers, often in groups.

A "new" technique was also developed at about this time, that of lightly touching sketch with gold or any colour, but even this so-called "new" technique owed a lot to similar developments in Persian Art. Paintings, however good they may be technically, sadly lack the essential vitality found in those of Akbar's period. Although most scholars feel that Mughal Art passed its zenith after the reign of Shahjehan, which came to end in 1658, yet it remained technically sound until the last years of Emperor Mohammad Shah, who died in 1748.

The gradual decline of the once glorious Mughal Empire saw the artistic moving away from Imperial Capital. It was an age when patronage was declining at Mughal Delhi and political upheavals were decimating princely courts; wandering artists found sanctuary and new patrons in the hill principalities. There, they developed new idioms, which blended the intricate and rather sophisticated Mughal style with more vigorous and energetic folk art of the hill people—this school known as "Pahari" (means 'hill'), generated a brief but exquisite renaissance of Indo-Pakistan miniature painting. Many fine examples of Pahari Art are to be found in Lahore Museum. Mughal paintings lost much of their glamour and refinement after Jehangir's death in 1627.

During the late 17th and 18th centuries this art migrated to regional centers such as in Rajput and Jaipur, where it prospered under the influence of the local culture. Jehangir (1605-27) had an artistic inclination and during his reign the Mughal painting further developed. Brushworks became finer and the colours lighter. He particularly encouraged paintings depicting events of his own life, individual portraits, and studies of birds, flowers and animals. The Jehangirnama, written during his lifetime, and which is a biographical account of Jehangir, has several paintings, including some unusual paintings like ones which depicts sexual union of a saint with a tigress, and fights between spiders.

During the reign of Shahjehan (1628-58), Mughal paintings continued to develop, but they gradually became cold and rigid. Themes including musical parties; lovers, sometimes in intimate positions, on terraces and gardens; and ascetics gathered around a fire, abound in the Mughal paintings of this period.

### *Decline*

Aurangzeb (1658-1707) did not actively encourage Mughal paintings, but as this art form had gathered momentum and had a number of patrons, the Mughal paintings continued to survive, but the decline had set into. A brief revival was noticed during the reign of Muhammad Shah (1719-48), and by the time of Shah Alam II (1759-1806), the art of Mughal painting had lost its glory. By that time, in the royal courts of the Rajput kingdoms of Rajputana, India, another school of Indian painting, namely, Rajput painting was taking shape.

## Rajput Paintings

Rajput painting, a style of Indian painting, evolved and flourished, during the 18th century, in the royal courts of Rajputana, India. Each Rajput kingdom evolved a distinct style, but with certain common features.

Rajput paintings depict a number of themes, events of epics like the Ramayana and the Mahabharata, Krishna's life, beautiful landscapes, and humans. Miniatures were the preferred medium of Rajput painting, but several manuscripts also contain Rajput paintings, and paintings were even done on the walls of palaces, inner chambers of the forts, havelies, particularly, the havelis of Shekhawait.

The colours extracted from certain minerals, plant sources, conch shells, and were even derived by processing precious stones, gold and silver were used. The preparation of desired colours was a lengthy process, sometimes taking weeks. Brushes used were very fine.

### *Schools*

Over a period of around 300 years, beginning from the 16th century, different schools of Rajput painting emerged, and notable among them are Mewar School, Bundi-Kota kalam, Jaipur school, Bikaner school, Kishengarh school, Marwar school, and Raagamala style of painting. Rajasthan's role in the development of Indian art has been very important. The decoration of dwellings and other household objects was but one aspect of the creative genius of the Rajasthani—the world of miniature paintings is perhaps the most fascinating and the distinctive styles that have existed here are renowned the world over. From the 16th century onwards there flourished different schools of paintings like the Mewar school, the Bundi-Kota kalam, the Jaipur, Bikaner, Kishengarh and Marwar schools.

Influenced by the surroundings, these medival paintings have their own unique styles—the hills and valleys, deserts, places and forts, gardens, court scenes, religious processions and those highlighting scenes from the life of Lord Krishna were the recurrent themes of these paintings. The Raagamala paintings and those based on Geeta Govinda are treasures of Rajasthan. It is widely believed that the miniature artists of Rajasthan were, practising and perfecting their, art as early as the beginning of the 16th century and were later employed by the Mughal courts, specially by the Great Mughal emperor

Akbar. Each school of painting had its distinctive features. For instance, the flowing rivers, dense forests, lush green fields of Kota-Bundi region were transferred to the paintings of that region. In palaces of Kota-Bundi are displayed the paintings depicting hunting scenes and animal fights.

Other than Nature, the figures of women here are graceful, with well proportioned bodies and sharp features. Colours used are mainly bright, with red prominently appearing in the background. Areas in the vicinity of this region, like Uniara, Indergarh and Sarola were also influenced by the Kota and Bundi kalam. The rulers of Amer-Jaipur were closest to the Mughals and had maintained political and social links with them. Therefore, it was only natural to find a strong Mughal influence in the paintings here. Examples of this can be understood in the paintings in the palaces of Amer, Bairat and Toda Rai Singh and much later in Samod, Achrol, Shahpura, Alwar and Tonk.

The Kishengarh school is best known for its Bani Thani paintings. A totally different style with highly exaggerated features—long necks, large, almond shaped eyes, long fingers and the use of subdued colours.

The originality of style can be credited to its royal patron—Raja Sawant Singh, better known as Nagari Das. The usual court scenes have also been painted here but it was Nagari Das and his love for the singer-poet Bani Thani that gave this tiny state the most refined and delicate paintings.

Jodhpur has a very strong folk tradition and here the figures are mainly robust warriors and dainty women. Paintings of the legendary lovers like Dhola-Maru on camelback, hunting scenes, which included innumerable horses, and elephants dominate the paintings of the Marwar region. Similarly, Bikaner too had strong Mughal influences and developed a style, which was a combination of both the local as well as borrowed styles.

The colours used by the miniature artists were made from minerals, vegetables, precious stones, indigo, conch shells, pure gold and silver. The preparing and mixing of colour was an elaborate process and it took weeks, sometimes months, to get the desired results. Very fine, specially created brushes were made for different kinds of paintings.

The landscape changed, the colours used were varied, paintings were done on paper and palm leaf to illustrate manuscripts, and on walls of palaces and the inner chambers of forts, havelies (the painted havelies of Shekhawati are well-known), and paintings were done on cloth. But the importance of miniatures has never diminished—even after all these years. Pure Rajput paintings and those influenced by the Mughal court provide an interesting insight into the lifestyle of the centuries and continue to fascinate the scholars to this day. Artists in Jaipur, Nathdwara and Kishengarh still work on miniatures and some of them produce excellent work. There have been several new developments but on the whole, the magical quality of the miniature continuous to live on.

In a different class but with several similarities are the cloth paintings of Rajasthan, which include the phads scroll paintings used by the Bhopas and the pichwais—cloth hangings used behind the deity in Vaishnava temples. Done in bright colours with bold outlines, these paintings have very strong religious traditions. And the artist who works on them considers himself to be a servant Of the Lord and puts in shraddha or devotion on each pichwai or phad that he paints. This art form is also done for commercial use.

Amber in Rajasthan was one of the first kingdoms to become the Vassal of Akbar but noticeably its painting style remained conventional like that of Malwa. However, the court portraitures were executed in markedly Mughal style. In 1728, Sawai Jai Singh shifted the capital from Amber to Jaipur. He and his successors patronised many artists. The paintings clearly showed inheritance from the Mughal source but the bold compositions and use of abstractions were distinctly regional.

During the late 18th and early 19th centuries, numerous works of art were produced that depicted episodes from the life of Krishna. The names of the artists that doted the royal courts are evident in the court records and inscriptions on paintings. Ragamala and devotional subjects remained the popular themes of the paintings in the 19th century and found patronage outside Jaipur court too.

## Deccan Paintings

### *Tanjore Paintings*

If ever Art has ardently wooed Beauty, nowhere is it more evident than in the paintings of Thanjavur. Every creation is truly a celebration of the beautiful. Rich, full bodied colours vie with exquisite filigree work to overwhelm the eye. The themes are figures of God, Krishna being the most frequently reproduced, but in various poses and depicting various stages of his life. Other Gods are depicted too. Today people are experimenting with birds, animals, building structures, etc.

Thanjavur, located in the rich delta of the river Cauvery between Tiruchirapalli and Kumbakonam had been the centre of economical and cultural activities under the Nayaks of Vijayanagar dynasty, Sultan of Bijapur and lastly by Maratha rulers. Though Thanjavur was not the birth place of this art, this style of paintings developed here during the 18th century under Maratha rulers. As people and artists migrated to Tanjore from Mysore, Andhra, Bijapur, Maharashtra and Gujarat, the theme and style came to be largely influenced by various schools of arts and religious requirements, also coming under some Western and Chinese influence.

Seasoned wooden planks were joined on which paper or a piece of cloth was fixed by using tamarind seed paste. Locally available stone powder and unboiled lime powder were used to prepare the surface. Outline was drawn by tracing the original hand drawn figures. Semiprecious and precious stones, cut glasses, etc., were placed to make the jewels for the figure. Apart from giving artificial gold colouring, gold and silver leaves were used to colour the costumes and jewellery and other decorative areas.

The pigments were prepared using locally available natual materials. The artists favoured bright luminous colours as the paintings were originally meant to be kept in poorly lighted rooms, temple, mutts and homes for worshipping. Tanjore style paintings are also drawn on glass by using different techniques. The characteristics of the Tanjore paintings are its brilliant colour scheme, decorative jewellery with stones and cut-glasses and its chubby larger-than-life figures.

A rare Tanjore style painting from the late 19th century depicting the ten Sikh Gurus with Bhai Bala and Bhai Mardana. Tanjore painting is an important form of classical South Indian painting native to the town of Tanjore in Tamil Nadu. The art form dates back to the early 9th century, a period dominated by the Chola rulers, who encouraged art and literature. These paintings are known for their elegance, rich colours, and attention to detail. The themes for most of these paintings are Hindu Gods and Goddesses and scenes from Hindu mythology. In modern times, these paintings have become a much sought after souvenir during festive occasions in South India.

The process of making a Tanjore painting involves many stages. The first stage involves the making of the preliminary sketch of the image on the base. The base consists of a cloth pasted over a wooden base. Then chalk powder or zinc oxide is mixed with water-soluble adhesive and applied on the base. To make the base smoother, a mild abrasive is sometimes used. After the drawing is made, decoration of the jewellery and the apparels in the image is done with semiprecious stones. Laces or threads are also used to decorate the jewellery. On top of this, the gold foils are pasted. Finally, dyes are used to add colours to the figures in the paintings.

## Mysore Painting

The delicate lines, the graceful delineation of figures and the discreet use of bright colours and lustrous gold describe the Mysore paintings. However, these have mythological themes for the subject and are known for their iconographic treatment of the deities as in the Vijayanagar School.

The Vijayanagar Empire [1336-1565 A.D] that held complete sway over south India developed an independent school of art and made lasting contribution to the development of Indian paintings. The Vijayanagar Artists contributed a good deal to the development of three distinct schools, namely the Deccani School [sultanate], the Mysore School and the Tanjore School. The Mysore school was at its zenith during the rule of Mummadi Krishnaraja Wodeyar [1799-1868 A.D], thanks to the royal patronage. The art gallery in the Jaganmohan palace at Mysore, Karnataka is a living tribute to the great love for paintings shown by this ruler.

### *Painting in the Deccan*

Portions of the Deccan, a vast plateau in south-central India, were conquered by Muslims from North India (primarily Turkish-speaking peoples from Persia, Central Asia, and Afghanistan) as early as the 14th century. A cosmopolitan mix of Indian Muslims and Hindus, Persians, Afghans, Turks, and Africans, residents of the Deccan maintained contact not only with nearby Persia but also with faraway Egypt, Iraq, Turkey, and Yemen. The extensive relationships that Deccani rulers fostered with the far-flung lands of Islam helped to distinguish their culture from that of India's other great Muslim rulers, the Mughals, who were more closely allied to Persia and Central Asia.

Rulers of the three major Deccani sultanates—Ahmadnagar, Bijapur, and Golconda—patronised painters. Although each state had its own style(s), they shared a general Deccani approach to painting, preferring lyrical portraits, Persian literary themes, and depictions of musical modes instead of historical events and realistic likenesses. Deccani artists worked in idioms that combined in varying proportions the delicate rhythms of Persia, the lush sensuality of South India, and exotic elements taken from Europe and Turkey. The results of their efforts were technically accomplished, lyrical pictures that conjure up the quiet enchantments of love, music, and poetry rather than the sober realities of life.

### *South Indian Painting*

The painters of South India maintained a distinctive regional identity until the late 19th century. Working in traditional formats (wall murals, illuminated manuscripts, miniature painting, as well as paintings on cloth, wood, glass, and ivory), artists served a variety of patrons, from Hindu nobles to military chiefs, in this politically shifting region. They worked in regional variants of the "late South Indian Style"—a highly mannered, vividly coloured idiom featuring compositions filled with elaborately ornamented figures that recall South Indian temple structures. By the 19th century, South Indian paintings became increasingly westernised, resulting in unexpected and often charming combinations of East and West, old and new.

## Chalukyan Paintings

### *The Imprint of Ajanta in Tibetan Art*

***Eva Fernanadez del Campo Barbadillo:*** The paintings of Ajanta are a landmark of transcendental importance in Indian art. Because they represent the only well preserved example of ancient mural painting, they are now considered an essential point of reference for the study of not only subsequent Indian art, but also the Buddhist art in the rest of Asia. The most representative part of the corpus of Ajanta paintings belongs to the 5th century AD, a time at which Indian culture reached its zenith, coinciding with the rule of the Gupta dynasty in Northern India which had alliances with and was related by marriage to the Vakataka dynasty of the Deccan.

The imprint of Ajanta is quite obvious in the rest of the paintings that were painted in India and Sri Lanka; however, it can also be observed, though somewhat diluted by time and distance, in the style of painting that spread from Central Asia, through China, up to Japan and South east Asia. This paper attempts to show to what extent Ajanta art also had an influence on Himalayan Art. At the same time the Ajanta paintings were being painted, or in the years immediately following this period, a numbers of caves were painted in the proximities of Ajanta and, in some of these, it is till today possible to see some surviving examples of polchromy. Not far from Ajanta we have the outstanding cave complexes of Aurangabad and Pittalkhora and, in the state of Madhya Pradesh, the large group of caves of Bagh.

From these primary locations, the pictorial tradition born in India spread in three directions: towards the northeast, through the international trade route links to the Silk Route; southward of India and, from there, towards Southeast Asia; and, finally, crossing the Himalayas till Tibet. The first line of expansion goes from India to Japan passing through Pakistan, Afganistan, Central Asia and China. Few remnants are to be found presently in Pakistan, although the discoveries of D.Facena in Butkara I prove the existence of a style of mural paintings, practically non-existent today in which the Indian tradition merged with the Greco-Buddhist tradition.

In Afganistan there are numerous examples of this type of painting, the most outstanding being Bamiyan, Kakrak and Foladi. Crossing the Pamir mountains along with trade caravans and Buddhist pilgrims, the pictorial tradition that had taken birth in India reached Central Asia and China where there are complexes having mural paintings such as Qizil, Dandan Oilit, Khotan and the very large Dun Hang complex, from where the Buddhist painting tradition reached the murals of Horyuji in Japan.

The second line of expansion of the Ajanta influence started with the conquests of the Chalukyas in the Deccan in the 6th century and the construction of their cities: Ahiole, Badami and Pattadakal, partly inspired by the paintings that they saw there, among which Ajanta must have left a deep imprint, as can clearly be seen in the paintings of cave number 4 in Badami.

From Badami the stamp of Ajanta spread towards the south in the same way that it reached Badami, namely through military conquests. The campaigns of the Pallava king Mahendravarman I on Chalukyan territory gave rise to, from the artistic point of view, significant cultural migration the Pallava king must have seen the magnificent Chalukyan paintings which inspired him to construct his own temples in Mahaballipuram and Kanchipuram.

According to texts written in those times, many temples and palaces were decorated with paintings but, unfortunately, only a few of them have survived till today and these are to be found in the temples of Kailashnatha and Vaikuntha Perumal in Kanchipuram, and the Telegirisvara temple in Panamalai.

In these paintings, although the separation in terms of time and geographic distance is considerable, the imprint of ajanta is still perceptible, and from there it must have travelled to the countries of southeast Asia. Pallava art, that was in turn inherited from Andhra, was the origin and inspiration of all the rest of Dravidian art, while in the Pandya period paintings were still to be found that bore an astonishing similarity to Ajanta. The technique employed in painting them was also the same. The third route of the spread of the mural painting tradition from India is the one that interests us, namely, the route affecting the Himalayan areas.

The Buddhist artistic tradition prevailed in India in isolated locations even after the revival of Hinduism in the 5th century and even after the Buddhist centres had disappeared from the south. These places, centered in northern India, were extremely important in the configuration of Tibetan art or lamaistic art. The most important among them were Bihar, Bengal, and Kashmir, from where this art spread much later, and where a technique of portable paintings was evolved that were used as covers for holy books These books were exported all over Asia, and their paintings were highly significant in the propagation of Indian iconography perpetrating the classical Gupta-Vakataka tradition.

However, as far as mural paintings is concerned, some samples have been preserved only in the trans-Himalayan valleys of the present-day Kashmir that geographically belong to Tibet. Yet it would seem natural that both Kashmir as well as Bihar also inherited the pictorial tradition of Ajanta and that this tradition travelled from there to Nepal and Tibet. By the XII century the waves of Muslim invaders must have demolished practically all the existing Buddhist monuments in this area making it very difficult to reconstruct the past of this region and determine exactly how long the Indian pictorial tradition survived there after the fall of the Gupta and Vakataka dynasties.

But the existence of monasteries clearly linked to the Ajanta style in the trans-Himalayan valleys of Laddakh and Spiti, has led a lot of scholars to believe that this tradition survived in

Kashmir from where the same artists must have spread it to Tibet. It would be logical to think that, from the X century onwards, many Buddhists were forced to retract further north and cross over to the other side of the Himalayas where the Islamic invaders had not reached.

In the Spiti and Laddakh valleys, situated on the Tibetan side of the Himalayas, but which today form part of the territories of the Indian states of Himachal Pradesh and Kashmir, we find the monastic complexes of Tabo and Alchi. The walls of both monasteries are covered with extremely well preserved paintings. These paintings are so closely related to the Indian paintings of Maharashtra that the Indian scholar M.N. Deshpande has even called them "the Ajanta of the Himalalayas".

The similarity between both manifestations of mural painting can be seen, first of all, in the technique, that is practically identical a base made of clay and organic materials covered with a layer of plaster and tempera painting; but, further, from the stylistic point of view, the similarities are also apparent. Traditionally, it is believed that mural painting spread both from the valleys of Kashmir, Spiti and Laddakh, as well as from Bihar, to the rest of the Himalayan regions where it met with the Chinese tradition in order to give rise to the painting of the great lamaistic monasteries. From this point of view, the role of Ajanta is important insomuch as it marks the beginning of the entire mural tradition, but here we shall try to show that Ajanta played a much more definitive role in Himalayan painting that is normally attributed to it. This affirmation is based on three ideas:

(i) The technical and stylistic similarities that exist between the Ajanta paintings and many of the lamaistic murals, as well as the evident iconographic coincidences.

(ii) The fact that in Ajanta some elements that are also characteristic in Tibetan art have been depicted for the first time.

(iii) The very clear link that exists between the Jokhang (the oldest monastery in Tibet) and the stone complexes of Maharasthtra.

There are many iconographic similarities that exist between Ajanta painting and Tibetan painting which are perfectly logical if one bears in mind that India is the birthplace both of Buddhism as well as its first artistic manifestations that, from very early times, spread to the rest of Asia thanks to the great international trade routes. Therefore, many of the Tibetan decorative elements, such as mandalas, imaginary and monstrous creatures and, of course, iconographies of Buddhas and Bodhisattvas along with their attributes, are actually inspired in Indian elements.

In the very beginning –and this can be observed in the sculptures on the first storey of the Jokhang in Lhasa—the images also have a strong Gupta flavour in them, as can be observed in the elegance of their forms, in the restraint and conceptual idealism that they portray, that clearly evokes Indian images of the IV and V centuries AD. This imprint of the Gupta dynasty is still evident in the Tibetan monasteries of the XI century, as in the case of Dratang where the figures, belonging to different ethnic groups (as in Ajanta) are arranged in a rather unconventional manner around the Buddha. This style, prevailing in the language of the Ajanta murals, is reminiscent of the cosmopolitan life of the palaces and also of the worldly and uninhabited private life of their inhabitants.

Likewise, it is very difficult to look at the Tibetan Bodhisattvas without remembering the images of the two Bodhisattvas on either side of the sanctuary of Vihara number 1 in Ajanta: Vajrapani and the famous Padmapani whose extraordinary strength and artistic qualities must have led to a definite impact on the entire art of expansion. Similarly, the naturalism of some scenes and the way plant motifs are dealt with cannot but –in some cases—remind us of how these same motifs were dealt with in Ajanta. The technique used in painting these murals is also very similar in both cases: tempera applied on a layer of plaster spread, in turn, over a base of organic materials.

In both cases, colour is applied in a large variety of tones, thus giving volume to the figure and modeling it after the red or black outlines have been drawn with freehand calligraphic brush strokes. Both in Ajanta as well as in the Tibetan paintings of the early temples it is possible to make out the drawing of the painting's guide lines under the coat of colour on the layer of plaster so much so that in many places a double line can be seen outlining the figures. This type of mural painting, although very widespread later on in Asia, actually originated in Ajanta. But, over and above all the influences of a general nature of Ajanta paintings on Tibetan art, it is essential to point out two definite elements in order to establish the connection between them: firstly, the scene in cave number 17 of the Ajanta complex known as "the Zodiac" and, secondly, the type of scenographic composition used in the murals.

On the veranda of Vihra number 17 in Ajanta, on the left hand side (occupying exactly the same position as the Wheel of Life in the Lamaistic monasteries) there is a highly deteriorated painting in which there is a circle divided into several sections and each section depicts different scenes. Ever since the first visit of Mr. Ralph to Ajanta in 1828, this painting has been known as "the Zodiac", and Foucher compared it to the Tibetan wheel of transmigration, as has also been stated later by Waddell. The Wheel of Life, or the Wheel of Transmigrations, depicts all those living beings that have not yet reached a state of spiritual liberation and describes the twelve causes of evil that obstruct the way to nirvana. According to Waddell, the outer circle of the painting in Ajanta depicts these twelve nidanas, or causes of existence.

In the diagrams corresponding to the drawings published by Schlingloff, D. and Waddell, L.A. some of the existing concomitance and differences between the veranda painting of Vihara 17 of Ajanta and the Tibetan Wheels of Life can be perceived. The connection between the two seems evident, both depict a figure holding a great radially divided wheel; in the case of Ajanta the arms and hands of the figure holding the wheel can still be distinguished, though the face and the lower portion have disappeared. Regarding the divisions on the wheel, while the Tibetan wheels have six, the Indian one has ten and, therefore, instead of showing the twelve nidanas in the outer circle, it should be showing twenty. Nevertheless, the motifs on the outer circle that can be made out can certainly be identified as the same as those of the Tibetan wheels: the monkey, symbol of the conscience that "in ignorant people springs uncontrolled from object to object"; the embraced lovers, that refers to sensual perceptions; the woman offering a glass of wine to the man, the symbol of desire, and the blind camel being led through the desert, as an allegory of unconscious desire.

The preserved portion of the Ajanta painting would correspond to what in the Tibetan wheels is the paradise of the gods, something that could also coincide perfectly with the scene depicted in the Indian art, though it must be born in mind that Indian art is much more naturalistic than Tibetan art and that the scene, while adhering to the style of Ajanta itself, is much closer to the cosmopolitan and mundane day-to-day life in the Vakataka palaces.

The second aspect that is considered definitive for purposes of highlighting the influence of Ajanta on Tibetan art is the type of compositions used in the paintings. The Ajanta murals are characterised by scenographic type compositions having no formal limits. The scenes are threaded together, one merging with the other, in such a way that there is narrative continuum in which the most important moments are framed either in architectural pavilions or else in circular compositions that attribute additional emphasis to them and make the spectator focus his attention on them.

This type of composition avoids both the linear sequence of the scenes and the classical western perspective of the inverted pyramid producing an effect that is more akin to cinema or Japanese makimono. If we take the example of the scene of Mahajanaka Jataka's dancing girl, in Vihara number 1 in Ajanta, an unmistakable similarity would be noted with the scene pertaining to Shalu (XI century to XIII century) which depicts a spinning dancer whose rotative movement looks similar to that of the Ajanta dancer. She is also surrounded by musicians that follow her with their eyes and gestures, though in a less subtle and more expressive manner than in Ajanta.

Surprisingly, the scene is being watched from the left hand side by an unabashed pair of lovers sitting in an architectural pavilion, very similar to those of Ajanta. Although both the clothing as well as the expressions of the figures originate from Pala art, the composition and the way the background is treated as if it were a stage backdrop decorated with little flowers, can be clearly linked to Ajanta. The type of composition used in Ajanta is absolutely original and easy to distinguish, and it is very probable that it shaped not only Tibetan mural painting but also the compositions used in Chinese and Japanese painting. Finally, we must highlight the very strong link that exists between Ajanta and the Jokhang, the oldest temple in Tibet, situated in Lhasa.

The construction of the Jokhang dates back to the first half of the VII century AD and is attributed to king Songtsen Gampo. Not only is it the oldest temple in Tibet but, also, it is the most sacred and venerated. Therefore, its influence on the construction of the rest of the Tibetan buildings is indisputable. The similarities existing between the first storey of Jokhang and the Ajanta caves are so many and so pronounced that it would seem appropriate to think that either the person who made the Tibetan complex personally saw the Indian complex, or else Nepal had similar structures made of wood that were inspired by the Indian ones and these served as a bridge to Tibet. The first similarity that is most striking is the organisation of space.

The Jokhang temple has a quadrangular foundation, with a square space in the centre surrounded by chapels among which the central and leading chapel is the sanctum sanctorum, the place that houses the most venerated image of Tibet: the Jowo Sakyamuni. This structure is exactly the same as the structure of the Viharas of Ajanta except for the fact that the side chapels in the Jokhang are not used as cells for the monks, as is the case in Ajanta, but are used as sanctuaries.

The reason behind this difference is possibly that, while the building was originally designed as an authentic Vihara, that is to say, as a monastery, with the passing of time the ells could no longer serve their intended purpose of housing the monks in the light of the pressing need to add new images of worship: Lamas and deities that gradually enriched the Buddhist pantheon.

Although it has been repainted and touched up on a number of occasions, the Jokhang offers some proof of what it must have been like in the early times that is extremely interesting for the topic under consideration. It is very significant to see how the oldest portions of the complex of Ajanta; among them we could mention the rows of lions carved in wood that go round the courtyard and, at times, are considered to be of Gupta origin. These lions have an unquestionable equivalent in the rows of lions carved in stone that appear on the door frame of cave number 1 in Ajanta, around the stupa of Chaitya number 26 and decorating, like atlantes, the jambs of the doorway of Vihara number 1.

The door frames that decorate this first storey of the Jokhang should also be compared to those of the main doors of the Ajanta caves, more particularly so the door frames of Vihara 1, that undoubtedly, at that time must have been the most attractive and lavish of them all. Another element that definitely connects the two monuments being talked about here, are the pillars. On the first storey of the Jokhang some pillars are still remaining that date back to the times of the temple's foundation; these pillars, having a square base and consisting of several geometrical structures placed one on top of the other and ending with a crown of an inverted lotus flower and a wide decorated abacus, are practically identical to those in Vihara number 1, especially as far as their decorative motifs are concerned: zebus, apsaras, kinnaras, yakshas and griffins.

As regards painting, it is very difficult to precisely gauge the influence of Ajanta on the jokhang due to the massive destruction it suffered during the Cultural Revolution. But, if we were to assume that some of the paintings could have been redone in keeping with the original designs, then one can also find similarities with Ajanta. Among the similarities we could underline the perspective of a moving focus, to which we have already referred when talking about compositions; this way of conceiving space gives rise to sceneries with small stages or pavilions, almost like theatrical platforms on which the moments of maximum tension in the story are painted.

But besides the organisation of the narrative highlights, there are some specific coincidences we can draw attention to the depiction, on the right hand side of the wall of feet, of some demoniacal characters that appear in the mural narrating the story of the construction of the Jokhang. These figures are literally copied from various characters appearing in Viharas number 17 and 16 in Ajanta: the former belong to Simhala Avadana, and the latter to a painting that has not been totally interpreted traditionally called "Devils in front of the Monastery", which could have some connection with the theme depicted in the Lhasa monastery. To conclude, it must be said that there is a strong link between the Ajanta caves and Tibetan art.

This influence could have been the outcome of a logical transmission through other Asiatic depictions that were closer to Tibet: Pala and Kashmiri art, Nepalese art and even the art of Central Asia, on which the imprint of Ajanta was firmly marked through the great transcontinental trade routes. Nevertheless, the strong resemblances that exist between Ajanta and the Jokhang, as well as the absence of similar buildings in the above mentioned regions, make us think that there was really a direct influence from Ajanta on the Tibetan temple and that, from there, it spread to the rest of the lamaistic art in the region. It is extremely difficult to venture a hypothesis on how this contact came about, although everything seems to indicate that the artists who started the construction work in Jokhang had personally seen the Ajanta caves.

## Regional Paintings

### *Warli Paintings*

Warli painting derives its name from a small tribe inhabiting the remote regions of Maharashtra, India. Folk imagination, beliefs and customs are spontaneously expressed in these monochromatic tribal paintings. From the cracked and unknown walls of the village of Warli, Warli, an Indian folk art painting, has travelled across borders and are now the cherished possessions of many a collector and art lover.

The philosophy of a way of life, especially those of tribal societies, is best depicted through colourful images. Trees, birds, men and women collaborate to create a composite whole in Tribal Paintings, and the paintings of the Warli tribe of Maharashtra are the most joyous celebration of that very philosophy.

The whims and moods of tribal life make for interesting themes, which is why Warli Paintings are much more than designs on walls, they are authentic depictions of a way of life.

### *Patachitra Paintings*

Patachitra is a vibrant folk art form native to Orissa, a state in eastern India. This famous ethnic painting was born out of the cult of Jagannath Dev—the presiding deity of Orissa. Incredible pictorial conceptions, characteristic conventions and vibrant colours make the Patachitra a unique treasure in the rich coffer of Indian traditional art. Executed primarily on cloth, using natural colours, these handcrafted paintings have charmed admirers from all over the world.

### *Phad Paintings*

Phad painting is a beautiful specimen of Indian cloth painting. Rajasthan in Western India is its place of origin. In the simplest term Phad can be described as a large painting on cloth, which venerates the deeds of a hero. The smaller version of phada is known as phadakye. Generally, the life events of Goga Chauhan, Prithaviraj Chauhan, Amar Singh Rathor, Tejaji, and many others were illustrated on the Phadas in the earlier times but today the stories from the life of Papuji, and Narayandevji are primarily depicted. For their unique beauty and chronicling character, Phada painting has come to be regarded as one of the most sought after folk paintings in the world of art and culture.

A eulogised Rajput inspired an art form in Rajasthan, which dazzles you with its vivacity. The bold greens and blues of the robust figures of Phad Paintings transcend time to recreate the story of the brave Rajput warrior Pabuji. Adorning a 30 feet long scroll, these paintings show Pabuji's victory and the life style of his time. The colours employed are generally vegetable dyes and are used in a fixed order starting from orange-yellow to brown, green, red and finally black.

### *Lepkashi Paintings*

Indian Handicrafts have made a name for themselves the world over. Ancient skills have been honed to perfection by craftsmen who have learnt the trade from their fathers, as did their fathers before them. This tradition continues over the centuries, safeguarding the wide and varied artistic wealth of India. Today, this tradition unfolds itself in an overwhelming variety of products, combining aesthetic appeal with utilitarian value. To satisfy modern tastes and meet international demand, design institutes have been giving a new look to these traditional crafts. A variety of products is available today in all their regional splendour.

These beautiful items are like a breath of fresh air in this age of mechanisation and mass production. The high calibre of skills exhibited in creating the products has stood the test of time. What's more, craftsmen have shown great ingenuity and flexibility in adapting to the requirements of the modern age.

Each region of India abounds in handicrafts reflecting the genius of its local craftsmen. Andhra Pradesh in the south has the distinction of having all important categories of handicrafts practised in their traditional locations spread over different parts of the state.

"Lepakshi", the well-known temple town in Andhra Pradesh, is a repository of stone sculpture and frescoes of a high order attained during the Vijayanagar period. Lepakshi as a name has thus aptly been chosen by the Andhra Pradesh Handicrafts Development Corporation as a name for its Marketing Wing. Lepakshi serves as a vital link between the lover and buyer of objects of beauty and the legendary handicrafts of Andhra Pradesh. "Lepakshi" Emporia have endeavoured to project the artistry and elegance of Andhra Pradesh Handicrafts in order to create an impact on markets within the country and abroad. We hope that after going though this page it will stimulate the interest and demand among the people for handicrafts from Andhra Pradesh

***Kalamkari Arts***

Kalamkari is the craft of painted and printed fabrics. It derives its name from kalam or pen with which the patterns are traced. It is an art form that developed both for decoration and religious ornamentation. In Andhra Pradesh, Kalamakari is done in Machilipatnam and Srikalahasti. There is evidence to show that block painted fabric resist dyed with indigo that was exported from India as early as 1938. The blocks of block printing were made by specialist block-makers, but sometimes the printers also made their own blocks. In Andhra Pradesh, block-printed fabrics come from Machilipatnam, Chirala, Vijayawada and Tuni.

***Thangka Paintings***

Crafts in India proudly presents a rich collection of traditional Buddhist Thangka paintings that originated between 7th and the 12th centuries. Its variety and iconography conveys much about the spiritual practice of Buddhists and the Tibetan worldview

***Mandana***

Auspicious wall paintings of Rajasthan and Madhya Pradesh, mandanas are meant to protect the home and hearth as well as to welcome gods into the house. Mud and cow dung are usually plastered on the walls which are then painted white. The women of the house paint symbols like the swastika, the sun or the tree of life in black and red. Auspicious diagrams are drawn on the floor with rice paste, coloured powder, flower petals or grains of rice, often with symbolic motifs set within floral and geometric patterns.

## Indian Folk Paintings

***15th to 19th Century :*** Until fifty years ago, it would have been inconceivable to plan an exhibition of the traditional folk paintings of India. At that time, folk paintings from most of the regions of the country were unknown, and even those somewhat familiar, had not yet found their way into the holdings of museums and private collections. Scholars engaged in the study of anthropology and the folklore of various regions of India did not consider it worthwhile to scrutinise and throw light on the painting or the other art expressions and crafts of the inaccessible terrain they were probing. Paintings made in the comparatively more frequented villages and centres of pilgrimage were termed “primitive”.

In actual fact, beginning with the 20th century the appreciation of Indian painting slowly became more reasoned from the Indian point of view. Before this time, in emulation of British art lovers and scholars, only Mughal painting was appreciated by connoisseurs in India. It was in 1916 that Ananda Coomaraswamy established Rajasthani and Pahari paintings on a pedestal of respect. Although compared to the refined Mughal work these were folkish and rougher in execution, their charm was more logically and enthusiastically interpreted by him, His writings added a fresh nuance to the aesthetic evaluation of all forms of Indian art and the significance of Indian art was firmly rehabilitated in the West. Hereafter, various other factors led art lovers to look also for the pictorial expressions of the village painters.

Initially, this search for folk painting was restricted to Bengal. It was due to the fact that the Bengalis were the first to note the significant changes that were taking place on the ‘modern art’ scene in Europe around 1900. The work of contemporary European painters in France and Germany had created a revolution in Europe’s art circles.

The modern painters had ignored perspective, used colour for its own sake or for symbolic purposes and had freely distorted and modified the human form. They had aimed at intense simplifications and had abandoned the natural in favour of the abstract or the geometric. These changes were taking place partly as reactions to the just discovered African sculpture on one hand and Japanese woodcut prints on the other. As Mrs. Archer mentions, “popular painting in Bengal seemed in this respect no different from Negro sculpture and it was in a mood of excited patriotism that certain Bengali writers, critics and painters began to reappraise Kalighat painting and at the same time to seek out and collect another distinctive form of village painting—the scrolls made by patuas in rural Bengal".

India's pioneer collector an art critic, Ajit Ghose, and the artist Mukul Dey, returned from London to Calcutta in the early 1920's. Both collected Kalighat painting which was still being made near the Kali temple at Calcutta. Ajit Ghose thus expressed (Rupam, 1926) his enthusiasm for Kalighat paintings, "there is an exquisite freshness and spontaneity of conception and execution in these old brush drawings". Similarity with Europe's modern art was detected also in the scroll paintings of rural Bengal and Ajit Ghose, in the same article, stressed their 'archaic simplicity', their 'largeness of style', their 'amazing boldness' and the dramatic effects which were achieved by their summary simplifications. Guru Saday Dutt, a senior Bengali official of the Indian Civil Service, toured the villages of Bengal in the 1930's. He made a large collection of folk arts and exposed to art lovers the charm of many more centres of rural Bengal's painting.

As 'folk' and 'popular painting' became more firmly established in its newly found position of respect, more centres of such paintings were gradually located, the immense pictorial strength of the work was increasingly noticed and their regional varieties put into art-chronological order. Added to this enthusiasm was the fact that in the early 1950's, in the post-Independence years after the abolition of the Indian States, miniatures coming from the Indian palace godowns flooded the art market. With a profitable art market, dealers began the search and sale of paintings other than those made for courts.

The term 'folk paintings' here encompasses pictures made in Indian villages, by both men and women, for ornamentation of their abodes, portrayals of their gods and for their various rituals; and, by local professional painters or artisans for use of the local people.

The term also includes pictures made in the bazars by hereditary painters to cater to the needs of the urban population, and those made at centres of pilgrimage by traditional professional painter families. All these paintings were produced in a variety of styles and themes. History, sociology and geography infused the painting of each region with local flavour. To some extent their style and quality depended on the materials available in the place in which they were executed 'These very factors help us to identify them region wise. And yet, through all the apparent diversity there runs an underlying unity which makes them 'Indian'.

Although Indian painting is often classified as belonging to court, temple and the art of the folk, it is not very appropriate to make such a division. Until the establishment of the Mughal rule in early 16th century, the courts of early India were not a closed society apart, and the painters for rulers and the richer people like bankers, merchants and zamindars were often the same. The quality differed only because of the material used and the time given for its execution. Both of which depended on the remuneration paid to the artist who was free-lance.

The idea of the exclusive court painters started with the Mughals and was followed by their feudatory rulers who adapted their mannerisms. It can be confidentally said that the energy, inventiveness and lyricism found in Akbari paintings were the features brought to the Mughal studios by the recruits from the hereditary painter families of Gujarat and other parts of India; they had originally been trained to work in a folkish style for small courts and others with modest means.

Paintings from Western India, chiefly Gujarat and southern Rajasthan, where the well-known and clearly identified styles of miniatures, chiefly of Jain themes, started from about the twelfth century, amply prove our point. Even after the establishment of the Gujarat Sultanate in the 15th century and the Mughal rule towards the end of the 16th century, work done in Western India retained its angular features, bright and boldly abstracted colour areas and full profiles. They can safely be classed folk. From this region, two very rare pages from a manuscript illustrating the Devi-Mahatmya (1-2) are displayed in this exhibition. These are very close in style to a manuscript dated AD 1485 and painted at Pipalner in Malwa, near Gujarat.

Among various other groups of paintings from Gujarat, the illustrations from the Bhagavata Purana the first of about 1600, and the second (14 and 15) of about 1625-50 may be termed 'folk'. Although Mughal costumes are depicted on some figures in both manuscripts, they were produced in a village or an urban centre by families of professional painters, whose style and strength of design changed very little in spite of their contact with Mughal artists or their work. They must have been proficient in producing manuscripts with a large number of illustrations. It is for this reason that both manuscripts have a studied uniformity of style and display an imaginative sense of space and design. This trait can be seen also in the Kathakalpataru The manuscript of about 1625 AD done somewhere in northwest recently. In all of them prevails a unique sense of colour and pattern, perhaps on account of Gujarat's love for colour and ornamentation.

Paintings from the Rajput and Central Indian centres are stylistically more individual. The love for the episodes from the Ramayana, Krishna Lila and local folk legends were an immense source of inspiration at the village level, both for the patron and the artist. The composition is simple, the treatment less sophisticated but more direct, and the colours are bright and symbolically used. Also noticeable is the touch of Mughal painting, and the use of Mughal fashions and manners at all courts, the rulers were Hindus spiritually, and painting at the folk level retained the use of local costumes and colour preferences.

Pahari painting, or the painting at the Rajput courts and their domains in the Punjab Hills, is a glorious facet of Indian painting. There are reasons to believe that their animated quality emerged out of the indigenous folk art. The power-charged style of Basohli, from about 1660, and the folkish work of Kulu and Mandi, from about 1675, set standards for other centres of Pahari painting. Little influenced by court painting, the pages from the early eighteenth century' Book of Omens' retain the sturdy primitive traits of folk painting done earlier in the region. In their simplicity of form, subdued use of colour, imaginative use of picture space and naive creativity, may be seen the best components of Indian folk paintings, displaying the intangible world of devout emotion with a tinge of playfulness.

One of the most ancient and significant forms of pictorial expression was employed by the traditional picture-showmen in parts of India for religious and ethical education, as well as for entertainment. Gujarat, Rajasthan, Bengal, Orissa, Maharashtra and Andhra Pradesh have had a long tradition of the narration of local legends, simultaneously illustrated by paintings. We have exhibited examples of scroll-painting from Andhra Pradesh and Bengal, and fifteen paintings on paper, used by the picture-showmen of southern Maharashtra. Andhra scroll paintings were executed on fine handwoven cotton; the scrolls of Bengal were done on paper; and, in examples from Maharashtra mill made paper was used.

The paintings of the scrolls of Andhra Pradesh, known examples of which date from about 1625, are of a fairly sophisticated style that can hardly be termed 'folk'. It is because the same artists were commissioned by the Hindu aristrocracy of the region. Each scroll painting narrates legends propagating the exploits of the progenitors only of a particular caste, and was shown only to people of that caste. Many such legends about 8 to 10 metres in length and about one metre in breadth. They were mostly vertical and episodes were divided into horizontal panels. There is a pervasive rhythmic unity in their total effect and a firm, vigorous line encloses areas of bright flat colour set against red ground. The costumes, ornaments and other details are South Indian.

The scroll paintings of Bengal and Bihar are smaller. There were several centres of their production and the style of painting varied from district to district. Yet, all of them were charged with a rhythmic expression, directness, freshness, a refined sense of bright colours and have used lively wiry line. They either narrate locally popular tales or the Krishna legend in Bengal. Another type of scrolls were made for Santhals of Bengal and Bihar, narrating legends favoured by them; one other group consisted of Chakshudan (restoration of sight);

they were made after a death in village home and portray the dead person.

The picture-showmen (Chitrakathis) of southern Maharashtra, of Pinguli village in Sawantwadi State, were least influenced by outside influences (40-50). The main feature of the large series of these paintings are the battle scenes; they are charged with superhuman vitality. In style, these paintings, produced all through the nineteenth century, are very original; they have a typical dramatic quality and bold and flat colour areas bound by a uniform studied line. In a way, they follow the tradition of leather puppets which the same family of painters produced. The choice of themes and various details befittingly express the preference of their audience, the Marathas. The subjects chosen were from Hindu religious legends.

In places of pilgrimage and at temples, shops of painters often existed where pilgrims could buy souvenirs. A fascinating style developed in the nineteenth century at the Kalighat temple in Calcutta, where apart from popular Hindu deities, even topical events were painted on ordinary machine-made paper. Executed in a boldly swift and casual manner they retain an exclusively original sweeping power and the monumentality. Using European water colours, the figures and other forms have an accentuated roundness on account of the use of modelling tone along the inside of the contours, completed by strong black outlines.

Around the Puri temple and nearby villages, painters produced paintings for visiting pilgrims. Although the most common subjects were the three cult images painted on primed cotton, the painters sometimes kept sketch books for taking orders from clients. Almost all Orissan manuscripts were written and painted on palm leaf, yet, in many exceptional cases, they were executed on paper. However, in the latter case, their style changed only slightly, the difference being due to the nature of the material used.

In the vast plateau of the Deccan, a variety of patrons and, consequently, styles of paintings existed. Apart from the scroll paintings discussed above, conservative painting of great originality, strength and distinct style was produced at the various small courts of the Deccan. Wanaparti, a Hindu state in south Deccan, was one such centre. The three pages from a Ragamala series from this place are very original in style and their unconventional use of colour. A notable fact about them is that they illustrate the south Indian Karnatak modes of music; all other Indian Ragamala sets are based on north Indian music.

While concluding this small note, we must inform the reader that many types of Indian folk paintings are not represented in this exhibition. Firstly, the wall paintings done on village homes in several parts of Gujarat and Orissa, and the paintings on the walls of the bridal chambers of Madhubani in Bihar and by the Warlis in Maharashtra and Bastar in Central India, though familiar to us, are, naturally, not possible to show. Secondly, since the Museum restricts its collection to work done before 1900 AD, the recent work of the Madhubani and Warli painters on paper, so much sought after today, was outside our scope. So also the Museum does not possess good examples of folk painting from South India, where it is restricted only to glass painting. Otherwise, this exhibition is fully representative of India's folk paintings, and is a manifest tribute to the unknown master painters whose creations our Museum intends to glorify.

### *Company Painting and Folk and Village Painting*

With the decline of the Mughal empire and provincial administrative structures in the 18th and 19th centuries, artists had to look beyond their traditional sources of patronage for work. They found ample opportunity in the increasing number of English residents in India during this time. Captivated by their exotic surroundings, these newcomers were eager to purchase paintings that depicted aspects of daily life, important historical monuments, and the subcontinent's plants and animals.

Indian artists were quick to accommodate these new patrons and, in the process, to modify traditional techniques to suit

Western tastes. The resulting "Company Painting" (named after the British East India Company which controlled much of the subcontinent during the 18th and first half of the 19th century) featured a more transparent handling of the watercolour medium; forms modeled with the use of light and shade; a subtler, more muted colour palette; and a Western concern for the illusion of spatial recession.Not all Indian painters, however, surrendered to Western aesthetic preferences. During the 19th and early 20th centuries, many lively, indigenous traditions continued in the form of folk and village painting. Produced for ritual and utilitarian use, these quickly rendered pictures featured immediately "readable" compositions with bold, simple colours, strong outlines, and an energetic use of pattern. They are barely touched by Western intrusions.

### *Folk Paintings*

Colourful designs, invariably tinged with mystic belief are found in rural folk paintings. They reveal the traditional aesthetic sensibility of the Indian village. The Madhubani paintings of Bihar, the Pata paintings of West Bengal and the Nirmal paintings of Andhra Pradesh are only a few from the vast gallery of Indian folk paintings. Epics, *puranas*, the Krishna-lila (antics of Lord Krishna), etc., are their main sources of inspiration. Gods and goddesses are depicted in all possible forms and actions, and are painted in varieties of technique and colour.

Indian folk painting is as old as the land, its trees, rivers, hills and humans. From time immemorial people or common 'folk' have articulated their instincts and sentiments through the medium of painting. Images have been sketched on pots and pans, on walls of village houses, on dried leaves and later on clothes and paper.

Executed in almost all possible ways, folk art paintings have been an integral part of Indian civilization. Evolving out of the cave paintings of pre-historic period, folk painting continues to be a dynamic tradition. Guided by no formal school, restricted by no orthodox norm, folk painting grows out of life and is sustained by life. Religious rituals, domestic beautification, familial celebrations, seasonal festivals are some of the inspirations of folk Indian paintings. Presently this immense treasure of folk paintings that was shrouded in anonymity and neglect, has been unearthed. Warli paintings, Madhubani paintings, Patachitra and other forms of traditional Indian folk art are internationally acclaimed possessions today.

### *The Discovery of Indian Folk Paintings*

It is commonly said that one refuses to see the beauty of ones own yard until one sees all there is to see in this world. So is the story of Indian Folk Paintings, this neglected art form was discovered by Indian scholars as late as the beginning of the 20th Century.

With the rise of Modern Art in Europe and its irreverence towards form and structure, Indian began to take notice of the vibrant motives that had adorned their own walls and courtyard for centuries. The simplicity that the proponents of Modern Art so keenly aspired for was so effortlessly achieved in Indian Folk Painting. Thus, Indian Folk Painting was now recognised for its true artistic value.

### *Madhubani Paintings*

Women of the Madhubani village of Bihar maintain a strange matriarchal tradition, they paint figures from nature and myth on household and village walls to mark the seasonal festivals, for special events of the life-cycle, and when marriages are being arranged they prepare intricately designed wedding proposals, and the technique of painting is safely and zealously guarded by the women of this village, for it is to be passed on by a mother to her daughter.

Women of this village have been practicing this art form for centuries but it came to the forefront only in the 1960s, when a drought hit the area and people had to think of an alternative non agricultural source of earning. Selling these traditional paintings on hand-made paper was the best alternative. Today they are one of the most celebrated Folk Arts of the world.

### *Pata Paintings*

The temple of Jagannath Puri in Orissa is a source of livelihood for many. For centuries peddlers, artists and food vendors have thronged the by lanes of Puri in search of a livelihood. Amongst them were the Pata Painters, who were commissioned by one of the Ganga Kings in the 12th century, to popularise the cult of Jagannath amongst the millions who visited the temple every year. The themes of these paintings were inspired by the Bhakti Movement (a cult religious movement of those times). Radha Kishna and Jagannath are lovingly depicted in bold colours. The Pata Painting are also practised on different media. The most popular items are Ganjapa playing cards, Masks, Toys of Jagannath, Balabhdra, Subhadra and miniature of Jagannath temple.

### *Nirmal Paintings*

Nirmal is a small town in Andhra Pradesh, it is famous for its wooden works and glased paintings. The paintings in bold colours derive their name from the village and are rich in variety and theme. The themes are generally from the epics—Ramayan and Mahabharata. The medium used is oil. The above-mentioned genres are just a few samples from the treasure trove called Indian Folk Paintings. Its will be virtually impossible to categorise each and every sample of Indian folk painting. For every time a motif is drawn in a courtyard or a wall of an Indian house, the tradition of Indian Folk Painting gets a new meaning.

### *Folk Paintings of Rajasthan*

In Rajasthan, the folk paintings are usually done on some specific occasions like marriage, birth ceremony and festivals. This tradition of folk paintings is found in villages and rural areas practised by various tribes. They are very original, fresh and done with raw-hand.

## Pahari Paintings

Rajput paintings in the region of the Punjab Hill states of North India, *i.e.* in the states of Himachal Pradesh, Jammu &

Kashmir and few areas in erstwhile Pakistan are known as Pahari paintings. Scholars have categorised Pahari paintings on the basis of geography and family style.

On the basis of geography two categories can be identified. One is the Basohli and Kulu style, and second is the Guler and Kangra style. While the former group shows influence of the Chaurpanchasika style and emphasises on the abstraction, bold lines, and conservative colours, the latter underscores on cooler colours and refinement.

Parallel can be drawn between the developments of the Pahari School and the Rajasthan School. However, there are certain punctuated gaps in the development of Pahari paintings, which the scholarly research is trying to fill in. The family relationship of the Hill Rajas with the royal court at Rajasthan had its marked influence on the painting traditions, which evolved in the Hill States. The influence of the Mughals, Gujarat, and Deccan were also conspicuous in these Indian paintings.

The growing popularity of vernacular literature with the emergence of Bhakti movement provided themes for the Pahari Paintings. Erstwhile Shaiva-Shakta themes in paintings were now accompanied by the vernacular poetry and folk songs adoring Krishna and Rama. Katha-vachaka (storyteller) played a significant role in broadening people's understanding of the religious texts like Puranans and Ramayana.

They held discourses in temples, market places and educated people on proper conduct and purity of life. While, the poets and performers from the plains visited hills and provided cultural performances. Thus, the vibrant social and cultural milieu provided endless themes to the painters. Unlike Rajasthani Paintings, which centered on portraitures, and depiction of splendid court life, Pahari paintings emphasised on love and devotional themes.

The royalty commissioned texts based on love themes and stories of Krishna. Gita Govinda (the Divine Love Song) and the tenth book of the Bhagavata Purana (the stories of Krishna) provided evergreen themes. While the Aranya Kanda, and the Lanka Kanda of Ramayana epic were repeatedly illustrated.

One of the early notable works of art was Devi Mahatmya manuscript, painted at Kangra in 1552. Besides this, Rasamanjiri, a 15th century Sanskrit text, penned down by Bhanudaata of Mithila in Bihar, was a significant illustrated work. The heroes (nayakas) and heroines (nayikas) and beauteous maidens of this rhetoric text personified subtle ecstasies of romance.

### *Painting in the Punjab Hills*

Like their counterparts in Rajasthan and Central India, the Rajput rulers of the Punjab Hills of North India were devout Hindus and fierce warriors, engaging in political intrigue, strategic marriages, and skirmishes over land holdings. The remoteness of the mountainous Punjab kingdoms insured that the Mughals, who entered the region during Akbar's reign, by geographic necessity accorded the Pahari (meaning "from the hills") rulers higher degrees of autonomy than elsewhere in India.

The stylistic trends and favoured subject matter of Pahari painting varied from state to state. Generally speaking, stories from sacred Hindu texts (again, with an emphasis on Krishna) as well as love poetry, Ragamala texts, portraits, and scenes of court life, were favorite subjects for paintings. The earliest pictures from the Punjab Hills had bold, abstract compositions, vid colours, and energetic lines. In later paintings, Mughal influence is seen in increased naturalism, refined detail, an elegant, subdued palette, and choice of secular subjects. New discoveries in recent years are expanding the scholarship and in some cases rewriting both the questions and answers about the development of painting in the Punjab Hills.

### *Kangra Paintings*

Every work of art is fragrant of its time, said Laurence Binyon. The religion of Vaishnavism provided Kangra painters with inspiration while in the ruler, Sansar Chand, they found a patron who honoured and encouraged them. It was in such happy circumstances that these artists created a style which combines elegance with nervous grace. There is delicacy and sensitivity in the line, combined with rare beauty of colour. For almost forty years these artists were aglow with inspiration and they created these memorable paintings which communicate the spiritual concepts of Vaishnavism so vividly.

Bihari Lal Chaube (1595-1663) was born in Govindpur, near Gwalior, and spent his boyhood at Orchha where his father, Keshav Rai, lived. His father was a Brahmana and his mother a Kshatriya, and he belonged to that mixed caste now known as Ray, which produced such well-known poets as Padmakar, Gwal and Dev. In 1607, his father left Orchha and settled with his wife's family in Mathura, the home of the Vrajabhasha dialect. Shah Jahan happened to visit Vrindavana, the holy city of Krishna.

Bihari had an opportunity of displaying his poetic talent in his darbar and won his appreciation. A broad-minded son of a Rajput mother, Shah Jahan patronised Hindu poets. For some time Bihari lived with Shahjehan at Agra, where he had an opportunity of meeting Abdur Rahim Khankhana, a well-known Hindi poet, who appreciated his poetry and encouraged trim. Shahjehan is said to have held a darbar at Agra at which his feudatories from various parts of India assembled, and among them was Mirza Jai Singh Kachhwaha, Raja of Amber, who was impressed by Bihari's poetry and invited him to Amber.

Jai Singh I (1625-1667), who is better known as Mirza Raja, was a mansabdar of six thousand soldiers of the Emperor Aurangzeb. He was instrumental incapturing Shivaji, the Maratha leader, whom he conveyed to the court of Aurangzeb. When he came to know that the pledge of safety given to Shivaji was likely to be broken, he abetted his escape.

Tod says that he had twenty two thousand Rajput cavalry at his disposal and had twenty two vassal chiefs who commanded under him. "He became so confident of his power that he would sit with them in darbar holding two glasses, one of which he would call Delhi, the other Satara, and dashing one to the ground would explain, 'There goes Satara; the fate of Delhi is in my right hand and this, with like facility, I can cast away'." The legend of the origin of the Sat Sai is as follows: Raja Jai Singh married a girl-wife, retired into his inner apartments with her and gave orders that anyone disturbing him with official business would be blown from a gun. This continued for about a year, and the administration of the kingdom fell into confusion. Apart from the ministers of the Raja, his senior Rani Anant Kumari, who was jealous of the young wife, could not tolerate neglect from her husband.

The senior Rani, as well as the ministers, consulted Bihari Lal who suggested the following scheme, which was carried out. He wrote down the famous verse of the Sat Sai commencing with nahin paraga, which, ostensibly praising the beauty of the young queen, alludes to her age and gave a clear hint as to the state of affairs.

*nahin paraga nahin madhur madhu*
*nahin vikasa yahi kal*
*ali kali hi saun bandhyau*
*again kaun haval.*

"There is no pollen; there is no sweet honey;
*nor yet has the blossom opened.*
*If the bee is enamoured of the bud,*
*who can tell what will happen*
*when she is a full-blown flower."*

This verse was concealed amongst the flower petals which were sent each day to the harem, to form the bed of the happy spouses. In the morning the paper remained stiff amidst the withered petals, and bruised the king's body. He drew it out, read it, and at once returned to a sense of his responsibilities. He went outside, held a public court, and summoned the ingenious writer of the verse. Bihari Lal appeared, and the king, to show his satisfaction, promised him a gold mohur for every doha he might bring him in this way. Bihari Lal wrote two or three dohas, and received on each occasion the promised reward, till some seven hundred in all had been composed. These were collected and made into a book.

Prince Azam Shah, third son of the Emperor Aurangzeb, who was a lover of Hindi poetry, called an assembly of poets and had the verses of the Sat Sai arranged according to the classification of Nayakas and Nayikas found in the works such as the Rasikapriya of Keshav Das. This was entitled the 'Azam Shahi' recension which was followed by Kavi Lallu Lal in his commentary of the Sat Sai called the Lal Chandrika, and published by Grierson (1896). He calls Bihari the 'mine of commentators'. Commenting on his poetry, he says, 'each verse is a perfectly polished jewel.' The verses of the Sat Sai are rich in poetic flavour, elegance, and subtlety of feeling. They have the quality of miniature painting for vividness. Brevity of expression is combined with richness of content and a power to elicit spiritual sentiment. They excel in refinement and grace.

The dramatic personae in these poems are Radha and Krishna, who are the Nayika and the Nayaka, and the sakhis, the maids of Radha. The sakhis carry messages between the lovers, they conciliate them when they quarrel, and among themselves they keep up a running commentary on the course of love. The paintings of the Sat Sai have some features in common with the paintings of the Gita-Govinda. Masterly drawing, with extraordinary sensitive line, dramatic design, and festal radiance of colour, is seen in both the series. Dashes of red in the horizon are another common feature. The clothing and the treatment of vegetation are also more or less similar in both the series. In the facial formula and the buildings and landscape, however, there is a difference.

The Gita Govinda is a forest idyll, and in its Kangra paintings, the drama of the loves of Radha and Krishna is played in the forest, or along the river bank. In the paintings of the Bhagavata Purana, the incidents in the life of the boy Krishna are depicted against the background of the forests of Vrindavana and the river Yamuna. It is the trees of the forest, and the current of the river which are most prominent in these paintings. On the other hand, in the paintings of the Sat Sai the background of architecture provides the setting for the love drama of Radha and Krishna. It is against the background of straight lines of walls, windows and balconies that the games of love are carried on by Radha and Krishna, watched by the sakhis.

The parallel straight lines and right angles create a compositional pattern of restfulness and calm. Against the repose of architectural compositions, we feel the restlessness of love. While the architectural setting has precision, the human forms have a fiuid grace, matching the elegance of a waterfall against the straight vertical lines of a mountain. And always there is a pair of confidantes discussing the course of love of the divine couple. When there is dissension or misunderstanding among the lovers, they are unhappy and have an expression of serious concern on their faces, and they are never tired of coaxing, cajoling, or giving advice. When the course of love runs smoothly, they are unrestrainedly happy.

The knitting together of form and colour into a coordinated harmony is essential of great art. In these Kangra paintings, form and colour are so blended that the effect is musical. To achieve such a harmony, the artist made use of both line and colour. The line which he used is the musical, rhythmical line, expressing both movement and mass. And what a rhythm the dancing line creates, a pure limpid harmony! This line was effectively supplemented by colours—the blues, yellows, greens, and reds—the pure colours of earth and minerals, which shine like jewels and have not been dimmed by the passage of time. The combination of fluid line and glowing colours ultimately produced an art which combines the beauty of figure with dignity of pose, set against the calm of the hills.

Another characteristic of these paintings is the manner in which dramatic relations and expectancy are expressed through design, as well as expression, on the faces of the lovers. Others are present, and, due to modesty, physical contact is not possible. Radha glances at Krishna with loving eyes through her veil, and on some pretext she moves away brushing her shadow with his shadow. The lovers are standing in the balconies of their houses facing each other. Their fixed gaze has provided a rope on which their hearts travel fearlessly like rope dancers.

Clad in white, the lady has gone into the moonlight to meet her lover. It is white everywhere and hidden in it only the fragrance of her body enables her sakhi to follow. The white radiance of the moon and its pale silvery light has been marvellously evoked by the artist.

The artist has shown considerable skill in painting night scenes. The night is pitch dark and the lane is narrow. The lovers, coming from opposite directions, brush against each other, and only the light touch of their bodies enables them to recognise each other. How brilliantly the artist has painted the inky sky, resplendent with stars. Against the background of a paddy field and her home stands the demure village beauty. Wearing a fillet, and holding a stick, stands she of slender waist, with eyes downcast, unconscious of her innocent charm and beauty.

We know that Manaku had a son, Khushala, and if Manaku died some time before 1800, it is likely that these pictures were painted by Khushala after his father's death. The work of the son is influenced by the father. The series on the Gita-Govinda is more complete, and more than one hundred and forty paintings exist. On the other hand, there are hardly forty paintings of the Sat Sai and about twenty drawings. The latter are in the collection of the Bharat Kala Bhavan, Varanasi, and are possibly late. It seems that the Sat Sai paintings were painted later than those of the Gita-Govinda and hence their date of composition is probably in the region of 1805.

The Kangra Miniatures of the Pahari School made a mark in the 18th century. Though influenced by the Mughals, the Kangra School retained its distinctiveness. The paintings were naturalistic and employed cool, fresh colours. The colours were extracted from minerals, vegetables and possessed enamel-like luster. Verdant greenery of the landscape, brooks, springs were the recurrent images on the miniatures. Texts of the Gita Govinda, Bhiari's Satsai, and the Baramasa of Keshavdas provided endless themes to the painters. Krishna and Radha as eternal lovers were portrayed rejoicing the moments of love. The Kangra miniatures are also noted for portraying the famine charm with a natural grace. The paintings based on Ragmalas (musical modes) also found patronage in Kangra. Some of the famous Kangra Ragmala Paintings include Ragini Gujari, Raga Lalit and Ragini Sorathi.

Kangra School in its later stage included scenes under star-studded skies and also portrayed storms with lightning running across the horizon. These features were conspicuously absent in the other schools of panting. Later, Kangra miniatures also depicted towns and cluster of houses in the distance but curiously mountains above the height of 13,000 ft were never made a part of the paintings. Kangra miniatures were adopted as a model of pictorial expression at many places of Pahari paintings including Chamba. The miniature artists faced hardships after they lost the patronage of the royalty, due to the changed political equations. Today, it is a dying art form as many of the artists have embraced other professions The classic miniatures of the yore are preserved in museums. However, reproductions of these miniatures are also available that can be made a part of private collection.

### *Basohli Paintings*

Basohli, situated on the bank of the Ravi River produced magnificent series of manifestations of the supreme goddess called Devi series. The Devi series was bold in execution and iridescent beetles were used in the illustrations as jewels. Another notable illustration was the romantic text of Rasamanjari, painted by artist Devidasa under the patronage of Raja Kirpal Pal (1678-95). Basohli rulers also patronised portrait paintings.

### *Basohli Origin*

The chief characteristics of the Basohli paintings were geometrical patterns, and use of bold colours to infuse vitality in the paintings. Besides the bold colours, lustrous enamel like colours were also employed. The decorative conventions and dramatic compositions where the figures were shown clad in rich costumes, stylised faces, and large bulging eyes lent unique individuality to these paintings.

### *Bilaspur*

Bilaspur, situated in Himachal Pradesh saw the rise of the paintings in the mid 17th century. The earlier paintings were portraitures that were succeeded by illustrations of the Bhagavata Purana, Ramayana, and Ragamala series in the 18th century. Besides these, painters at Bilaspur also executed paintings on rumal (coverlets) for rituals and ceremonies.

***Chamba***

Located in Himachal Pradesh, the painting traditions of the region showed close resemblance to the Mughal style. The influence of Deccan and Gujarat were also conspicuous in the paintings. In the late 17th century, influence of Basohli style became, evident, however it was lost out to the Guler painting tradition, which became dominant in the region. Dashavatara, attributed to the mid 18th century, executed by artist Mahesh was a significant work from this school. The illustration work based on the on the life of Krishna and the story of Usha and Annirudha from the Bhagavata Purana were other notable works of art. Besides paintings, decoration on rumals (coverlets) usually bearing a design related to the life of Krishna were brilliantly executed by court artists before they were worked in fine silk by ladies of Zenana (Chamber of females).

***Garhwal Paintings***

Molu Ram was a noted artist from Garhwal. His earlier work reflected the influence of Mughal style while his later work can be interpreted as cruder version of Kangra traditions. Himself a poet, his pictures often carried his own verses and exact dates. One of the splendid works of this region was the work of art based on Shiva-Parvati.

***Guler Kangra Style***

In a span of one and a half centuries, around 1800, dramatic changes in the painting traditions led to the development of mature Guler-Kangra style. The decorative and stylised treatment of various motifs in flat, and cut out forms became more naturalistic in the new style. The difference was visible in the treatment of eyes and modeling of the face. This painting style introduced naturalistic landscapes. The illustrated Gita Govinda, from this genre, showed landscapes, and used shading. Scholars noted that the shading device appeared all over the grassy plains of the several paintings of the series. However, this feature was absent in the earlier Pahari paintings.

The other significant development of this period was the emphasis on the graciousness and femininity of Indian women.

The facial types of women were well modelled and shaded so judiciously that it provided porcelain like delicacy.

***Guler***

Painting in Guler began earnestly in the 18th century. The family of Pandit Seu was well noted for their fine body of work. Ramayana dated 1720 and a series of collection in Reitberg Museum were few of his classic work. His work laid the foundation of the Kangra style, which was evolved and refined, from the artists of his family subsequently.

***Jammu***

The painting traditions of Jammu in the late 18th century and early 19th century showed close resemblance with the Kangra type. Recent research has indicated that Shangri Ramayana of the late 17th and early 18th centuries was produced in Jammu and not in Kangra as it was earlier believed to be.

***Jasrota***

Jasrota, located in Jammu and Kashmir, saw some noteworthy works of art executed by Nainsukh of Guler. Under Raja Balwant Singh (1724-63), Nainsukh produced portraits, court scenes, events from the prince's life as well as allegorical scenes.

***Kangra***

In the second half of the 18th century, Kangra style characterised with the lyrical and refined qualities developed. Under Maharaja Sansar Chand, Kangra became the main centre of Pahari Painting. Artists from the family of Pandit Seu produced finest works of art in this school. Bhagavata Purana, Gita Govinda, Nala Damayanti, Ragamala, and Satsai (Seven Hundred verses) were some of the notable works of art. Sansar Chand also commissioned many durbar scenes of himself and his nobles but these were in a stiffer and formal style.

***Kulu***

A series of portraits of the Kulu rulers have been executed outside Kulu. Shangri Ramayana dated 1690 –1710 ascribed to Kulu, exhibited four distinct styles. However, new scholastic research indicates that this work was not produced in Kulu but at Jammu. The other notable works of art were a Bhagavata Purana and two Madhumalati manuscripts.

### *Mandi*

Mandi, a small kingdom south of Kulu saw the emergence of an individualised style under Raja Sidh Sen (1684-1727). Portraits patronised by him depicted the ruler as a gigántic figure with exaggerated enlarged heads, hands and feet. The same painting tradition continued in the reign of his successor Shamsher Sen (1721-81). It is interesting to note that both the rulers have been depicted as incarnations of Shiva in the paintings commissioned by them. Mention must be made of Sajanu, an artist who produced splendid work characterised by geometric compositions and delicate naturalistic details.

### *Mankot*

Painting traditions at Mankot located in Jammu and Kashmir closely resembled to the Basholi type. Portraitures were common in the mid-17th century. The paintings in this region were characterised with the use of bright colours and boldly rendered subjects. Bhagavata Purana and Ramayana were few of the significant works of this region. In the later period the style showed greater naturalism and use of muted colours.

### *Nurpur*

Nurpur, in Himachal Pradesh can be described as a stopover between Chamba and the Punjab plains. Chamba painters often stayed there, which resulted in cultural exchange between their counterparts at Nurpur. This is manifested in the certain common idioms used in the paintings of both regions. One of the earliest paintings was of the ruler and his brother at worship. This work carried a strong Mughal influence. The Nurpur style employed bright colours and mostly flat backgrounds. However, in the later period the paintings used muted colours.

# Bibliography

Ali, A. Yusuf : *A monograph of Silk Fabrics*, Allahbad, 1900.

Anand, Mulk Raj : *Kama Kala: Some Notes on the Philosophical Basis of Hindu Erotic Sculpture*, Nagel, New York, 1962.

Anand, Mulk Raj : *The story of India*, Kutub, Bombay, 1948.

Baldinger, Annemarie, Seiler : *Classification of Textile Techniques,* Calico Museum of Textiles, Ahemdabad, 1979.

Barpujari, H.K. : *The comprehensive History of Assam,* Publication Board of Assam, 1993.

Barve, V.R. : *Complete Textile Encyclopedia*, Russi Lal Publishers, Bombay, 1967.

Beny, Roloff : *India*, McGraw-Hill, New York, 1969.

Bernier, Francois : *Voyages de Francois Bernier...Contenant la Description des Etats de Grand Mogul. Ou Il Est Traite des Richesses, des Forces de la Justice, & des Causes Principales de la Decadance des Etats de l'Asie, & de Plusiers Evenemens Considerables*, P. Marret, Amsterdam, 1724.

Bhavnani, Enakshi : *Folk and Tribal Designs of India*, Taraporevala, Bombay, 1974.

Chandra, Pramod : *Bundi Painting*, Lalit Kala Akademi, New Delhi, 1959.

Chattopadhyay, Kamaladevi : *The Glory of Indian Handicrafts*, Indian Book Company, Delhi, 1976.

Desai, Devangana : *Erotic Sculpture of India: a Sociocultural Study*, Tata McGraw-Hill Pub. Co., New Delhi, 1975.

Dhamija, Jasleen : *The Survey of Embroidery Traditions' in Textiles and Embroideries of India*, Mark Publications, Bombay, 1965.

Elwin, Verrier : *The Art of Northeast Frontier of India*, Northeast Frontier Agency, Shillong, 1959.

Forman, Werner : I*ndian sculpture; masterpieces of Indian, Khmer, and Cham Art,* Spring Book, London, 1962.

Fortune, Robert : *Visit to the Tea-Districts of China and India; Including Sung-Lo and the Bothea Hills; With a Short Notice of the East India Company's Tea Plantations in the Himalayan Mountains,* J. Murray, London, 1852.

Fraser, James : *The History of Nadir Shah (formerly called Thames Kuli Khan, The Present Emperor of Persia)*, A. Millar, London, 1742.

Fraser, James : *The History of Nadir Shah (formerly called Thames Kuli Khan, the Present Emperor of Persia)*, A. Millar, London, 1742.

Greenbie, Sydney: *The Romantic East; India, Indo-China, China and Japan,* R. M. McBride & Co., New York, 1930.

Heber, Reginald : *Narrative of a Journey Through the Upper Provinces of India, from Calcutta to Bombay, 1824-25,* J. Murray, London, 1828.

Houghton, Ross C. : *India Speaks with Richard Halliburton*, Grosset & Dunlap, New York, 1933.

Houghton, Ross C. : *Women of the Orient: An Account of the Religious, Intellectual, and Social Condition of Women in Japan, China, India, Egypt, Syria, and Turkey, Cincinnati, Hitchcock and Walden*, Nelson and Phillips, New York, 1877.

Hussain, Majid : N.S. Olaniya : *Encyclopedia of India: Arunachal Pradesh & Mizoram*, Rima Publications, 1994.

Iyer, D.S.V. : *Looms in Textiles and Embroideries of India*, Mark Publications, Bombay, 1965.

Khanadalavala, Karl : *Pahari Miniature Painting*, New Book Co., Bombay, 1958.

Mackenzie, Helen : *Life in the Mission*, Redfield, New York, 1856.

Marshall, John Hubert : *Mohenjo-daro and the Indus Civilization*, A. Probsthain, London, 1931.

Maurice, Thomas : *The History of Hindostan: Its Arts, and its Sciences, as Connected with the History of the Other Great Empires of Asia, During the Most Ancient Periods of the World,* W. Bulmer and Co., London, 1799.

Mill, James :*The history of British India*, Baldwin, Cradock, and Joy, London, 1826.

Minturn, Robert Bowne : *From New York to Delhi, by Way of Rio de Janeiro, Australia and China,* Appleton, New York, 1859.

Mudaliar, M.P. Nachimuthu : *Manipur, Naga and Assam Fabrics', in Textiles and Embroideries of India*, Mark Publications, Bombay, 1965.

Nyori, Tai : *History and Culture of the Adis*, Omsons Publications, 1993.

Panchani, Chandra Sheikhar : *Arunachal Pradesh: Religion, Culture & Society, Konark Publishers*, New Delhi, 1989.

Paulinus, A. Sancto Bartholomaeo : *A Voyage to the East Indies: Containing an Account of the Manners, Customs, etc., of the Natives, with a Geographical Description of the Country,* Appleton, New York, 1859.

Philipa, Scott : *The Book of Silk*, Thames and Hudson Ltd, 1993.

Randhawa, Mohindar Singh : *The Krishna Legend in Pahari Painting*, Lalit Kala Akadami, New Delhi, 1956.

Rawson, Philip S. : *Erotic Art of the East*, Putnam, New York, 1968.

Rennell, James : *Memoir of a map of Hindostan*, W. Bulmer and Co., London, 1793.

Riefstahl, Rudolph Meyer : *Persian and Indian Textiles from the Late Sixteenth to the Early Nineteenth Century, an Album of Thirty Six Plates,* E. Weyhe, New York, 1923.

Robertson, William : *An Historical Desquisition Concerning the Knowledge Which the Ancients Had of India*, Cadell and Davies, etc., London, 1817.

Saraf, D.N. : *Indian Crafts- Development and Potential*, Vikas Publishing House, Delhi, 1982.

Skinner, Thomas : *Adventures during a Journey Overland to India, by way of Egypt, Syria and the Holy Land*, R. Bentley, London, 1837.

Speltz, Alexander : *The Colored Ornament of All Historical Styles; a Treasury of Examples Reproduced in Facsimile from Water-Colour Drawing*, B.T. Batsford, Ltd., London, 1915.

Tagore, Rabindranath : *Drawings and paintings of Rabindranath Tagore*, Lalit Kala Akademi, New Delhi, 1987.

Tennant, Rev. William : *Indian Recreations: Consisting Chiefly of Strictures on the Domestic and Rural Economy of the Mahomedans & Hindoos*, Longman, Hurst, Rees and Orme; etc., London, 1804.

Terry, Edward : *A Voyage to East India:Within that Rich and Most Spacious Empire of the Great Mogul,* J. Wilkie, etc., London, 1777.

Wolff, Joseph : *Narrative of a mission to Bokhara, in the years 1843-1845,* Pub. for the Author, London, 1846.

Wright, Caleb : *India and its Inhabitants*, Brainerd, Cincinnati, 1853.

Yazdani, Ghulam : *Ajanta: Monochrome Reproductions of the Ajanta Frescoes Based on Photography*, Swati Publications, Delhi, 1983.

Yazdani, Ghulam : *Ajanta: the Colour and Monochrome Reproductions of the Ajanta Frescoes Based on Photography*, Oxford University Press, London, 1955.

# Index


**A**

Abstraction, 126, 230.
Arjuna, 21, 47.
Arts, 2, 8, 11, 18, 32, 40, 72, 73, 74, 76, 77, 81, 84, 86, 91, 136, 154, 155, 158, 167, 182, 183, 187, 196, 204, 219, 221, 228.
Aswamedha, 47, 51.
Authority, 197.

**B**

Balarama, 19, 67, 90.
Bansuri, 92, 148, 149.
Bhakti Movement, 13, 230.
Bodhisattvas, 173, 211.
Brahma, 3, 5, 6, 121, 153.
Buddha, 45, 172, 192, 211.
Business, 158, 232.

**C**

Cave Paintings, 145, 171, 227.
Celebrations, 78, 103, 165, 227.
Ceremony, 43, 51, 62, 167, 168, 229.
Chakra, 56.
Chronology, 189, 190.
Classical Dance, 1, 2, 8, 12, 39, 46, 53, 56, 70, 72, 73, 74, 77, 78, 79, 80, 83, 84, 85, 91, 94, 96, 98, 99, 165.
Classical Music, 107, 108, 109, 110, 112, 115, 118, 124, 128, 136, 140, 141, 150, 151, 171, 193.
Company, 161, 226.
Crafts, 218, 219, 220.
Culture, 1, 13, 17, 46, 47, 49, 50, 53, 57, 62, 149, 153, 157, 160, 162, 175, 176, 179, 180, 181, 184, 195, 196, 200, 206, 207, 217.

**D**

Dance Costumes, 57.
Department, 50.
Dhrupad, 109, 110, 112, 113, 114, 115, 117, 118, 119, 129, 130, 131, 132, 133, 134, 135, 136, 137, 138, 139, 142, 145.
Drum, 4, 11, 18, 19, 30, 31, 57, 64, 66, 79,

100, 101, 114, 133, 134, 135, 136, 146, 147, 148.

## E

Education, 224.
Enjoyment, 25, 46, 95.
Ethics, 3.
Evolution, 49, 120, 121, 156.
Exertion, 24.

## F

Faith, 9, 54.
Film Industry, 159, 161, 162, 167, 169.
Folk Dances, 2, 46, 50, 51, 63, 64, 72, 85, 102, 103, 165.
Friends, 34.

## G

Gandharva, 46, 47.
Ganesha, 75, 88, 122.
Gardens, 200, 201.
Gharana, 13, 15, 113, 128, 129, 130, 131, 132, 134, 135, 136, 137, 138, 142, 146.
Gita Govinda, 84, 90, 230, 234, 236, 238, 239.
Government, 44, 51, 167, 168.
Guidance, 196.
Gunas, 22, 26.
Gupta Art, 191.

## H

Harappa, 105.
Harishchandra, 159, 160.
Harmonium, 39, 98, 118, 129, 139.
Hindu Deities, 225.
Hindu Mythology, 205.
Hindu Scriptures, 145.

## I

Idealism, 211.
Illusion, 227.
Independence, 150.
Indian Art, 172, 178, 180, 182, 201, 207, 213, 220.
Indian Cinema, 158, 161, 162, 168, 169.
Indian Folk Paintings, 219, 228, 229.
Indian Music, 107, 108, 110, 114, 129, 140, 141, 142, 143, 144, 146, 148, 150, 151, 171, 226.
Indian Paintings, 171, 172, 180, 205, 207, 210, 227, 230.
Indian Parallel Cinema, 168.
Indian Philosophy, 154.
Indian Society, 145.
Indian Theatre, 18, 153, 154, 156, 157.
Indra, 3, 26, 130, 137.
Interpretation, 20, 85, 107, 115.

## J

Jainism, 41.
Jewellery, 12, 70, 79, 174, 175, 191, 204, 205.

## K


Kalidasa, 155.
Kapila, 12.
Katha, 230.
Kathak, 2, 12, 13, 14, 15, 16, 17, 46, 71.
Kshatriya, 231.
Kuchipudi, 2, 39, 40, 41, 44, 46, 71, 82, 99.


## L


Lakshmi, 2, 191.
Legends, 2, 37, 53, 76, 77, 155, 178, 194, 223, 224, 225.
Liberation, 84, 97, 160, 212.
Literature, 2, 3, 17, 24, 59, 73, 76, 77, 84, 90, 94, 106, 154, 172, 183, 205, 230.


## M


Mahadev, 87.
Mahesh, 238.
Manipuri, 2, 45, 46, 47, 48, 49, 50, 51, 52, 53, 54, 55, 56, 57, 58, 59, 61, 62, 63, 65, 66, 67, 71.
Meditation, 43, 185.
Miniature Paintings, 179, 181, 192, 193, 194, 201.
Mithila, 47, 230.
Modern Instruments, 139.
Mohiniattam, 2, 68, 69, 70, 71, 72, 73, 74, 75, 76, 77, 78, 79, 80, 81, 82, 83.
Mughal Painting, 186, 195, 196, 197, 200, 220, 223.
Musical Instruments, 35, 39, 92, 102, 140, 142, 148.


## N


Narada, 106.
Narayana, 36, 40, 42, 73, 80, 81, 82.
Nataraja, 4, 87, 160, 161.
Natya Krama, 6.
Navigation, 122.
Nirvana, 212.
North Indian Classical Music, 112, 115.
Notation, 120, 128.


## O


Odissi, 2, 69, 71, 80, 81, 83, 84, 85, 86, 87, 89, 90, 91, 92, 93, 94, 95, 96, 97, 98.
Opinion, 18.
Ornaments, 3, 40, 57, 58, 79, 98, 101, 190, 191, 224.


## P


Pahari Paintings, 220, 229, 230, 237, 238.
Pilgrimage, 177, 220, 221, 225.
Prayer, 9, 19, 33, 96, 99, 100.
Puranas, 18, 51, 54, 153, 227.

## R

Raag, 110, 115.
Rajput Painting, 200, 201.
Rama, 2, 16, 18, 26, 73, 151, 178, 193, 230.
Ravana, 16, 21, 27.
Realisation, 43.
Regional Cinema, 160.
Rituals, 7, 62, 83, 153, 221, 227, 237.
Rock Paintings, 172, 187.

## S

Saints, 29.
Salvation, 44, 76, 97.
Sankirtana, 63, 65.
Sanskrit Literature, 59.
Santoor, 130, 144.
Sarangi, 66, 118, 130, 134, 142.
Saraswati, 75, 131, 145.
Sattriya, 98, 99, 100.
Shakuntala, 16.
Shishya, 11, 15, 121.
Sitar, 16, 83, 92, 109, 113, 130, 140, 141, 150.

## T

Taal, 56, 110, 111, 112, 113, 117, 135.
Tabla, 13, 14, 15, 16, 17, 92, 112, 117, 118, 130, 131, 134, 136, 138, 145, 146, 147, 150.
Tanpura, 92, 98, 143.
Theatre, 13, 17, 18, 21, 82, 94, 153, 154, 155, 156, 157, 158, 166.
Treatment, 59, 160, 205, 223, 234, 238.

## U

University, 118, 121.
Upanishads, 95, 151.

## V

Vaishnavism, 13, 42, 99, 231.
Vajrayana, 175, 176.
Vandana, 14, 66.
Vedic Literature, 106.
Veena, 69, 83, 87, 124, 129, 130, 131, 140, 144, 145.
Videha, 47.

## W

Wall Paintings, 176, 179, 180, 185, 219, 226.
Weapons, 189.
Wisdom, 5, 34.
Witness, 30.
Worship, 2, 8, 11, 41, 42, 46, 87, 88, 90, 92, 102, 185, 214, 240.

## Y

Yakshas, 215.
Yamuna, 234.
Yoga, 15.

❑❑❑

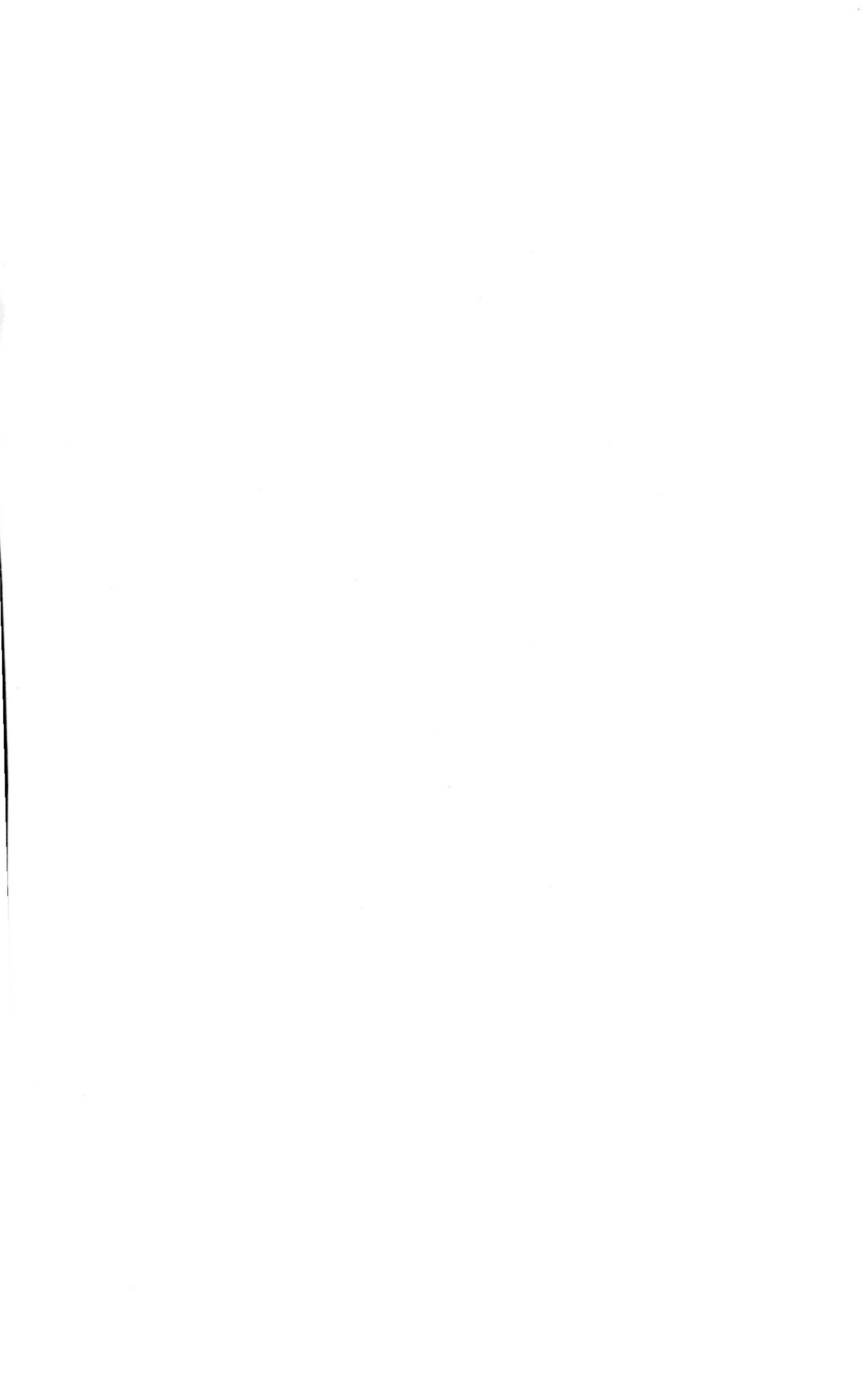